Englisch

LÖSUNGEN
zu den Units,
Exam preparation Seiten
und Extra grammar

Lösungen zu den Units, Exam preparation Seiten und Extra grammar

Unit 1: Between school and work

Seite 5

Springboard

1 1 The boy in photo 1 wants a moped.
2 The boy in photo 2 wants a mobile phone.
3 The girl in photo 3 wants an MP3 player.
4 The boy in photo 4 wants a TV.
5 The girl in photo 5 wants a mountain bike.
6 The girl in photo 6 wants a dog.

2 Roberta wants an MP3 player. Jim wants a moped. Maria wants a mountain bike. Theresa wants a dog. Tarkan wants a mobile phone. Henry wants a TV.

3 Freie Übung

Seite 6

Text 1: Extra money is useful

1 a) 1 richtig; 2 falsch; 3 falsch; 4 falsch; 5 falsch; 6 richtig
b) 7 false; 8 false; 9 true; 10 false

2 1 newspaper; 2 supermarket; 3 animal clinic; 4 snow; 5 cage; 6 clothes

Seite 7

3 1 friendly; 2 buy; 3 mother; 4 out of work; 5 love; 6 a lot (of); 7 save; 8 everything; 9 give; 10 useful

4 1 Theresa likes animals.
2 She enjoys her job in the animal clinic.
3 Mr and Mrs Scott don't work.
4 Does Jim Scott get pocket money? – No, he doesn't.
5 Do you love animals, too? – Yes, I do.

5

WHO?	WHEN?	WHERE?	DOES WHAT?	LIKES/ DOESN'T LIKE?
Jane	weekends	fast food restaurant	cooks hamburgers	likes
Yussef	Thursday afternoons	uncle's shop	sells fruit and vegetables	likes
Carmen	Friday + Saturday evenings	bank	cleans offices	doesn't like
Edgar	weekends	supermarket	cuts up cardboard boxes	doesn't like

6 Lösungsvorschlag
Jane works in a fast food restaurant at the weekend. She cooks hamburgers there. She likes it because the people are OK and the work isn't too hard.
Yussef works in his uncle's shop on Thursday afternoons. He sells fruit and vegetables. He is always busy because Thursday is market day. He likes his job and only works one or two hours.
Carmen cleans offices in a bank on Friday and Saturday evenings. She doesn't like it. The money is good but it is scary when she is alone in the bank at night. Edgar works in a supermarket at the weekend. He cuts up cardboard boxes. He thinks the work is boring but his boss says he can have a better job in five or six weeks.

Seite 8

Text 2: Does school really prepare us for life?

1 1 a; 2 a; 3 c; 4 b

2 1 c; 2 b; 3 a; 4 c; 5 b

Seite 9

3 1 to; 2 of; 3 after; 4 about; 5 for

4 1 E; 2 A; 3 G; 4 B; 5 D

5 Freie Übung

Lösungen zu den Units, Exam preparation Seiten und Extra grammar

Seite 10
Job profile: Veterinary assistants

1 Lucy – animal clinic; John – zoo; Barbara – farm

2
2. He or she holds animals for the vet.
3. He or she talks to pet owners about their pets.
4. He or she files information about animals on a computer.
5. He or she gives the animals food and water.
6. He or she washes the animals.

Seite 11
Managing situations: Emailing and telephoning

1 2, 5, 6, 3, 1, 4

2
2. Mrs Thompson – 879 046 – dog, Ben – 2.45 p.m.
3. Miss Watson – 978 665 – cat, Sammy – 3.00 p.m.
4. Mr or Mrs Miller – 765 938 – cat, Napoleon – 3.30 p.m.
5. Mr Preston – 897 554 – snake, Albert – 4.00 p.m.

3 Freie Übung

Seite 12
Extra material: Albert wakes up!

1
1. Lucy is always careful with snakes.
2. She doesn't know if Albert is poisonous.
3. Lucy puts the snake into a transport box.
4. She gives the transport box to Ramon, the other assistant.
5. He opens the box because he wants to look at the snake.
6. The snake goes around his arm.
7. Ramon shouts for help because he is afraid.
8. Lucy moves towards the snake.

2 Freie Übung

Unit 2: Friends

Seite 13
Springboard

1 Freie Übung

2 1 Angus; 2 Fiona; 3 Ian; 4 Cary; 5 Tom; 6 Irene

Seite 14
Text 1: Q & A with Big Ed

1 1 Edwina; 2 Neil; 3 Brenda; 4 Billy

2 1 C; 2 H; 3 B; 4 D; 5 A; 6 G; 7 F; 8 E

Seite 15

3 1 Brenda; 2 Edwina; 3 Billy; 4 Neil

4 1 b; 2 c; 3 a; 4 b

5 1 was; 2 happened; 3 Did you have; 4 shouted; 5 told; 6 did he say; 7 had; 8 found; 9 lied; 10 told; 11 belonged; 12 wasn't; 13 didn't you tell; 14 thought; 15 needed

Seite 16
Text 2: An unexpected friend

1 1 false; 2 true; 3 true; 4 false; 5 not in the text; 6 true; 7 false; 8 false; 9 not in the text

Seite 17

2
1. After school, Samantha Denny delivers an evening newspaper to people's homes.
2. Last year Sam didn't miss a single day of work.
3. She won the 'Top Round' competition and the prize was a weekend in Dublin.
4. Sam couldn't do her newspaper round on Friday and Saturday because she was sick.
5. The prize this year is a weekend in Tenerife.
6. Sam was bitter because she wouldn't win the prize and the end of the year was only 10 days away.

(3) 1 pain; 2 article; 3 evening; 4 competition; 5 round; 6 marketing

(4) 1 bad; 2 winner; 3 sick; 4 win; 5 hard; 6 the end; 7 happy; 8 wonderful; 9 morning

(5) *Lösungsvorschlag*
Samantha Denny trägt Zeitungen aus. Letztes Jahr hat sie an einem Wettbewerb teilgenommen und gewonnen, weil sie das ganze Jahr keinen einzigen Tag krank war. Ihre Belohnung war ein Wochenende in Dublin. Dieses Jahr hat Samantha aber Bauchschmerzen und hat zwei Tage bei der Arbeit gefehlt. Sie denkt, dass sie den diesjährigen Wettbewerb nicht gewinnen kann. Dann ruft ihre Kollegin Rita an. Sie hat mit ihrer Chefin gesprochen und hat vereinbart, dass Rita Samanthas Zeitungen austragen würde, wenn beide Mädchen sich den Preis teilen können. Die zwei Mädchen fahren für ein Wochenende nach Teneriffa.

(6) Freie Übung

(7) *Lösungsvorschlag*
The best thing that happened to me last year was my birthday. I had a really nice party. My best friend lives in a town far away but he came to the party as a surprise. We had a lot of fun.

Seite 18

Job profile: Airport personnel

(1) 1 B; 2 D; 3 A; 4 C

Seite 19

Managing situations: Mediation

(1) 1 C, 2 G, 3 F, 4 B, 5 D, 6 A, 7 H, 8 E

(2) *Lösungsvorschlag*
1 She needs the nursery. Nehmen sie die Rolltreppe bis zur nächsten Etage und gehen Sie rechts lang. Der Wickelraum ist gegenüber dem Buchladen.

2 They need information about hotels / a hotel room. Der Hotelinformationsschalter ist im Erdgeschoss am Terminal 2. Der Bus fährt alle zehn Minuten.

3 She needs the luggage lockers. Sie sollten den Fahrstuhl dort drüben benutzen und dann bis zum Keller fahren. Die Gepäckschließfächer sind gegenüber dem Fahrstuhl.

Seite 20

Extra material: A holiday in Tenerife

(1)
1 The colour of the sand is black.
2 Martin met the girls on his first day on holiday in Tenerife.
3 The two girls come from Hartlepool in the north of England.
4 The girls laughed at his school CD because all the speakers are from the south of England and they talk in a funny way.
5 No, the girls' hotel is on the other side of the town.
6 Martin and the girls want to meet on the beach at 10 o'clock. They want to look around the harbour and visit an old castle.

Seite 21

Exam preparation

(1)
1.1 Steve and his father kept crocodiles, snakes and lizards in their zoo.
1.2 Steve became well known in Queensland because he caught crocodiles in towns and cities and took them to quiet rivers.
1.3 His honeymoon was unusual because he took his new wife to catch crocodiles.

Seite 22

(2) 2.1 richtig; 2.2 falsch; 2.3 falsch; 2.4 richtig; 2.5 falsch; 2.6 true; 2.7 true; 2.8 false; 2.9 true; 2.10 false

Lösungen zu den Units, Exam preparation Seiten und Extra grammar

3
- **3.1** Steve Irwin learned about crocodiles when he helped his father at the zoo when he was little.
- **3.2** Steve's zoo became popular because his visitors liked watching the feeding of the crocodiles.
- **3.3** Steve became very rich when he made the TV series "The Crocodile Hunter" and "The Ten Deadliest Snakes in the World".
- **3.4** Some naturalists didn't like Steve's films because they made the animals seem more dangerous than they were and because they thought Steve was only interested in making money.

4 4.1 e; 4.2 b; 4.3 g; 4.4 c; 5 a

Unit 3: Partners

Seite 23

Springboard

1 1 waiter/waitress; 2 caterer; 3 barista; 4 cook; 5 bakery assistant; 6 barman

2 1 cook; 2 caterer; 3 waiter/waitress; 4 barista; 5 barman; 6 bakery assistant

3
1. A waiter serves meals to restaurant guests.
2. A caterer delivers food to firms and private homes.
3. A barista makes coffee in a café.
4. A cook cooks food in a restaurant kitchen.
5. A bakery assistant sells bread and cakes in a baker's shop.
6. A barman mixes cocktails in a hotel bar.

Seite 24

Text 1: Barista of the month

1
1. Dean didn't like the hard work or the dirt.
2. Dean thought the barista's job was a good job because it was clean, warm, he could wear normal clothes and it was a good place to meet people.
3. The real job was hard work because he had to learn lots of things very fast.
4. Dean stayed in the job because one of the waitresses helped him.

2
1. When he was a dustman, Dean collected rubbish.
2. Buckstar has a branch in Manchester City Centre.
3. A coffee bar is a good place to meet people.
4. In his first few weeks, Dean made a lot of mistakes.
5. Dean's girlfriend helped him with the handbook.

Seite 25

3 1 richtig; 2 falsch; 3 falsch; 4 falsch; 5 false; 6 true; 7 false; 8 false

4 1 D; 2 F; 3 A; 4 H; 5 B

5 1 in; 2 with; 3 at; 4 after; 5 for; 6 to

Seite 26

Text 2: Their first flat

1
1. Maureen and Dean are looking for a bigger flat because they want to move in together.
2. They are looking for flats in their local newspaper.
3. When they find the advert, they call and make an appointment.
4. Dean doesn't like Mrs Chapman's flat because it's too small.
5. Maureen doesn't like it because the rooms are dark and dirty.
6. They won't look at another flat today because Maureen is tired and hungry.

Seite 27

2
1. Maureen is reading a newspaper.
2. Maureen and Dean are looking at a map.
3. Maureen and Dean are waiting for a bus.
4. Maureen and Dean are looking around a flat.

Lösungen zu den Units, Exam preparation Seiten und Extra grammar

5 Maureen and Dean are talking about the flat.

3 1 C; 2 E; 3 D; 4 A; 5 B

Seite 28

Job profile: Jobs in a restaurant

1 1 B; 2 D; 3 A; 4 E; 5 C

2
1 Jane is at the market. She is buying fruit and vegetables.
2 Jane is answering the phone and making reservations.
3 Jane is talking to the cook. They are planning meals.
4 The restaurant is busy. Jane is helping the waitresses.

Seite 29

Managing situations: Giving directions

1 Names: Times: Number of guests:
Chapman   7.30 p.m.   2
Matheson   8 p.m.   5
Whittaker   7.15 p.m.   4
Ryder   6.30 p.m.   6

2 *Lösungsvorschlag*
Turn right when leave station, walk along New Street, over river, cross Gart Street into Bridge Street, at crossroads turn left into Hill Road, King Street is second street on right

3 Freie Übung

Seite 30

Extra material: First dates

1 Bob and Kathryn; Louise and Gordon; John and Doreen; Rachel and Robert

2 *Lösungsvorschlag*
When I go on a first date, I suggest we go to the cinema. I prefer to talk a bit first and then if I don't like my date, I don't have to talk to him during the film. But if I do like him, we can have something to drink afterwards and have fun.

Unit 4: Old world and new world

Seite 31

Springboard

1 1 C; 2 D; 3 B; 4 A

2 *Lösungsvorschlag*
This is a photo of the new castle in Stuttgart. The kings of Württemberg lived here. It is opposite the old castle.

Seite 32

Text 1: New Scousers

Seite 33

1
1 professional woodworker, trained bricklayer and stonemason, plasterer, house painter
2 German workers have a good reputation because people respect their qualifications.
3 The synagogue on Princes Road needs a lot of repairs and renovation.
4 Dieter's job won't be easy because the old ceilings he has to repair have complicated designs.
5 The Albert Dock job is interesting because the new restaurant has to look like the old pumphouse.

2 1 F; 2 D; 3 A; 4 E; 5 B

3 1 had to; 2 can; 3 couldn't; 4 can; 5 had to; 6 can not; 7 can; 8 will have to

Seite 34

Text 2: A new business

1 1 false; 2 true; 3 false; 4 false; 5 true

Seite 35

2
1 Andreas no longer lives in Karlsruhe, he lives in Perth in Australia.
2 When he arrived, he started work in a garage.
3 During the Outback trip, Andreas travelled in an old Land Rover.

Lösungen zu den Units, Exam preparation Seiten und Extra grammar

4 After the Outback trip, he decided to buy an old Land Rover and fit it with things you need in the Outback.
5 Next year he wants to rent a bigger workshop and employ another mechanic.

3 1 trailer; 2 flashlight; 3 battery; 4 tent; 5 sleeping bag; 6 gas cooker

4
Name:	Kathy
Age:	17
Leisure:	judo, reading, listening to music, horse riding
Job plans:	veterinary assistant

Name:	Basir
Age:	17
Leisure:	football, collecting football shirts, cars, motorbikes
Job plans:	mechanic

Name:	Liam
Age:	16
Leisure:	fishing, reading (thrillers), music
Job plans:	baker

Name:	Audrey
Age:	16
Leisure:	swimming, jogging, snooker
Job plans:	bus driver or professional snooker player

5 Freie Übung

Seite 36

Job profile: A car mechanic

1 1 tyre; 2 wheel; 3 windscreen; 4 engine; 5 steering wheel; 6 clutch; 7 brake; 8 accelerator; 9 lights; 10 exhaust

2
1 At work a mechanic should always wear safety glasses to protect his eyes.
2 He should wear protective gloves to protect his hands.
3 He should wear protective boots to protect his feet.
4 He should wear a safety helmet to protect his head.
5 He should wear ear protectors to protect his ears.
6 He should wear a cup mask to protect his lungs.

Seite 37

Managing situations: Operating instructions

1
1 Die Maschine kann Holz und Metall bohren.
2 Bevor Sie eine Holzschraube festdrehen, müssen Sie ein Probeloch bohren.
3 Mit dem ‚adjusting ring' wechseln Sie die Funktion der Maschine.
4 Bevor Sie Stahl anbohren, sollten Sie eine Einbuchtung ins Metall machen.
5 Eisen und Messing brauchen keine Bohrflüssigkeiten beim Bohren.

Seite 38

Extra material: Safety rules

1 1 concentrate on; 2 clean and well lit; 3 the rain or wet conditions; 4 safety glasses or goggles; 5 loose clothes; 6 power source; 7 power cord; 8 materials and purpose

Seite 39

Exam preparation

1
1.1 The posters were so shocking because Isabelle looked like a living skeleton with very thin arms and legs.
1.2 The Nolita campaign was a campaign by an Italian clothes firm against size zero models.
1.3 Isabelle ate just one square of chocolate a day and a cup of tea without sugar.

Seite 40

2 2.1 falsch; 2.2 richtig; 2.3 richtig; 2.4 falsch; 2.5 richtig; 2.6 true; 2.7 false; 2.8 true; 2.9 false; 2.10 true

Lösungen zu den Units, Exam preparation Seiten und Extra grammar

3
3.1 Photos of Isabelle Caro shocked people because she looked like a living skeleton.
3.2 The campaign warned young girls about anorexia and trying to look like a size zero model.
3.3 Anorexia helped Isabelle's career because she stayed thin and got lots of modelling jobs.
3.4 The doctors at the hospital thought Isabelle would die because she was in a coma for four days and needed seven blood transfusions.

4 4.1 b; 4.2 e; 4.3 a; 4.4 g; 4.5 d

Seite 41

5 5.1 stick; 5.2 coma; 5.3 dying; 5.4 fat; 5.5 more

6 6.1 **1** saw; **2** turned; **3** organized; **4** has become; **5** will want
6.2 **1** since; **2** from; **3** many; **4** healthier; **5** young

Seite 42

7 *Lösungsvorschlag*
75% der Leute, die ein Tattoo machen lassen, wollen dieses später entfernen lassen. Louis Malloy ist ein professioneller Tätowierer und gibt Leuten Rat, die überlegen ein Tattoo machen zu lassen. Bevor man ein Tattoo stechen lässt, sollte man gut darüber nachdenken; man behält das Tattoo lebenslang. Man sollte u. a. überlegen wie groß es sein soll und wo man es stechen lassen will. Es ist ratsam kein billiges Tattoo zu kaufen und man sollte immer einen professionellen, erfahrenen Tätowierer wählen. Das Studio muss sauber sein und man sollte das Tattoo gut nachbehandeln lassen.

8 *Lösungsvorschlag*
1 I like tattoos. I think they look really nice. Lots of celebrities like David Beckham and Robbie Williams have them so it is fashionable at the moment.
2 I don't like tattoos. I think they look horrible. Also a tattoo is for life, it is difficult to remove them. A tattoo might look good now but they don't look good when you are old.

Seite 43

9 9.1 Turn right and walk along Station Street. Take the second turning on the left into Old High Street. Cross Green Way and the bank is then on the right.
9.2 Um diese Kasse zu benutzen, muss man weniger als 7 Waren haben.

Seite 44

10 10.1 d; 10.2 g; 10.3 e; 10.4 a; 10.5 h; 10.6 b; 10.7 f; 10.8 c

11 Freie Übung

Unit 5: Media stars

Seite 45

Springboard

1 Kate Moss – Rimmel; Thomas Gottschalk – Haribo; Franz Beckenbauer – O2; Penelope and Monica Cruz – Mango

2 Freie Übung

Seite 46

Text 1: James Dean – a media icon

1 1 actor; 2 uncle; 3 farm; 4 short; 5 cheap; 6 crash

2 1 James Dean was born in 1931.
2 He lived in Indiana until 1949 when he went to New York.
3 Although he was a good actor, he only worked as an 'extra' in cheap films.
4 His first big role was (in 1955) in the film 'East of Eden'.
5 In the same year he acted in 'Rebel Without a Cause' and 'Giant'.
6 James died in a car crash on the 30th of September, 1955.

Lösungen zu den Units, Exam preparation Seiten und Extra grammar

3 1 short; 2 good; 3 short; 4 cheap; 5 east; 6 young; 7 handsome; 8 dangerous; 9 love

4 Freie Übung

Seite 47

5 1 Ted got up at 5.30 a. m. yesterday. / Yesterday Ted got up at 5.30 a. m.
2 In 1942 my parents moved into a small apartment in Skipper's Lane.
3 Yesterday afternoon we drove to a beach near Dover on the south coast.
4 Our coach arrived at our hotel in Madrid yesterday afternoon at 6.15 p. m. / Yesterday afternoon at 6.15 p. m. our coach arrived at our hotel in Madrid.
5 Our club meets at 4.30 every Thursday afternoon.

6

Name	Date of birth	Place of birth	Date of death	Place of death
James Dean	8th February, 1931	Marion, Indiana	30th September, 1955	Cholame, California
Charlie Chaplin	16th April, 1889	London, England	25th December, 1977	Vevey, Switzerland
Marlene Dietrich	27th December, 1901	Schöneberg, Germany	6th May, 1992	Paris, France
Elvis Presley	8th January, 1935	Tupelo, Mississippi	16th August, 1977	Memphis, Tennessee

Seite 48

Text 2: The Beckhams Ltd

1 1 G; 2 K; 3 A; 4 C; 5 F; 6 H; 7 I; 8 E

Seite 49

2 *Lösungsvorschlag*
Die Familie Beckham ist sehr berühmt und deswegen ist sie bei Werbefirmen begehrt; die Firmen bezahlen Millionen, damit die Beckhams in Werbespots mitspielen. Die Beckhams nutzen ihr Geld aber auch für wohltätige Zwecke. Zum Beispiel kaufen sie Rollstühle für behinderte Kinder, die sich diese nicht leisten können. Die Beckhams haben auch der Wohltätigkeitsorganisation Malaria No More geholfen. Diese will Moskitonetze an jede arme Familie in Afrika verteilen. Diese Moskitonetze kosten nur $10 pro Stück aber, sie schützen eine Mutter und ihr Kind fünf Jahre lang. David Beckham hat ein Video für Malaria No More gedreht und viele Leute haben es gesehen und Millionen von Dollar dafür gespendet.

3 1 Ollie Rycraft needed a special wheelchair but his parents couldn't afford it.
2 People watched the video clip on TV or on the internet.
3 Poor families in Africa can't afford bed nets, so 'Malaria No More' buys the bed nets for them.
4 David plays football and Victoria sings.
5 When the Beckhams support a charity, millions of people will donate money to it. / Millions of people will donate money to a charity when the Beckhams support it.
6 The Beckhams are media icons because lots of people admire them. / Because lots of people admire them, the Beckhams are media icons.

Seite 50

Job profile: Roadies

1 1 tour manager; 2 rigger; 3 driver; 4 beautician; 5 lighting/sound technician; 6 cook

2 1 D/G; 2 J/B; 3 H/A; 4 C/E; 5 L/I; 6 K/F

Seite 51

Managing situations: Safety at work

1 1 This means don't enter this room. 2 This is where you can find a first aid box. 3 You must wear a safety helmet here. 4 This is where you can find an emergency exit. 5 Be careful! The substances here are toxic. 6 This means don't smoke. 7 Be careful! The floor here is slippery. 8 You must wear safety goggles here.

2 *Lösungsvorschlag*
Heute Morgen gegen 10.30 ist unser Lehrling Martin hingefallen. Er befand sich vor der Hauptwerkstatt, wo der Boden ein wenig nass war. Es war keine Warntafel angebracht, sodass er ausgerutscht und hingefallen ist. Er hat sich sein rechtes Bein verletzt.

Seite 52

Extra material: Stars who care

1 1 Landmines are horrible because they kill and injure thousands of people a year, even after the wars are over.
2 Angelina Jolie supports refugee charities, the campaign to ban landmines and is an ambassador for the United Nations.
3 We should pay a fair price because thousands of small farmers in Africa could then earn enough money to feed their families.
4 You can buy foods with fair trade labels and complain to supermarkets which don't sell fair trade products.

2 Freie Übung

Unit 6: Shopping

Seite 53

Springboard

1 1 deodorant; 2 mascara; 3 vitamin tablets; 4 lipstick; 5 nail polish; 6 headache tablets; 7 shampoo; 8 toothpaste; 9 plaster

2 bodycare: deodorant, shampoo, toothpaste; cosmetics: mascara, lipstick, nail polish; healthcare: vitamin tablets, headache tablets, plasters

3 88 p; £ 1.80; 95 p; £ 1.10; 15 p; £ 1.99

Seite 54

Text 1: Likes and dislikes

1 1 false; 2 true; 3 false; 4 true; 5 true

Seite 55

2 1 especially; 2 impatient; 3 sensible; 4 size; 5 (not) much; 6 bargains

3 1 look around; 2 walk into; 3 have to; 4 try on; 5 spend on; 6 talk about

4 1 going; 2 walking; 3 looking; 4 carrying; 5 doing; 6 shopping

5 Freie Übung

Seite 56

Text 2: Is it an original or a copy?

1 1 Designers do not like copies because they aren't as good as the original products.
2 There is sometimes no difference between designer products and the copies because they use the same materials.
3 Some designers close their factories in Europe because they can make their products more cheaply in factories in Asia.
4 Some Italian designers use Chinese workers because they are cheaper than Italian workers and work longer hours.

Lösungen zu den Units, Exam preparation Seiten und Extra grammar

2 1 earn; 2 factory; 3 outsourcing; 4 firm; 5 immigrant

Seite 57

3 1 guarantee; 2 pirate; 3 cheaper; 4 designers; 5 factories; 6 longer; 7 less; 8 workers; 9 Italian; 10 immigrants

4 *Lösungsvorschlag*
1 I think pirate copies are OK because the originals are too expensive. Many people can't afford real ones. We should buy copies because they are cheaper. The designers earn a lot of money anyway.
2 I disagree with pirate copies because it's not fair for the designers. They don't make any money from copies but it is their design. We shouldn't buy pirate copies because the originals are often better quality.

5 1 cheaper; 2 more expensive; 3 prettiest; 4 more; 5 taller, thinner; 6 more complicated; 7 most famous; 8 best

Seite 58

Job profile: Sales assistant

1 B, E, G, C, D, F, A

2 Freie Übung

Seite 59

Managing situations: Talking about jobs & directions

1 1 right; 2 Baker Street; 3 Low Road; 4 High Street; 5 bank

2 Freie Übung

3 1 The boutique is open from 9 until 5.30 Monday to Saturday and from 10 until 4 on Sunday.
2 John's main jobs are sorting the clothes out, helping customers, counting money and cleaning the shop.

4 Freie Übung

Seite 60

Extra material: The January sales

1 *Lösungsvorschlag*
1 Ted and Lucy see an advert for the sales in the paper. They decide to go early to get a good place.
2 Ted and Lucy join the queue. There are already a few people there.
3 Ted and Lucy wait patiently in the queue. They drink tea because it is cold.
4 The store unlocks the doors and there's a great rush. Lucy and Ted decide to meet outside later.
5 Ted and Lucy come out of the shop with a lot of purchases. Ted has bought a digital camera.
6 Ted already had a camera but this one is better.
7 Ted shows Lucy what else he has bought. He got a jacket, shoes and a T-shirt.
8 Ted asks Lucy what she bought. She has a lot of bags.

Seite 61

Exam preparation

1 1.1 peaceful; 1.2 landlord; 1.3 poor; 1.4 quiet; 1.5 old

Seite 62

2 2.1 1 are; 2 looks; 3 is going; 4 received; 5 will get
2.2 1 the same; 2 better; 3 more comfortable; 4 many; 5 his

3 *Lösungsvorschlag*
Andy Clipston hat die alte Dorfkneipe gekauft, um sie abzureißen. Er baute sie aber sieben Monate später wieder auf. Es war genau dieselbe, nur weiter von der Autobahn entfernt. Er hatte Angst, dass die Autobahn die Kneipe zerstört und wollte sie retten. Andy ist nun Wirt der Kneipe und musste alles über Bier und wie man eine Kneipe führt lernen. Die neugebaute Kneipe ist jetzt Treffpunkt für

viele Vereine wie ein Billiardverein und es gibt jeden Freitag und am Wochenende Musik, sowie britische und thailändische Küche. Die Kneipe hat jetzt einen Preis gewonnen – sie ist zur besten neugebauten Kneipe gewählt worden.

④ *Lösungsvorschlag*
1 I think that the pub is more important. It is the place where people go to see friends and neighbours. It is also often where different clubs and sport teams meet. Discos are just for young people.
2 In my opinion, a disco is more important. It is good that young people have somewhere to go, especially in small villages. Often, there are only older people in a village pub.

Unit 7: Food and exercise

Seite 63

Springboard

① Freie Übung

② protein: sausage, ice cream, peanuts, sardines; carbohydrates: bread; vitamins: cucumber, orange juice, strawberries; fat: sausage, ice cream, chocolate

③ Freie Übung

Seite 64

Text 1: A healthy lifestyle

① 1 nutrition; 2 overweight; 3 lifestyles; 4 exercise; 5 lean

Seite 65

② 1 Overweight teenagers need to change their lifestyle, exercise and eat healthily.
2 In a special course teenagers learn about exercise, physical activity and healthy food.
3 Healthy food contains less fat, sugar and salt and more vitamins and fibre.

③ 1 has helped; 2 has worked; 3 have started; 4 have just moved; 5 has written; 6 has just seen

④ Freie Übung

Seite 66

Text 2: Captain Cook and a space flight to Mars

① *Lösungsvorschlag*
Eine lange Reise in einem Raumschiff und eine Reise in einem alten Segelschiff hat eine Gemeinsamkeit – gesundes Essen. Auf beiden Reisen ist es problematisch, genügend Vitamine zu bekommen. Das war auch früher ein Problem für Segler. Nach einigen Monaten ohne frisches Essen wurden sie krank – ihre Haut wurde schwarz, ihre Haare und Zähne fielen aus, viele starben. Captain Cook fand jedoch eine Lösung. Seine Segler aßen frische Eier zum Frühstück, die sie in Öl frisch hielten. Sie aßen auch viel Sauerkraut, da es viele Vitamine enthält. Es gab auch ‚Grog' zu trinken, eine Mischung aus starkem Rum und Wasser. Dazu bekamen die Segler saubere Kleidung, viel Schlaf und organisierte Freizeitaktivitäten.

Seite 67

② 1 died; 2 simple; 3 big; 4 long; 5 disinfected; 6 more

③ 1 voyage; 2 sailor; 3 leisure

④ 1 that/which; 2 who/that; 3 which/that; 4 that/who; 5 which/that; 6 which/that

⑤ 1 He was born on 27th of October, 1728 in Marton, a village in the north of England.
2 First he was a farmworker and then a shop assistant.
3 He found his next job in Whitby. He became a sailor.
4 A 'cat' was a small ship that took coal to London.
5 When he left Whitby, James was 27.

Lösungen zu den Units, Exam preparation Seiten und Extra grammar

Seite 68

Job profile: Fitness trainer

1 1 head; 2 neck; 3 arm; 4 chest; 5 back; 6 leg; 7 foot; 8 knee

2 head: hair, face, teeth; torso: chest, stomach; arm: hand, elbow; leg: foot, knee etc.

Seite 69

Managing situations: Telephoning

1 1 A; 2 B; 3 G; 4 C; 5 H/I; 6 D; 7 K/L; 8 E; 9 F; 10 J

2 *Lösungsvorschlag*
A Good morning. Pep Fitness Studio.
B Good morning. James Smith speaking.
A Louise here. How can I help you?
B Can you put me through to Mr Hope, please?
A I'm afraid he isn't available. He's in a meeting. Would you like to leave a message?
B Thanks. Can you ask him to call me back, please? My number is 654 789.

Seite 70

Extra material: A new TV programme

1 Freie Übung

Unit 8: Adventures in Australia

Seite 71

Springboard

1 1 Captain James Cook; 2 Aborigines; 3 boomerang; 4 didgeridoo; 5 the 'Outback'; 6 Ayer's Rock/Uluru; 7 the Great Barrier Reef; 8 koala bear

2 Freie Übung

Seite 72

Text 1: German girls find lost boy

1 1 police officer; 2 motorbike; 3 tracker dog; 4 waitress; 5 water pump; 6 sheep

Seite 73

2 1 Glen wasn't in his class, so the school called the police.
2 Two police officers arrived and called for more help and then organized a search.
3 On the first day they searched until it became dark.
4 Two German waitresses camped in the outback because they wanted to start their search early.
5 They rode to the sheep farm first because they needed water.
6 Glen ignored the two girls because he was playing with his playstation.

3 1 careful; 2 carefully; 3 angry; 4 angrily; 5 quickly; 6 quick; 7 well; 8 good

Seite 74

Text 2: Solo around the world

1 1 Jesse Martin is famous because he sailed solo around the world when he was only 17.
2 Jesse's voyage, which took eleven months, started and finished in Melbourne.
3 Jesse nearly ran into a big tanker because it was night and he didn't see it.
4 After he returned home from his voyage, Jesse ate a hamburger and then he wrote a book about his voyage.
5 'Lionheart' is the name of the boat that Jesse sailed around the world in and it's also the name of his book about the voyage.

Seite 75

2 A, F, E, D, B, C

3 1 Are; 2 Was; 3 Did; 4 Do; 5 Have

4 1 No, he didn't. 2 No, he wasn't. 3 Yes, they have. 4 Yes, it was. 5 No, he hasn't.

Lösungen zu den Units, Exam preparation Seiten und Extra grammar

Seite 76

Job profile: A woodworker

1 1 Seven people work at Oyster Bay Boatbuilders – the boss, a secretary, four woodworkers and the apprentice, Desmond.
2 He enjoys building boats in the old traditional way and he likes sailing, too.
3 He has Certificate 1 and 2 in woodworking. He is studying for Certificate 3 and hopes to start Certificate 4 next year.

2 He needs a saw to cut the timber.
He needs a drill to make holes in the wood.
He needs a nail to hold pieces of timber together.
He needs a chisel to carve the wood.
He needs a tape measure to measure the timber.
He needs a hammer to put the nails in the wood.

Seite 77

Managing situations: Small talk at a party

1 1 D; 2 C; 3 F; 4 A; 5 H; 6 G; 7 B; 8 E

Seite 78

Extra material: A job abroad

1 1 false; 2 true; 3 true; 4 false; 5 false

2 *Lösungsvorschlag*
Dear Sir or Madam
I am Thomas Frey from Germany and I am interested in your Australia working holidays programme. My English is quite good but I would like to improve it by working in Australia. I have always been interested in the country and think working is a good way to see the country. I would be interested in different types of work, for example bar work, office work and working on a farm.
I hope to hear from you soon with more details about the programme.
Yours faithfully
Thomas Frey

Seite 79

Exam preparation

1 1.1 Stephanie has worked for the Fire Department for almost seven years.
1.2 Stephanie's husband is also a firefighter in a nearby town.
1.3 Stephanie works ten days a month.

Seite 80

2 2.1 falsch; 2.2 richtig; 2.3 falsch; 2.4 falsch; 2.5 richtig; 2.6 false; 2.7 true; 2.8 true; 2.9 false; 2.10 true

3 3.1 Stephanie's fellow firefighters treat her like any other member of the team.
3.2 Stephanie is an important role model for her daughters because she is a female firefighter.
3.3 Being a firefighter is a good job for working mothers because they only have to work ten days a month.
3.4 Firefighters must be fit and strong because they have to lift and carry heavy things.

4 4.1 c; 4.2 f; 4.3 g; 4.4 b; 4.5 d

Seite 81

5 5.1 role model; 5.2 survivor; 5.3 light; 5.4 weak; 5.5 easy

6 6.1 1 started; 2 trains; 3 works; 4 is; 5 will arrive
6.2 1 her; 2 many; 3 better; 4 because; 5 more

Seite 82

7 *Lösungsvorschlag*
Jason ist auf das Dach geklettert, weil sein Ball dort war. Er ist ein Abflussrohr hochgeklettert, aber war dann nicht mutig genug, hinunterzuklettern. Seine Freunde holten seinen Vater, der mit einer Leiter versucht hat, nach oben zu gelangen. Die Leiter war aber zu kurz und er musste die Feuerwehr anrufen. Die Feuerwehr konnte Jason dann hinunter bringen. Dies war nicht das erste Mal –

Lösungen zu den Units, Exam preparation Seiten und Extra grammar

sein Vater musste Jason schon einmal von einer hohen Brücke retten. Sein Vater sagt, dass Jason nicht verstehe, wie gefährlich solche Situationen sein können.

8 *Lösungsvorschlag*
1 I think Jason was brave to go up on the roof. There are a lot of children today who are scared of a lot of things but he was not afraid. He only wanted to carry on with his game.
2 I think Jason was stupid when he climbed onto the roof. He did not stop to think about how dangerous the situation was. He could have really hurt himself. His health is more important than his ball.

Seite 83

9 9.1 Come out of the station and turn right. Walk along Station Street and take the second turning on the left, Museum Road. Walk past the art gallery on the left and the museum on the right and then the theatre is on the left.
9.2 B

Seite 84

10 10.1 e; 10.2 b; 10.3 g; 10.4 c; 10.5 d; 10.6 h; 10.7 f; 10.8 a

11 *Lösungsvorschlag*
Dear Sir or Madam
My name is Silke Hartmann and I am 17 years old. I live in Pforzheim in Germany. I speak quite good English and would like to get some experience working in a British bank. I have already had some experience as a receptionist here in Germany and think I will be good in the job.
I hope to hear from you soon.
Yours faithfully
Silke Hartmann

Extra grammar

Seite 87

Simple present

a) 2 Brad travels to the film studio by car everyday.
3 He does most of his work in America.
4 He sometimes flies to other countries.
5 Most days he works 8 or 9 hours.
6 He likes his job but he doesn't like being famous.
7 He doesn't talk to journalists very often.
8 He doesn't give many interviews.

b) 1 has; 2 play; 3 don't work; 4 Do you enjoy; 5 rains; 6 don't go

Seite 88

Present progressive

a) 2 Fatima is talking to Paul.
3 Cecelia is drinking a cola.
4 Matthew is putting his jacket on.
5 David is looking for a CD.
6 Amelia and her friend are arguing.
7 Leah is eating a piece of cake.
8 I am sitting on the sofa.

b) 1 is working; 2 helps; 3 is George doing; 4 likes, is learning; 5 is talking, are

Seite 89

Simple past

a) 1 used; 2 was; 3 opened; 4 barked; 5 scared; 6 fell; 7 started; 8 tried; 9 appeared; 10 was

b) 1 bought; 2 ate; 3 took; 4 saw, went; 5 found, knew

c) 1 didn't like; 2 didn't go, didn't have; 3 didn't like; 4 didn't come; 5 didn't finish

Seite 90

Present perfect

a) 1 for; 2 since; 3 since; 4 since; 5 for; 6 for

b) 1 has worked; 2 have been; 3 have eaten; 4 has seen; 5 have moved

Lösungen zu den Units, Exam preparation Seiten und Extra grammar

c) 1 Have you already eaten today?
2 No, I haven't eaten yet.
3 Has Michaela read this book already?
4 Have Jan and Oskar already seen this film?
5 I have known Susan for years.

Seite 91

Questions and short answers

a) 2 Do you have many DVDs?
3 Were you at the party yesterday?
4 Has she lived here long?
5 Can you sing well?
6 What are you doing?
7 Has he been to England?
8 Are you going to the supermarket now?

b) 1 No, I haven't. 2 Yes, I did. 3 Yes, he is. 4 No, I can't. 5 No, I don't. 6 Yes, I can. 7 No, I'm not. 8 Yes, I have.

Seite 92

Modal verbs

a) 1 must; 2 cannot; 3 has to; 4 can; 5 could; 6 had to

b) 1 D; 2 F; 3 H; 4 C; 5 A; 6 B; 7 E; 8 G

Seite 93

-ing form

a) 1 listening; 2 organising; 3 writing; 4 making; 5 studying; 6 building

b) 1 C; 2 A; 3 E; 4 B; 5 D

c) 2 Tony likes playing the guitar.
3 Do you like playing football?
4 My father doesn't like reading.
5 Do you like going to the cinema?
6 We don't like going to the dentist.
7 My mother likes buying shoes.
8 Matthew is good at cooking.

Seite 94

Relative pronouns

a) 1 B; 2 A; 3 B; 4 A; 5 B

b) 1 who; 2 which; 3 which; 4 who; 5 who

Seite 95

Adjectives and adverbs

a) 1 well; 2 expensive; 3 good; 4 great, wonderful; 5 happy; 6 hard; 7 beautiful; 8 slowly

b) 1 tired, badly; 2 fast, dangerous; 3 loud, properly; 4 well, well; 5 hard, difficult; 6 new, really, friendly; 7 extremely, nice; 8 quickly

Seite 96

Comparison of adjectives

a) 2 Madonna is older than Britney Spears.
3 The Nile is longer than the Thames.
4 Gold is more expensive than plastic.
5 Metal is heavier than paper.
6 Scotland is smaller than France.

b) 2 the thinnest; 3 the tallest; 4 the nicest; 5 the most intelligent; 6 the most annoying; 7 the shortest; 8 the richest

c) 1 most expensive; 2 bigger; 3 prettiest; 4 better; 5 smaller; 6 worst

Seite 97

Word order

a) 1 A; 2 B, 3 B; 4 A; 5 A

b) 1 so; 2 when; 3 but; 4 or; 5 because

Seite 98

Prepositions

a) 1 B; 2 A; 3 B; 4 B; 5 A; 6 B

b) 1 on; 2 to; 3 for; 4 at; 5 before; 6 on; 7 behind; 8 from; 9 with; 10 up

Englisch

Pete Oldham

Job Fit Englisch wurde geplant und entwickelt von der Redaktion Moderne Fremdsprachen des Cornelsen Verlags, Berlin.

Verfasser:	Pete Oldham, Barsinghausen
Beraterinnen:	Gabriele Holtermann, Ludwigsburg
	Margarete Nawaz, Pforzheim
Projektleitung:	Jim Austin
Verlagsredaktion:	Kari-ann Seamark
Redaktionelle Mitarbeit:	Leah Holroyd, Fritz Preuß
Gesamtgestaltung und technische Umsetzung:	Klein & Halm Grafikdesign, Berlin
Bildredaktion:	Gertha Maly
Umschlaggestaltung:	Klein & Halm Grafikdesign, Berlin
Titelfoto:	F1 online/PBY
Illustrationen:	Oxford Designers & Illustrators

Erhältlich sind auch:
Audio-CD   ISBN 978-3-06-450275-8
Handreichungen für den Unterricht   ISBN 978-3-06-020085-6

www.cornelsen.de

1. Auflage, 1. Druck 2009

Alle Drucke dieser Auflage sind inhaltlich unverändert
und können im Unterricht nebeneinander verwendet werden.

© 2009 Cornelsen Verlag, Berlin

Das Werk und seine Teile sind urheberrechtlich geschützt.
Jede Nutzung in anderen als den gesetzlich zugelassenen Fällen bedarf
der vorherigen schriftlichen Einwilligung des Verlages.
Hinweis zu den § 46, 52a UrhG: Weder das Werk noch seine Teile dürfen ohne eine
solche Einwilligung eingescannt und in ein Netzwerk eingestellt oder sonst öffentlich
zugänglich gemacht werden.
Dies gilt auch für Intranets von Schulen und sonstigen Bildungseinrichtungen.

Druck: CS-Druck CornelsenStürtz, Berlin

ISBN 978-3-06-450274-1

 Inhalt gedruckt auf säurefreiem Papier aus nachhaltiger Forstwirtschaft.

Vorwort

Der Übergang von der Schule ins Berufsleben stellt einen wichtigen Lebensabschnitt dar. **Job fit Englisch** soll Ihnen diesen Übergang erleichtern. Das Lehrwerk trainiert gezielt Ihre Kommunikationsfertigkeiten für das Berufsleben. Damit festigt der Kurs auch die notwendigen Kompetenzen der Stufe A2 des europäischen Referenzrahmens.

Acht Units befassen sich mit dem Umfeld Jugendlicher, mit Lebensgewohnheiten, Freizeit, Freunden, Landeskunde und Beruf. Eine *Springboard*-Seite bietet einen lockeren Einstieg in jede Unit. Der ‚In dieser Unit lerne ich'-Kasten vermittelt, was in der Unit auf Sie zukommt und der ‚Ich kann'-Kasten am Ende der Unit hilft Ihnen, Ihre Fähigkeiten einzuschätzen. Auf Doppelseiten werden spannende allgemeine und berufsbezogene Texte mit abwechslungsreichen Übungen angeboten; grammatische Grundstrukturen werden auch wiederholt und gefestigt. Die Sonderseiten *Job profile* bieten Einblicke in den englischsprachigen Berufsalltag. Für leistungsstärkere Klassen gibt es abschließend eine *Extra material*-Seite, die anspruchsvollere Texte und Übungen beinhaltet.

Exam preparation-Seiten bieten zusätzliche Materialien, um Ihre Prüfungsfertigkeiten zu trainieren. Zur Weiterarbeit steht außerdem im Anhang ein zusätzlicher Grammatikteil zur Verfügung. Hier gibt es weitere Erklärungen und Übungen, um das Wissen zu festigen.

Lerntipps, Wörterverzeichnisse und eine Liste unregelmäßiger Verben erleichtern ebenfalls Ihre Arbeit. Die eingelegten Lösungen erlauben Ihnen, selbstständig und eigenverantwortlich zu lernen.

Wir hoffen, dass Ihnen die Arbeit mit dem Buch Freude bereitet und wünschen Ihnen viel Erfolg!

Content

Unit	Grammar	Job profile	Managing situations	Extra material	Page
1 Between school and work	Simple present	Veterinary assistants	Emailing & telephoning	Albert wakes up!	5
2 Friends	Simple past	Airport personnel	Mediation	A holiday in Tenerife	13
Exam preparation					21
3 Partners	Prepositions Present progressive	Jobs in a restaurant	Giving directions	First dates	23
4 Old world and new world	Modal verbs	Car mechanic	Operating instructions	Safety rules	31
Exam preparation					39
5 Media stars	Word order	Roadies	Safety at work	Stars who care	45
6 Shopping	-ing form Comparison of adjectives	Sales assistant	Talking about jobs & directions	The January sales	53
Exam preparation					61
7 Food and exercise	Present perfect Relative pronouns	Fitness trainer	Telephoning	A new TV programme	63
8 Adventures in Australia	Adjectives & adverbs Questions & short answers	Woodworker	Small talk at a party	A job abroad	71
Exam preparation					79

Lerntipps 85

Extra grammar 87

Irregular verbs 99

Grundwortschatz 100

Chronologisches Wörterverzeichnis 104

Alphabetisches Wörterverzeichnis   Deutsch – Englisch 116

Alphabetisches Wörterverzeichnis   Englisch – Deutsch 121

Between school and work

Unit 1

Springboard

> **In dieser Unit lerne ich, …**
> - über Wünsche zu sprechen;
> - eine Meinung zu vertreten;
> - über regelmäßige Handlungen zu sprechen (*simple present*).

1 Look at the photos. What do these young people want?

The	girl / boy	in photo	one two …	wants	a TV. a mountain bike. an MP3 player. a mobile phone. a dog. a moped.

2 Listen to the CD and make notes. Now you can say who the young people in the photos are and what they want.

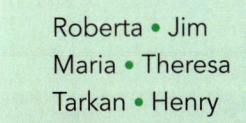

Roberta • Jim
Maria • Theresa
Tarkan • Henry

Roberta wants a …   *Jim wants a …*

3 What things do you want?

I want a/an …   *I also want a/an …*

Text 1: Extra money is useful

Theresa Galvan:
I work in an animal clinic at weekends. I'm an animal attendant. I help Ramon and Lucy, the veterinary assistants. I clean the cages and give the animals food and water. All the people here are friendly and I like animals. I buy clothes with my money. I want to wear what I like and not what my mother likes!

Jim Scott:
My parents can't give me pocket money because they are out of work. So I deliver newspapers in the morning. I also walk dogs in the afternoon. I love dogs and we have a lot of fun. At weekends I do garden work. I spend some money on clothes but I save the rest because I want a moped.

Henry and Roberta Davenport:
Our parents buy our clothes and everything we need for school. They also give us pocket money. But extra money is always useful. That's why we do jobs for our neighbours. For example, they give us a list and we go to the supermarket for them. We also wash cars in the summer and clear snow in the winter. We wash their dogs, too – but only the small ones!

 a) Aussagen über den Text. Sind sie richtig oder falsch?

1 Theresa Galvan arbeitet in einer Tierklinik.
2 Sie ist Tierarzthelferin.
3 Ramon und Lucy sind Tierpfleger.
4 Theresa kauft Make-up und CDs.
5 Beide Eltern von Jim Scott haben gute Stellen.
6 Jim trägt Zeitungen aus, führt Hunde spazieren und macht Gartenarbeit.

b) Statements about the text. Are they true or false?

7 Jim wants a mokick.
8 Henry and Roberta Davenport don't get pocket money.
9 They wash their neighbours' cars and do their shopping.
10 They wash dogs – the bigger the better!

2 Look at the photos. Find the English names in the three texts.

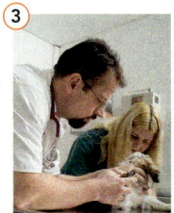

Unit 1

3 Look at the three texts and find the opposites of these words.

(Theresa)
1 unfriendly (line 3)
2 sell (line 4)
3 father (line 5)

(Jim)
4 in work (line 7)
5 hate (line 8)
6 a little (line 9)
7 spend (line 10)

(Henry and Roberta)
8 nothing (line 12)
9 take (line 13)
10 useless (line 14)

Grammar

Remember: simple present

- Wir benutzten das *simple present*, um regelmäßige Handlungen zu beschreiben.
  I **work** in an animal clinic.

- Die drei Stolpersteine sind:
  ▶ die 3. Person Singular (*he/she/it*): Theresa **works** in an animal clinic.
  ▶ die Bildung von Fragen: **Do** Ramon and Lucy **work** with Theresa? – Yes, they **do**.
  Does Theresa **enjoy** her work? – Yes, she **does**.
  ▶ Verneinungen: Ramon and Lucy **don't help** Theresa, she helps them.
  Theresa **does**n't **buy** make-up with her money.

- Signalwörter sind: *always, often, at six o'clock, on Monday,* usw.

4 Complete the sentences with the correct form of the verbs in brackets.

1 (like)   Theresa … animals.
2 (enjoy)   She … her job in the animal clinic.
3 (not work)   Mr and Mrs Scott … .
4 (get)   … Jim Scott … pocket money? – No, he … .
5 (love)   … you … animals, too? – Yes, I … .

▶ Mehr Übungen zum Thema *simple present* finden Sie auf Seite 87.

5 Copy this table into an exercise book. Then listen to the CD and make notes.

WHO?	WHEN?	WHERE?	DOES WHAT?	LIKES/DOESN'T LIKE?
Jane	*weekends*			
Yussef		*uncle's shop*		
Carmen			*cleans offices*	
Edgar				*doesn't like*

6 Now use your notes and write about these four people and their jobs.

- Exchange texts with a partner and check each other's work. Look for spelling and grammar mistakes and missing information.
- A final check: Listen to the CD again. Is everything correct?

Text 2: Does school really prepare us for life?

5 Jane, Marco, Henry and Sally are friends at school. They often sit together and talk after lunch.

	Marco	I want to leave school and get a job. School is a waste of time.
	Henry	I want a job, too – but a good job. A school qualification will help me.
5	Marco	I know that. But I'll never need some of the things we learn. What good are algebra and geometry? I'll never need them in a job.
	Sally	You're right. Things like that are no good for us.
	Jane	We learn them because they're in the final exam and we want to pass it.
10	Marco	Yes, but that isn't a good reason.
	Sally	Not every subject is useless. We learn Spanish. That's useful. It means we can look for jobs in Spain, too.
	Marco	Yes, OK. Not everything is useless.
	Sally	What would you change, Marco? Can you give us some examples?
15	Marco	Yes. We should learn more about life after school. Practical things that will help us.
	Henry	OK. Let's make a list of practical and useful topics. What do we want to learn about?

1 Statements about the text. Choose the correct answer.

1 Henry thinks
   a) a school qualification is useful.
   b) all qualifications are useful.
   c) a school qualification is useless.

2 Jane
   a) wants to pass the final school exam.
   b) isn't interested in the final school exam.
   c) thinks she can't pass the final school exam.

3 Sally thinks
   a) all school subjects are useful.
   b) only Spanish is a useful school subject.
   c) other school subjects are useful, too.

4 Marco thinks
   a) all school subjects are useless.
   b) some school subjects are useless.
   c) all school subjects are useful.

2 Odd one out: Which word doesn't fit?

1 a) job   b) work   c) play
2 a) algebra   b) Spanish   c) geometry
3 a) Africa   b) the USA   c) Spain
4 a) subject   b) topic   c) time
5 a) exam   b) life   c) qualification

Unit 1

3 Complete these sentences with the words below.

> about • after • for • of • to

Some pupils want … **(1)** leave school because they think it's a waste … **(2)** time. They think school subjects are useless and they won't help them find a job … **(3)** they leave school. They think school subjects should be … **(4)** more useful things. They also think school exams are too difficult … **(5)** them.

4 Match the beginnings (1–5) with the endings (A–G). Two endings do not match.

1 Marco wants to leave school because …
2 He thinks their school subjects should …
3 Henry thinks a school qualification …
4 Sally thinks Spanish is useful because …
5 Jane just wants to …

A teach them more about life after school.
B you can look for jobs in Spain.
C so that they have something to do.
D pass the final exam.
E he thinks it's a waste of time.
F his parents need the money.
G will help to find a good job.

5 a) Work with a partner and make a list of all your school subjects.

woodwork	Holzarbeit
metalwork	Metallarbeit
domestic science	Hauswirtschaft
technical drawing	Technisches Zeichnen
information technology	Computertechnik
religious education	Religionsunterricht

b) How useful are your school subjects? Use the scale below and give each subject a number. Add all the numbers together. What is the total?

0: useless, 1: almost useless, 2: useful – but only a little,
3: mostly useful, 4: very useful

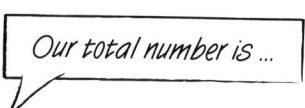

c) Compare your list with others.

Only a few people think that … is …   *Most people think that … is …*

d) What do you think? Is school useful? Why (not)?

Job profile: Veterinary assistants

1 Read the texts and say where you think these veterinary assistants work.

farm • animal clinic • zoo

Lucy: "There are two of us and we are like nurses in a hospital for animals. We talk to the pet owners about their pets. We file the information on our computer and send it to the vets. We also help them when they examine the animals. We clean the animals and their cages and give them food and water."

John: "This little tiger thinks I'm his mother! His real mother doesn't want him. That sometimes happens with young tigers and then I have to feed them with a bottle. This is one of my favourite jobs. But I also have to keep everything clean and that's hard work."

Barbara: "I work for a typical country vet. We look after the farm animals. I hold the animals for the vet. Small animals are no problem, but cows and horses can be difficult. This job isn't always easy, but it's healthy – I'm in the fresh air all day. And every day is different!"

2 Look at the pictures and say what jobs the veterinary assistants do.

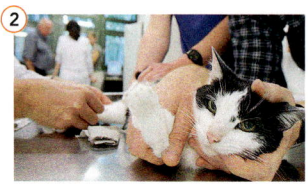

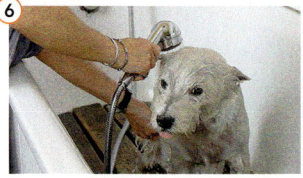

A veterinary assistant	gives	the cages.
	files	animals for the vet.
	talks to	pet owners about their pets.
	holds	information about animals on a computer.
He/she	cleans	the animals food and water.
	washes	the animals.

1 A veterinary assistant cleans the cages.
2 He/she …

Managing situations: Emailing and telephoning — Unit 1

1 Lucy Snowdon saw the job as an animal attendant on the internet and she wrote an email to the clinic. Rewrite it in the right order.

1. My email address is at the end of this email. I look forward to hearing from you.
2. Dear Dr Webster,
3. I like animals and I know how to look after them because I have pets of my own – a dog and a cat.
4. Yours sincerely, Lucy Snowdon
5. I would like to work in your clinic as an animal attendant.
6. I'm sixteen and when I leave school I want to work with animals. I want to be a veterinary assistant.

2 Lucy got the job. Now listen to the instructions that Dr Webster gives her and take notes. The first one is done for you.

1 Mr Dodd   830 156   rabbit: Snowy   2.30 p.m.

> Bei einem Anruf geben viele Briten ihre Telefonnummer an und nicht ihren Namen. Die Telefonnummern werden oft in dreier Gruppen ausgesprochen, z. B.: 801 339:
> 801   eight – oh – one
> 339   double three – nine

3 Pair work: Look at Lucy's first call and take over the roles. Then take over the roles in the other three calls.

A	B
Hello. This is 830 156.	Hello. Am I speaking to Mr Dodd?
Yes. Who is this?	Good morning, Mr Dodd. My name is Lucy Snowdon. I'm an animal attendant at the clinic.
Oh, is this about Snowy, my daughter's rabbit?	Yes. Snowy is fine, Mr Dodd. You can pick her up this afternoon at 2.30. Is that OK?
Yes, 2.30 is fine. I'll be there.	OK, I'll see you at 2.30, Mr Dodd.
Thanks for the call. Bye.	Bye.

Ich kann jetzt …
- über Wünsche sprechen;
- eine Meinung vertreten;
- über regelmäßige Handlungen sprechen (*simple present*).

Wie schätzen Sie sich ein? Können Sie das, oder möchten Sie weiter üben?

Extra material: Albert wakes up!

The snake is still asleep after the operation. That's good, Lucy thinks. She isn't afraid of snakes, but she is always very careful. Is this a poisonous snake? Lucy doesn't know. She measures it – 125 centimetres. She writes this into the
5 snake's file. His name is Albert. What a strange name for a snake! But what type of snake is Albert? There is nothing in the file because Albert is a new patient. I must ask Mr Preston when he comes for Albert at 4 o'clock, Lucy thinks. She puts fresh straw in Albert's transport box. Then she lifts
10 Albert very carefully and puts him into the box. She carries the box into the waiting room and gives it to Ramon, the other veterinary assistant. "This is Albert, Mr Preston's snake. He'll be here in twenty minutes. Please ask him what kind of snake Albert is. We need to know if he is poisonous."

15 Lucy is busy in another room when she hears a loud shout. "Help!" It's Ramon! She runs into the waiting room. Ramon is behind the desk and Albert is around his right arm. The snake moves its head slowly from side to side and hisses. Ramon is white with fear. "I j-j-just wanted to look a-at it!" Albert moves closer to his face and hisses louder. "Don't move," Lucy says, "and don't shout – just stay very still." Slowly, very slowly she moves closer. Just then the doorbell rings …

1 Put the verbs into the correct order to write a summary of the story.

Lucy	goes	always careful with snakes.
She	shouts	if Albert is poisonous.
Lucy	gives	the snake into a transport box.
She	doesn't know	the transport box to Ramon, the other assistant.
He	is	the box because he wants to look at the snake.
The snake	opens	around his arm.
Ramon	moves	for help because he is afraid.
Lucy	puts	towards the snake.

2 What do you think happens next? Write an ending to the story.
Compare your ending with your classmates' endings and decide which one is best.

3 Read the following text and draw a garter snake.

Fact file: Garter snake

This snake comes from New England, USA. It is brown with yellow stripes. It has a thin stripe down the middle of the back and a broad stripe on each side. There is a line of black spots between each stripe. Garter snakes eat small rats and worms.

Friends

Unit 2

Springboard

> **In dieser Unit lerne ich, ...**
> - Informationen weiterzugeben;
> - über Probleme mit Freunden zu sprechen;
> - über vergangene Ereignisse zu berichten (*simple past*).

1 Talk about the photos.

I can see ... *There is ...* *There are ...*

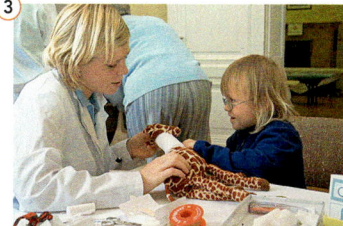

2 Listen to the CD. Who is talking? What do they do with their friends? Match the names with the photos.

Angus • Cary • Fiona • Ian • Irene • Tom

Tom is photo number ... . *... is photo number ... .*

3 What do you do with your friends?

At weekends we ... *After school we sometimes ...*

Text 1: Q & A with Big Ed

8. Most teenage magazines have a problem page where they print letters from readers and an "expert" gives advice. Here are some letters to Big Ed.

My boyfriend smokes and I hate it! He smells like an ashtray! When I asked him to stop, he just laughed at me. He said I was an old woman. What do you think?
5 *Brenda (Belfast)*

My friend has an alcohol problem. Last week his dad found a bottle of vodka in his school bag. He told his dad that it belonged to me. His parents are now very angry with
5 me. They told me never to come to their house again. My friend says that I should help him because we're friends. But I'm worried because his parents could tell the school or call my parents. What should I do?
10 *Billy (Everton)*

I often hang out with my friends. We look around the shops in the city centre. But now my friends have a new game they call "sneak a treat". One of them asks the shop assistant
5 a question. Then when the assistant isn't looking, the others steal something – a packet of chewing gum, a magazine or some make-up. Sometimes the things they steal are really silly – like a box of paper clips. They think it's
10 fun, but I don't. I don't want to get into trouble, but I don't want to lose my friends.
Neil (Bradford)

My parents are very old-fashioned. When I was fourteen I had to be home by 9 p.m. I'm now sixteen and my parents say that I have to be home by 10 p.m. or there will be big
5 trouble. My parents think this is a sensible "curfew" for a girl of sixteen. I disagree. I think it shows that they don't trust me.
Edwina (Brighton)

1. Link these photos with the letters.

1

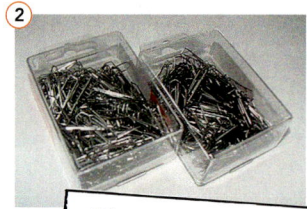
2

3

4

Photo number ... goes with ...'s letter.

2. Complete these sentences.

1. Brenda has a problem with
2. He smokes
3. Billy is worried about
4. His friend has
5. Neil doesn't want to
6. His friends steal
7. Edwina disagrees with
8. She thinks that they

A. get into trouble.
B. his friend.
C. her boyfriend.
D. an alcohol problem.
E. don't trust her.
F. her parents.
G. things for a game.
H. too much.

Unit 2

9 ③ Listen to Big Ed's advice and say whose letter he is answering.

Number 1 is his answer to …

④ Choose the correct meaning.

1. Advice is a helpful … .
   a) warning   b) tip   c) wink

2. Parents are … .
   a) a husband and wife   b) a man and a woman   c) people with children

3. You can find a paper clip in … .
   a) an office   b) a woman's ear   c) an exercise book

4. A curfew is … .
   a) an Irish dance   b) a time limit   c) a small dog

Grammar

Remember: simple past

- Die Vergangenheitsform ist bei allen Personen (*I, you, he,* usw.) gleich.
  *Billy **had** a problem, so he **wrote** to a magazine.*

- Es gibt regelmäßige und unregelmäßige Vergangenheitsformen.
  *Big Ed **answered** his letter and **gave** him some good advice.*

- Fragen und Verneinungen werden mit **did** gebildet.
  ***Did** Billy **take** the advice? – Yes, he **did**. He **talked** to his father.*

- Signalwörter sind: *yesterday, last week/month/year, two hours ago, in 2007,* usw.

▶ Eine Liste der unregelmäßigen Verben finden Sie auf Seite 99.

⑤ Pair work: Write the dialogue into an exercise book. Use the simple past forms of the verbs in brackets. Then take over the roles and act them.

Billy   Dad, I (**be**[1]) at Jim's house yesterday. Something bad (**happen**[2]).
Mr A   Oh? (**you/have**[3]) an argument with Jim?
Billy   No. Jim's dad (**shout**[4]) at me and (**tell**[5]) me never to come to their house again.
Mr A   Why (**he/say**[6]) that, Billy?
Billy   Jim (**have**[7]) a bottle of vodka in his school bag and his dad (**find**[8]) it.
          Jim (**lie**[9]) and (**tell**[10]) his dad that the vodka (**belong**[11]) to me!
Mr A   That (**not be**[12]) very nice of him. Why (**you/not tell**[13]) his father the truth?
Billy   Because I (**think**[14]) that Jim (**need**[15]) my help.

▶ Mehr Übungen zum Thema *simple past* finden Sie auf Seite 89.

Text 2: An unexpected friend

Last Friday afternoon Sam groaned with pain. She had a really bad stomach ache. She looked at the newspaper article on the wall above her bed. It was from last year.

Local girl wins weekend in Dublin

Samantha Denny, 15, delivers our evening newspaper to people's homes. And this year she is the winner of our 'Top Round' competition. Through wind, rain and snow, Samantha delivered the Evening Standard to all the houses on her round – from Monday to Saturday for a whole year. She didn't miss a single day. Our marketing manager, Mrs Alison Romney, presented Samantha with her prize: a weekend in Dublin.

Sam called Mrs Romney and told her that she was sick and had to stay in bed. She couldn't do her newspaper round that evening.

The pain was still bad on Saturday morning and Sam had to call Mrs Romney again. Sam now had two sick days, so she wouldn't win the competition. This year the prize was a weekend in Tenerife. Rita Benton would win it now – she only had one sick day. Sam was bitter – so much hard work and the end of the year was only ten days away!

Just then Sam's mobile phone rang. It was Rita Benton!
"Hi, Sam. How are you feeling?"
She hopes I'll still be sick on Monday, Sam thought. She wants to make sure.
"I feel much better today, Rita. I'll be fine by Monday. You must be very happy. You'll be in sunny Tenerife soon."
"Oh, yes! We'll have a wonderful time!"
"We? I don't understand."
"Well, Mrs Romney called me on Saturday morning. She wanted me to do your newspaper round. I told her I would do it, but only if we could both win the prize. We can go to Tenerife together!"
"That's wonderful. Thanks, Rita."

1 Are these statements a) true, b) false or c) not in the text?

1. Sam delivers morning newspapers.
2. She was sick on Friday and couldn't do her newspaper round.
3. Sam wasn't sick for a single day last year.
4. She won a competition last year and stayed in Dublin for a week.
5. Sam met her boyfriend, Liam, when she was in Dublin.
6. Sam was sick on the 20th and 21st of December.
7. Mrs Romney is a reporter with the newspaper.
8. Rita Benton called Mrs Romney.
9. Sam and Rita were good friends before they went to Tenerife together.

Unit 2

2 Finish the sentences with information from the text.

1. After school, Samantha Denny delivers …
2. Last year Sam didn't …
3. She won the 'Top Round' competition and the prize was …
4. Sam couldn't do her newspaper round on Friday and Saturday because …
5. The prize this year is …
6. Sam was bitter because …

3 Find the word in the text.

1. When you are hurt, you are in … .
2. A text in a newspaper is an … .
3. The … is the part of the day between afternoon and night.
4. When you win a … , you get a prize.
5. People who deliver things to houses in a small area have a … .
6. A … manager sells the things that his/her firm makes.

4 Look at the text and find the opposites of these words.

1 good (line 1)	4 lose (line 13)	7 sad (line 19)
2 loser (line 5)	5 easy (line 15)	8 terrible (line 21)
3 healthy (line 10)	6 the start (line 15)	9 afternoon (line 23)

5 Verfassen Sie einen Text, der die Hauptaussagen des Textes wiedergibt. Die Fragen helfen Ihnen dabei.

- Was hat Samantha im Jahr vorher gewonnen und wofür?
- Warum glaubt Samantha, den Wettbewerb in diesem Jahr nicht mehr gewinnen zu können?
- Was hat Rita Benton mit ihrer Chefin, Frau Romney, vereinbart?

6 Pair work: Find out more about your partner. Ask questions and answer them.

Where were you born?   *When did you start school?*   *What was your favourite subject last year?*

7 What was the best/worst thing that happened to you or your family last year? Write 30–40 words in complete sentences.

> Here are some useful words:
> surprise – Überraschung   important – wichtig   fire – Brand
> to surprise – überraschen   sickness – Krankheit   death – Tod
> serious – ernst   accident – Unfall

Job profile: Airport personnel

Heathrow is Europe's biggest and busiest airport. It employs hundreds of people.

1 Read these job descriptions and then match them to the photos below.

1
- unload bags from planes and take them to the terminals
- collect suitcases from terminals and load them onto the planes

2
- give information to passengers
- make announcements
- deal with complaints

3
- guard the airport buildings, planes and runways
- search aircraft
- check passengers and their luggage*

4
- clean planes and offices
- use floor cleaning machines
- remove graffiti from walls

(*luggage = Gepäck)

A Security officers

B Luggage handlers

C General cleaners

D Information assistants

Managing situations: Mediation — Unit 2

1 Which sign should you look for if you …

1 … lose something?
2 … need a plane ticket?
3 … want a haircut?
4 … want to buy some presents?
5 … need a hotel room?
6 … need a bus?
7 … want to check in your luggage?
8 … need information about a flight?

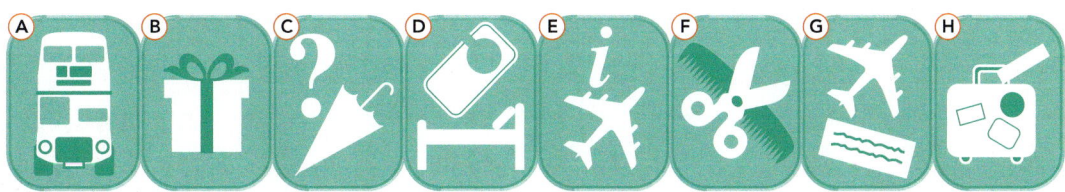

2 You're at the airport information desk. Three people need help because they can't speak English. Can you help them?

Step 1 Listen to the CD. What does the person want?
Step 2 The information assistant doesn't speak German, so you must tell her what the person wants in English. But not everything – just the important things. For example:
He/She wants a …
He/She needs a …
Step 3 Now listen to the CD again.
The information assistant is giving you the information to pass on in German.
A good tip: Make notes! The information below will also help you.
Step 4 Jetzt geben Sie die Informationen auf Deutsch weiter.

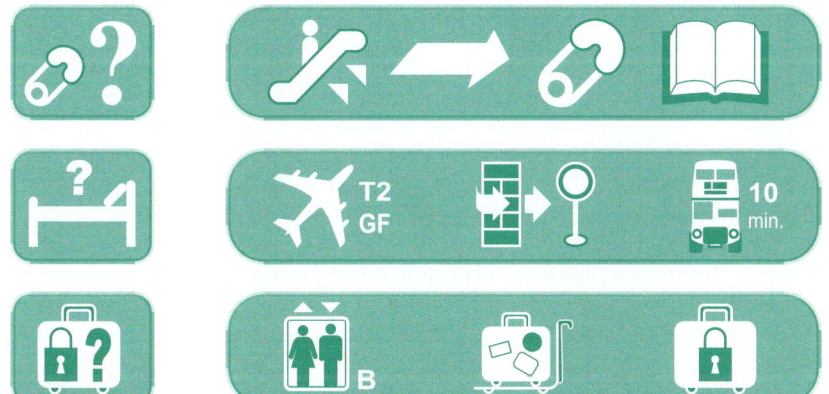

Ich kann jetzt …

- Informationen weitergeben;
- über Probleme mit Freunden sprechen;
- über vergangene Ereignisse berichten (*simple past*).

Wie schätzen Sie sich ein? Können Sie das, oder möchten Sie weiter üben?

Extra material: A holiday in Tenerife

1 Read Martin's email and answer the questions in English.

Lieber Erich,

wer hätte gedacht, ich würde Anfang Januar am Strand liegen? Es ist herrlich warm hier auf Teneriffa und der Strand ist vom Hotel nur 15 Minuten entfernt. Der Sand sieht komisch aus – er ist fast schwarz! Man kann aber schön darauf liegen, nur das Meer ist etwas zu kalt zum Schwimmen.

5 Gleich am ersten Tag habe ich zwei nette Mädchen kennengelernt. Sie sind Engländerinnen und heißen Sam und Rita. Sie sind Zeitungsreporterinnen oder so etwas Ähnliches. Sie kommen aus einer Stadt namens Hartlepool. Ich glaube, sie liegt irgendwo im Norden Englands. Sie sind nett, aber sie sprechen komisch – ganz anders als das Englisch auf der CD unseres Englischlehrwerks. Ich habe eine CD dabei (ich hatte wirklich vor, etwas zu lernen!) und ich habe sie ihnen vorgespielt. Sie
10 haben sich gekrümmt vor Lachen. Sie sagen, dass nur die Südengländer so gestelzt sprechen, und sie werden mir richtiges Englisch beibringen. Ich habe nichts dagegen – zwei nette ‚Lehrerinnen', das ist besser als die blöde CD!

Sam und Rita wohnen in einem Hotel in der Calle Iriarte, das ist am anderen Ende der Stadt. Wir wollen uns morgen wieder hier am Strand treffen. Sie sagten 'after breakfast' und ich sagte 'OK.
15 About 7.30'. Sie dachten, ich mache einen Witz. Für sie ist 'after breakfast' so etwas wie 9.30! Wir treffen uns hier also um 10 Uhr. Wir wollen uns im Hafen umsehen und die alte Burg besuchen. Sie heißt Castilio San Felipe und muss sehr alt sein.

Bis bald,
Martin

1 What colour is the sand on the beach?
2 When did Martin meet Sam and Rita?
3 Where do the girls come from?
4 Why did they laugh at Martin's school CD?
5 Is the girls' hotel near Martin's hotel?
6 What do they want to do the next morning?

Exam preparation

I Textarbeit

Text 1: Steve Irwin – Crocodile Hunter

When he was only 9, Steve helped his father to catch wild crocodiles, snakes and lizards for their zoo. He became well known in Queensland when he helped to catch crocodiles near towns and cities and <u>relocate</u> them to quiet rivers
5 away from people.

Steve took over his parents' zoo and made it one of the most popular zoos in Australia. Visitors loved watching the feeding of the crocodiles. Steve became an expert on Australian reptiles and in 1992 he made his first nature film for Australian television. Steve
10 wanted to protect all wildlife, but especially the animals that people are often frightened of: crocodiles and snakes. He campaigned on television programmes and in articles in newspapers and magazines. He called himself a "wildlife <u>warrior</u>".

In 1992 Steve had an unusual <u>honeymoon</u> – he took his new wife to catch wild crocodiles. A friend of Steve's made a film of the hunt. It showed Steve <u>wrestling</u> with crocodiles and it
15 became the first film in the TV series "The Crocodile Hunter". Steve also made the TV series "The Ten Deadliest Snakes in the World". These TV films were a big success all over the world. They made Steve very famous and very rich, too. Some <u>naturalists</u> thought he was more interested in making money than saving animals. Others thought his films were bad because they made the animals seem more dangerous than they really were.

20 On September 4, 2006 Steve died as he had lived – in front of a camera. He swam too close to a stingray and it <u>stabbed</u> him through the heart and killed him.

266 words

Annotations

line 4 relocate – *umsiedeln*
line 12 warrior – *Krieger(in)*
line 13 honeymoon – *Flitterwochen*
line 14 wrestle – *ringen*
line 17 naturalist – *Naturforscher(in)*
line 21 stab – *erstechen*

1 Questions on the text
Answer in complete English sentences, please.   Punkte

1.1 What reptiles did Steve and his father keep in their zoo?   2P
1.2 How did Steve become well known in Queensland?   2P
1.3 Why was his honeymoon unusual?   2P

Exam preparation

2 **Aussagen über den Text** 10 P

Kreuzen Sie (in einem Heft) an, ob folgende Aussagen richtig oder falsch sind.
Kreuzen Sie nur an, wenn Sie sicher sind. Falsches Ankreuzen führt zu Punktabzug.
Im Zweifel kreuzen Sie nichts an.

- **2.1** Steve Irwins Vater betrieb einen Zoo.
- **2.2** Es gibt keine Krokodile in Queensland.
- **2.3** Steve wurde zuerst in den USA berühmt.
- **2.4** Steve jagte Krokodile auf seiner Hochzeitsreise.
- **2.5** Steve war bei allen Naturforschern beliebt und respektiert.
- **2.6** Steve worked with his father as a child.
- **2.7** Steve sometimes caught crocodiles by wrestling with them.
- **2.8** Steve's first TV films were about dangerous snakes.
- **2.9** Steve earned a lot of money with his nature films.
- **2.10** Steve died when a crocodile killed him.

3 **Finish the sentences** 4 P

Use **only** information from the text, please.

- **3.1** Steve Irwin learned about crocodiles when …
- **3.2** Steve's zoo became popular because …
- **3.3** Steve became very rich when …
- **3.4** Some naturalists didn't like Steve's films because …

4 **Matching** 5 P

Match the beginnings 4.1–4.5 to five of the endings a)–g) according to the text.
Two endings do not match.

- **4.1** Working in his father's zoo helped
- **4.2** Steve wanted to help animals
- **4.3** Steve became rich
- **4.4** Steve and his wife hunted crocodiles
- **4.5** A stingray attacked and killed Steve

- **a)** when he swam too close and frightened it.
- **b)** that people are afraid of.
- **c)** on their honeymoon.
- **d)** than saving animals.
- **e)** Steve to become an expert on reptiles.
- **f)** because it was angry.
- **g)** after the success of his nature films.

Partners

Unit 3

Springboard

In dieser Unit lerne ich, …

- nach dem Weg zu fragen;
- eine Wegbeschreibung zu geben;
- eine Reservierung zu machen.

1 Jobs with food and drink. Match the jobs and the photos.

barista • waiter/waitress • bakery assistant • caterer • cook • barman

The person in photo … is a …

2 Listen to the CD and say who the people are talking to.

1 The man is talking to a …
2 The woman is talking to a …
3 The man and his son are talking to a …
4–6 …

3 Write a sentence about each of the jobs above.

	makes	coffee in a café.
	sells	food in a restaurant kitchen.
A waiter	delivers	bread and cakes in a baker's shop.
A …	cooks	food to firms and private homes.
	mixes	meals to restaurant guests.
	serves	cocktails in a hotel bar.

23

Text 1: Barista of the month

⑬

BUCKSTAR NEWS

Our Barista of the Month is Dean Turvey. Dean 'the Bean' was a finalist in this year's UK Barista Championship. He's 18 and he works at our branch in Manchester City Centre.

Why did you become a barista, Dean?

Well, I was a dustman – I collected rubbish. The money was good, but the work was hard and I didn't like the dirt. I always needed a hot bath after work. Then I had dinner, watched TV and went to bed early. That was no life!

So you wanted a nice, clean job?

That's right. I read about the barista job online. It was in a nice, warm building, I could wear normal clothes and I wouldn't get dirty. And a coffee bar is a good place to meet people.

And was it your dream job?

No, it wasn't at first. The work was hard. I had to learn a lot – different types of coffee, how to use the espresso machine and so on. And I had to learn it fast – when 20 people want 20 different things, you can't stop and look in the handbook. I made lots of mistakes in the first few weeks. Some customers complained and the shop manager wasn't happy. I nearly gave up two or three times.

But you didn't. And now you are one of our best baristas. What happened?

I met Maureen. She's a waitress here. We met after work and Maureen helped me learn the handbook. Things got better – I made fewer mistakes and I worked faster. Now Maureen and I are together.

What are your plans for the future, Dean?

I want to win the UK Barista Championship. Then I want to go on a Buckstar training course with Maureen. We both want to earn more money. Then we can find a flat and move in together.

❶ Answer these questions in complete sentences.

1. Why didn't Dean like his job as a dustman?
2. Why did Dean think the barista job was a good job?
3. How was the real barista job different to Dean's dream?
4. Name one reason why Dean stayed in a job that was very difficult for him.

❷ Finish the sentences with information from the text.

1. When he was a dustman, Dean …
2. Buckstar has a branch in …
3. A coffee bar is a good place to …
4. In his first few weeks, Dean …
5. Dean's girlfriend helped …

Unit 3

3 Sind die folgenden Aussagen richtig oder falsch?

1. 'Buckstar' ist der Name einer Kette, die Kaffee verkauft.
2. Dean leitet die Filiale im Manchester City Centre.
3. Im Jahr zuvor hat Dean es bis zur Endrunde der nationalen Barista-Meisterschaft geschafft.
4. Deans letzte Stelle war schlecht bezahlt.
5. Dean worked in an office in his last job.
6. Dean thought the barista job would be easier than it was.
7. Dean knew all the different types of coffee when he started work at the coffee shop.
8. Dean wants to marry Maureen, his girlfriend, as soon as possible.

4 Match the beginnings 1–5 to five of the endings A–H. Three of the endings do not match.

1. Dean didn't like
2. He was a dustman and
3. The money was good,
4. Dean wanted a job where
5. But the barista job

A. but it was hard work.
B. wasn't an easy dream job.
C. people wanted different things.
D. his last job.
E. the handbook was very difficult.
F. the work was hard and dirty.
G. many customers complained to the manager.
H. he could work inside and meet lots of people.

Grammar

Remember: Prepositions

- Präpositionen sind Verhältniswörter. Präpositionen sagen etwas aus über räumliche Beziehungen:
  *Dean works **at** our branch in Manchester City Centre.*

- oder über zeitliche Beziehungen:
  *Dean always needed a hot bath **after** work.*

5 Complete the sentences with one of the following prepositions.

after • at • for • in • to • with

1. The Starlight café was … an old building.
2. I always have a biscuit … my coffee.
3. I usually sit … a table near the window.
4. I often go there … work.
5. I sometimes stay there … hours.
6. Other times I go … the cinema afterwards.

▶ Mehr Übungen zum Thema *prepositions* finden Sie auf Seite 98.

Text 2: Their first flat

(14) Dean and Maureen both live in small, one-room flats. They want to move in together, so they are looking for a bigger flat. They find this advert in their local newspaper:

> 55 sqm: bedroom, living room, dining room/kitchen. Near Victoria Station.
> Rent £350 per month + 4-months' deposit. Contact Mrs Chapman 0161 801339.

5 Maureen calls and makes an appointment.

Dean and Maureen are at the flat. Mrs Chapman owns it and she is showing them around.
"It's perfect for a young couple. There's a bedroom, a living room, a bathroom and a kitchen. The kitchen is big enough
10 for a small table, so you could use it as a dining room, too."
Maureen goes into the empty kitchen. There is a small window, but it is very dirty.
"And the rent is £350 a month, Mrs Chapman. Is that right?"
"That's right, dear. That includes heating, too. Plus four
15 month's deposit."
"We'll think about it, Mrs Chapman. Thank you for showing us around."

Afterwards Dean and Maureen go to a pub.
"I didn't like it, Maureen. It was too small."
20 "Yes, and the rooms were too dark. And they were dirty, too."
"The only good thing about it was the rent. We could afford £350."
"You are forgetting the four month's deposit and the empty kitchen, Dean. No way!"
"Yeah, you're right. But will we ever find a good flat that we can
25 afford?"
"Yes, we will, Dean. But not today. I'm tired and hungry."
"Me, too. I'll go to the bar and order something to eat. Are chicken sandwiches OK with you?"
"Yes, that's fine. And we'll buy an evening newspaper later. We
30 can look for some flats and visit them tomorrow."

1 **Finish the sentences with information from the text.**

1. Maureen and Dean are looking for a bigger flat because …
2. They are looking for flats in their …
3. When they find the advert, they call and …
4. Dean doesn't like Mrs Chapman's flat because …
5. Maureen doesn't like it because …
6. They won't look at another flat today because …

Unit 3

Grammar

Remember: present progressive

- Diese Zeitform (Verlaufsform) gibt es nicht im Deutschen. Sie beschreibt, was gerade geschieht:
  What **are** you **doing**? – I **am cooking** a meal.
  (Was machst du gerade? – Ich koche gerade eine Mahlzeit.)

- Die Verlaufsform der Gegenwart wird so gebildet:
  am/is/are + **ing**-Form des Verbs (z. B.: try – trying, happen – happening, look – looking)
  Verneinung: **am not/isn't/aren't** + **ing**-Form

- Signalwörter sind: *at the moment, now, just, at present,* usw.

2 What is happening in these pictures?

1 read/newspaper • 2 look at/map • 3 wait for/bus • 4 look around/flat • 5 talk about/flat

▶ Mehr Übungen zum Thema *present progressive* finden Sie auf Seite 88.

1 Maureen is … a newspaper.

3 Maureen and Dean go to an estate agent (*Immobilienmakler*) for help. Complete the dialogue with sentences from the box.

Estate agent:
1 Good morning. Can I help you?
2 Oh, we can certainly help you find a flat. To buy or to rent?
3 Do you prefer any particular part of Manchester?
4 Do you have any children or pets?
5 And how much rent can you afford?

Maureen and Dean:
…
…
…
…
…

A No, we haven't. There's just the two of us.
B Around £350 a month.
C I hope so. We're looking for a flat.
D Yes, it should be in or near the city centre because of our jobs.
E We want to rent first. Perhaps we'll buy a flat later.

Job profile: Jobs in a restaurant

1 Match the photos to the statements below.

1. Jane Foskill: manager
2. Barry Haynes: chef
3. Toby Boswell: barman
4. Pia Umberto: kitchen assistant
5. Sue Cox, Ann Ryan: waitresses

A I know a lot about beer, wine and cocktails. I make sure that the waitresses get the right drinks for their guests.
B I make sure everyone does their job properly. When there's a problem, I deal with it.
C Our guests want their food and drinks quickly. We like to get tips, so we make sure all our guests are happy.
D I cook meals from 5.30 p.m. to 11 p.m. I also make sure that we always have enough food.
E I clean the kitchen in the morning and the evening. I make sure there are always enough clean plates.

2 What is Jane doing? Use the key words under the pictures.

1. buy • fruit and vegetables
2. answer the phone • make reservations
3. talk to • plan
4. busy • help

1 Jane is at the market. She is buying …

Managing situations: Giving directions   Unit 3

1 Listen to the four callers and make a list of the reservations. Note down the names, times and number of guests.

2 Some of the guests need directions to the restaurant. Listen to Jane, take notes and then follow the route on the map.

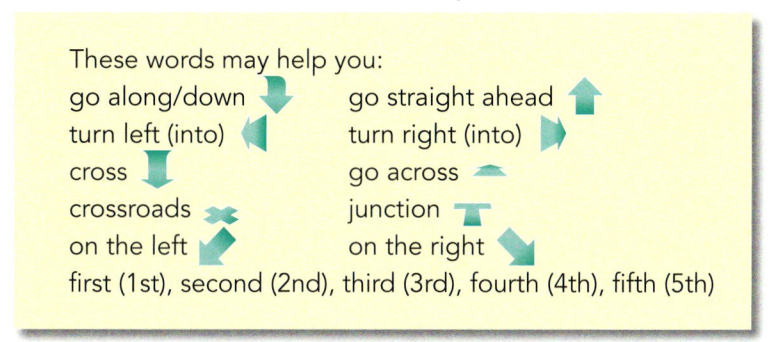

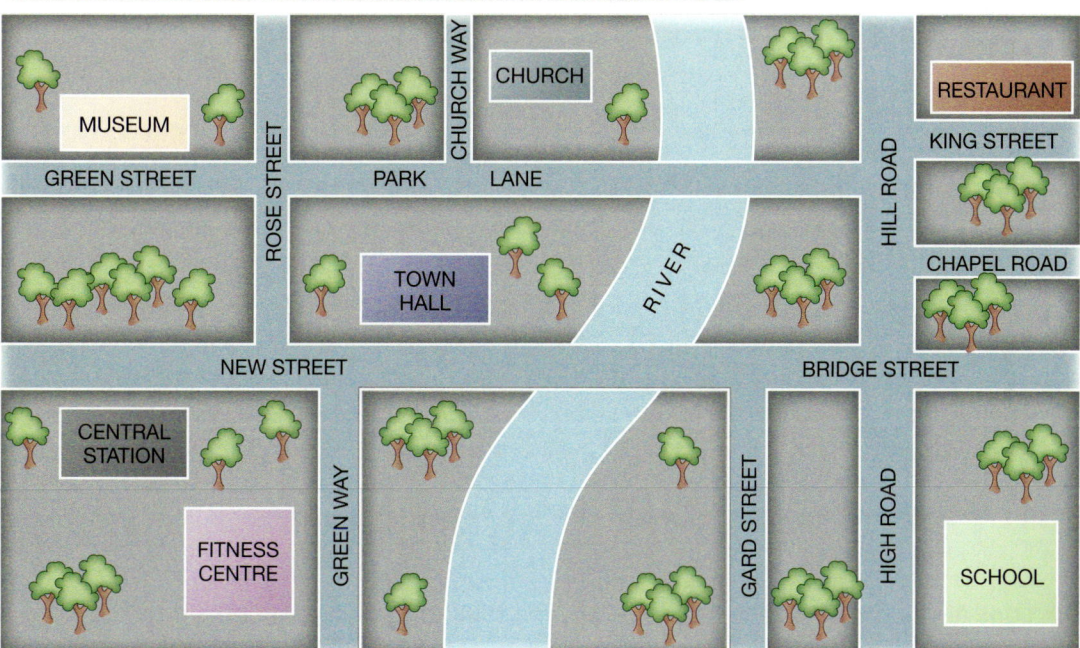

> These words may help you:
> go along/down ⬇   go straight ahead ⬆
> turn left (into) ⬅   turn right (into) ➡
> cross ⬇   go across ⬆
> crossroads ✳   junction ⊤
> on the left   on the right
> first (1st), second (2nd), third (3rd), fourth (4th), fifth (5th)

3 Work with a partner, take over the roles of Jane and the caller and act out similar dialogues. The words and phrases from above may help you.

Ich kann jetzt …

- nach dem Weg fragen;
- eine Wegbeschreibung geben;
- eine Reservierung machen.

Wie schätzen Sie sich ein? Können Sie das, oder möchten Sie weiter üben?

Extra material: First dates

Melinda: A friend organized a treasure hunt*. There were eight girls and eight boys. My friend wrote the boys' names on a card and put them into a bag. Then the girls picked a card out of the bag. My partner was Derek. We didn't win the treasure hunt, but we had a lot of fun and he asked me to meet him again. (*Schnitzeljagd)

Robert: When I go out with a girl for the first time, I suggest* something simple like a nice walk along the canal. We can talk and get to know each other and there's no stress. (*vorschlagen)

Kathryn: I love animals, so for a first date I always suggest the zoo. I feel more comfortable when there are lots of people around. I usually know after an hour whether* I want to go out with him again. (*ob)

Gordon: There's a big lake near here and I have a little boat there. I like fishing*, it's outside and it's quiet. I like quiet girls, too. I always ask my first date to go fishing with me on the lake. Girls hate it. They don't like boats and worms and they want to talk all the time. It's interesting to see how long they can keep quiet. (*angeln)

Doreen: My boyfriend wanted to take me to a hamburger restaurant because that was his favourite food. Anyway, I took him to a supermarket and we bought minced beef, fresh salad, onions, tomatoes and good bread rolls. Then we went to my flat and I showed him how to make hamburgers. He thought that was really cool. Now we often choose a recipe*, buy what we need in a supermarket and cook the meal together. It's fun, it's cheap and it's a good training course for boyfriends. (*Kochrezept)

1 Look at the people in the box. Who do you think they should go on a date with?

> Bob / likes animals • Louise / likes sailing
> John / likes cooking • Rachel / likes going on walks

2 What do you like to do on a first date? Write 30–40 words in complete English sentences.

> These words and phrases may help you:
> alone – *allein*   prefer – *vorziehen*
> avoid – *vermeiden*   suggest – *vorschlagen*
> comfortable – *bequem*   invite – *einladen*

Old world and new world

Unit 4

Springboard

In dieser Unit lerne ich, …
- meine Stadt zu beschreiben;
- über Arbeitsabläufe zu berichten;
- über Freizeit und zukünftige Pläne zu sprechen.

Liverpool is a World Heritage city with a long and interesting history. It is a multi-cultural city with people from all over the world. People who live there are called 'Scousers'.

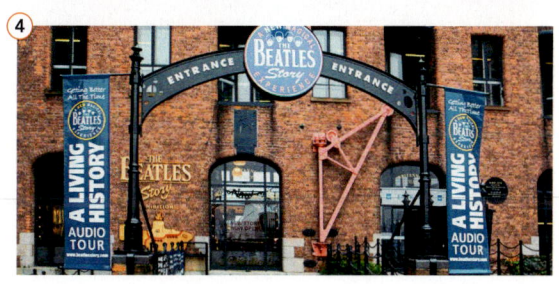

17 **1** Match the photos from a tourist guide with the following descriptions. Then listen to the CD and check your answers.

- **A** Step back in time and see how Liverpool's most famous band, The Beatles, became popular.
- **B** The many cafés, pubs and restaurants on the historic Albert Dock are now a popular tourist attraction.
- **C** The ACC Liverpool is a modern arena for sports and concerts. It opened in 2008.
- **D** Liverpool has been a port for a long time and in the Maritime Museum you can learn about the old ships and Captain Cook's voyages.

2 Make a tourist guide for your town or area. Find photos of interesting places and then write one or two sentences about each one.

Text 1: New Scousers

(18) Reporter This is Radio Merseyside and I'm Sandra Preston. Our guests on 'Liverpool Today' are four young people from Germany. Would you like to introduce yourselves?

5 **Ingrid** Of course. I'm Ingrid Böning from Kaiserslautern. I'm a professional woodworker. I can make all sorts of things with wood.

Thomas I'm Thomas Michler from Munich and I'm a trained bricklayer and stonemason.

10 **Dieter** I'm Dieter Schäfer. I'm from Mannheim. I'm a plasterer.

Jan I'm Jan Büsing from Kiel and I trained as a house painter.

Reporter Last year you started your own building firm: Meisterwerk Unlimited. Why did you choose a German name for a building firm in Liverpool?

15 **Dieter** Well, Germans have a very good reputation here. We've all got the German 'master certificate' and people respect our qualifications. They know we'll do a good job. Lots of British workers don't have any qualifications.

Reporter Do you get lots of jobs?

Ingrid Yes, actually. We're helping to renovate the Princes Road Synagogue. It's a
20 beautiful old building, but it needs a lot of repairs. I'm making the new window frames, seats and furniture.

Jan I worked there last week. I had to match modern paint to the old colours.

Dieter I'll be there next week. I'll have to repair some old ceilings. They have complicated designs, so it won't be an easy job.

25 **Thomas** Yes, and I repaired some of the old brick and stone walls. Now everything looks like new. I did a good job – they won't have to repair them again for another hundred years!

Reporter And where are you working now?

30 **Ingrid** I'm working with Jan in an old church on Nelson Street.

Dieter Thomas and I are working in an old building on Albert Dock. It was once a pump house but it's going to be a restaurant and pub.

35 **Thomas** It's an interesting job because it has to look like an old pump house. It may look old, but it must be warm and comfortable!

- In Germany two-thirds of all school-leavers have a vocational qualification.
- In the United Kingdom only one out of ten pupils leave school with a vocational qualification.
- The UK doesn't have anything similar to the German 'master certificate'. Many young people in Britain still learn 'on the job'.

Unit 4

1 Answer these questions on the text.

1. Name the jobs that the four young people do.
2. Why do German workers have a good reputation in Liverpool?
3. What is wrong with the synagogue on Princes Road?
4. Why won't Dieter's job be easy?
5. Why is the Albert Dock job interesting?

2 Match the beginnings (1–5) to five of the endings (A–G). Two endings do not match.

1. Ingrid works
2. The young Germans have
3. Many British workers
4. The synagogue
5. The pump house on Albert Dock

A don't have qualifications.
B will become a restaurant.
C have a 'master certificate'.
D their own building firm.
E needs renovation work.
F with wood.
G not many jobs.

Grammar

Remember: modal verbs

- Im Englischen benutzen wir modale Hilfsverben nur in Verbindung mit einem Vollverb.

Visitors **can** *enjoy a meal and a drink in the Brewery Tap pub.*
They know we **will** *do a good job. It* **won't** *be an easy job.*
It **may** *look old, but it* **must** *be warm and comfortable!*

simple past form
could
would – wouldn't
might – had to

- Die beiden Formen **must** und **have to** sind austauschbar. Da **must** keine *past-* oder *future-*Form hat, benutzen wir **had to**, **didn't have to** (past) oder **will have to**, **won't have to** (future):   I **had to** match modern paint to the old colours.
   They **won't have to** repair the walls again for another hundred years!

3 Complete the sentences with the correct forms of *can* or *must/have to*.

The guests on Liverpool Today … **(1 must/have to)** introduce themselves and describe their work. Not everybody … **(2 can)** do this well. For example, the guests in the last programme were also German, but they … **(3 can)** speak English very well. All four said that they … **(4 can)** do skilled restoration work. For their last job in a synagogue they … **(5 must/have to)** do a lot of specialized jobs. They think that many British workers … **(6 not can)** do these jobs as well. They have started their own building firm so that they … **(7 can)** work together. They get more jobs every month and soon they … **(8 must/have to)** work longer hours and at the weekend.

▶ Mehr Übungen zum Thema *modal verbs* finden Sie auf Seite 92.

Text 2: A new business

- Most Australian cities are on the coast. The centre of Australia ('the outback') is very dry.
- People who drive across the outback must be very careful, have the right equipment and carry lots of water and fuel.

(19) Andreas Trautman:

I'm a car mechanic and I live in Perth. When I first came here, I worked in a garage – I did exactly the same work I did in Karlsruhe. Then two years ago, I went on an Outback trip. I wanted to see more of Australia. The tour guides drove old Land Rovers. Four cars always
5 travelled together for safety. The roads were very bad and there was often no road. The biggest problems were the heat, the flies and the dry sand and dust. Even cars with four-wheel drive got stuck in the sand. Then one of the other cars had to pull them out. Sometimes we had to dig them out and that was hard work in that heat. The drivers
10 also had to change the air filters a lot.

Anyway, that gave me an idea. I bought an old Land Rover and a trailer. Then I fitted all the things a driver needs for the outback: a radio, a satellite phone, GPS, air conditioning, a spare battery, special air filters, extra fuel tanks, water tanks, etc. It took me nearly a year and all my money! I sold the Land Rover though and I made a good profit. That was the start of my busi-
15 ness. Now I employ two Polish mechanics – they work hard and do good work. We can produce four 'outback fit' cars a month. We now do other SUVs, too. We also sell camping equipment like gas cookers, flashlights, tents and sleeping bags. Business is good – next year I'll rent a bigger workshop and employ another mechanic. And the year after that … Well, we'll see.

① Are the following statements true or false?

1. Andreas started a different job when he moved to Perth.
2. The roads in the outback are not good to drive on.
3. He can't afford another mechanic.
4. Andreas only makes 'outback fit' Land Rovers.
5. Andreas' business is making a lot of money.

Unit 4

2 Finish the sentences using information from the text.

1 Andreas no longer lives in Karlsruhe, he …
2 When he arrived, he …
3 During the Outback trip, Andreas travelled …
4 After the Outback trip, he decided …
5 Next year he wants …

3 Look at the illustrations. Find the names of the equipment in the text.

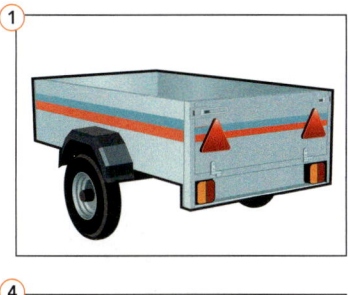

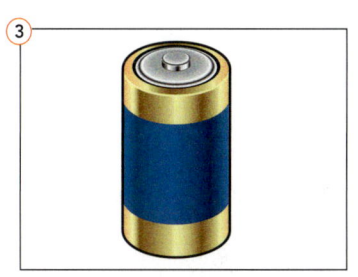

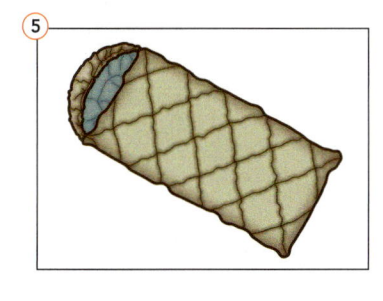

Number one is a …

4 Copy Kathy's profile card. Then listen to Kathy on the CD and complete it. Do the same with the other three people on the CD.

Name:	
Age:	17
Leisure:	
Job plans:	veterinary assistant

5 Introduce yourself and talk about your interests and plans for after school.

Hi. I'm …

In my free time I like to …

When I leave school, I would like to …

35

Job profile: A car mechanic

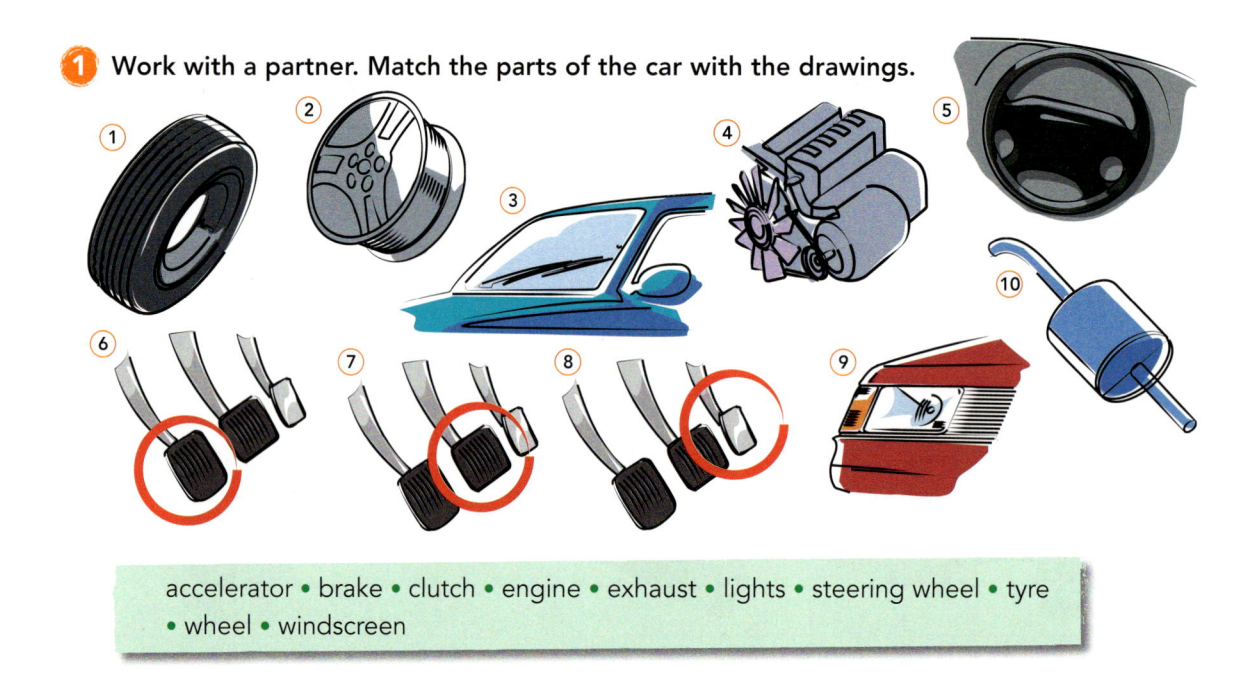

1 Work with a partner. Match the parts of the car with the drawings.

accelerator • brake • clutch • engine • exhaust • lights • steering wheel • tyre • wheel • windscreen

2 Write a sentence about each of these safety items. The words in the box can help you.

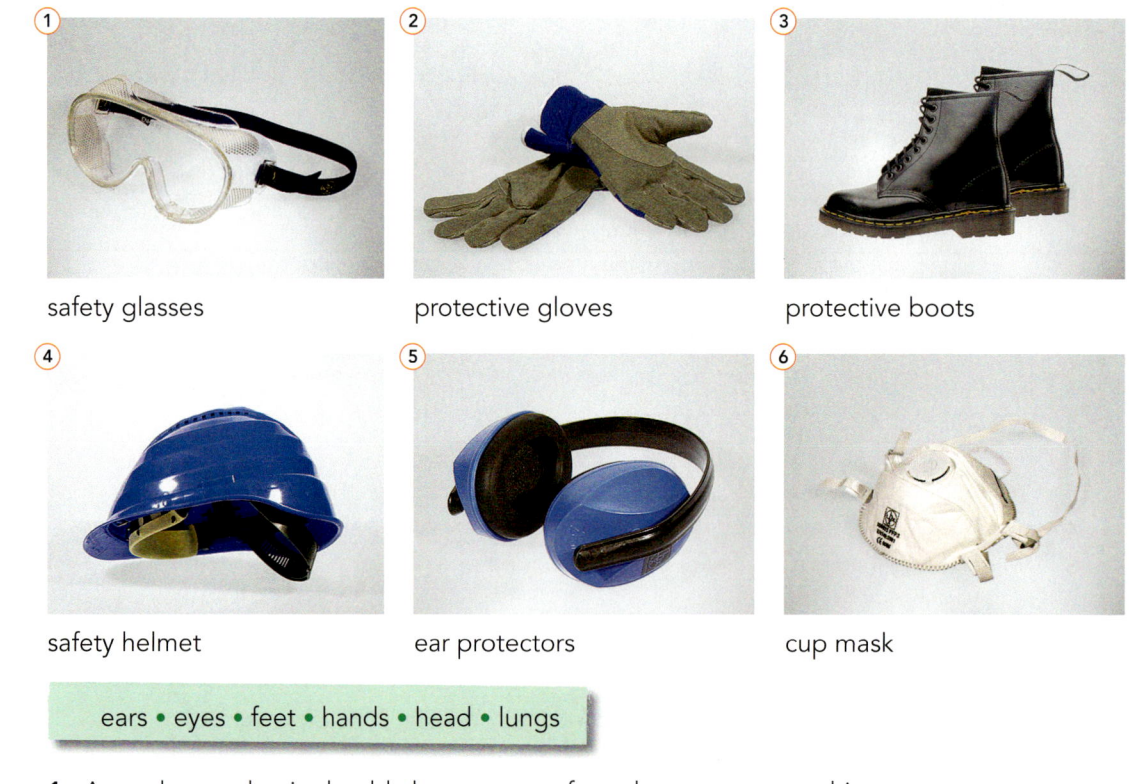

1. safety glasses
2. protective gloves
3. protective boots
4. safety helmet
5. ear protectors
6. cup mask

ears • eyes • feet • hands • head • lungs

1. At work a mechanic should always wear safety glasses to protect his …
2. He should wear … to protect his …

Managing situations: Operating instructions — Unit 4

1 Read the operating instructions and then answer the questions. The photos may help you.

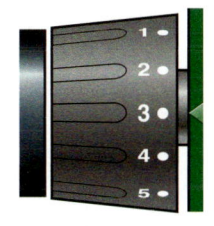

Use as a screwdriver

Place the driver bit in the screw head and apply pressure (*Druck*) to the machine. Start the machine slowly and then increase the speed gradually.

NOTE

5
- Make sure that the driver bit is straight or you may damage the screw and/or bit.
- When using wood screws, drill test holes first. This will make the work easier and can stop the wood splitting.

Use as a drill

First, turn the adjusting ring so that it points to the drill symbol. Then proceed as follows:

10
- **Drilling in wood**
  When drilling in wood, it is best to use a drill with a guide screw. The guide screw makes drilling easier by pulling the bit into the wood.

- **Drilling in metal**
  To stop the bit from slipping when starting a hole, make an indentation
15 (*Einbuchtung*) with a centre-punch and hammer.
  Place the point of the bit in the indentation and start drilling.
  Use a cutting lubricant when drilling metals, apart from when drilling iron and brass (*Messing*). These metals should be drilled dry.

1 Nennen Sie die beiden Funktionen dieser Maschine.
2 Was müssen Sie tun, bevor Sie eine Holzschraube festdrehen?
3 Welche Funktion hat der ‚adjusting ring'?
4 Was sollen Sie tun, bevor Sie Stahl anbohren?
5 Welche Metalle brauchen keine Bohrflüssigkeit beim Bohren?

Ich kann jetzt …

- meine Stadt beschreiben;
- über Arbeitsabläufe berichten;
- über Freizeit und zukünftige Pläne sprechen.

Wie schätzen Sie sich ein? Können Sie das, oder möchten Sie weiter üben?

Extra material: Safety rules

1 Complete the safety instructions with the phrases in the box.

> clean and well lit • concentrate on • loose clothes • materials and purpose •
> power cord • power source • safety glasses or goggles • the rain or wet conditions

Power tools
General safety rules

Failure to follow these instructions may result in electric shock, fire and/or serious injury.

1. Children and pets should be at a safe distance when you are using your power tools. You need to … the work you are doing. Distractions can cause accidents.

2. Keep your work area … . Accidents happen more often in untidy, dark areas.

3. Do not use power tools in … . Water can increase the risk of electric shock.

4. Use safety equipment. Always wear … to protect your eyes. You may also need dust masks, ear protectors and thick gloves.

5. Dress properly. Remember that … , jewellery or long hair can be caught in the tool and cause serious injury.

6. Disconnect the power tool from the … when you are not using it.

7. Do not use a tool with a damaged … . Be careful not to cut through the cord while you are using the tool.

8. Read the instructions carefully before you use it. Make sure that you only use the tool for the appropriate … .

Exam preparation

I Textarbeit

Text 1: Size Zero

Giant billboard posters which showed the body of French model Isabelle Caro shocked and horrified millions of people. Isabelle is a living skeleton with arms and legs as thin as sticks. She is 27 and weighs less than 32 kilos.
5 The photos on billboards and in fashion magazines were part of a campaign by the Italian clothes firm, Nolita, against size zero models. Isabelle has suffered from anorexia for the last 15 years. "I hope this campaign will show young girls how dangerous anorexia is. This is
10 what will happen to any young woman who tries to look like a size zero model."

Isabelle's career as a model started when she was thirteen. She was the ideal 'size zero' – tall and very thin. "The problem was, my body didn't want to stay thirteen
15 forever. So I ate one square of chocolate a day and a cup of tea without milk or sugar. I often had painful cramps and stayed in bed for most of the day. I felt terrible, but I got lots of modelling jobs."

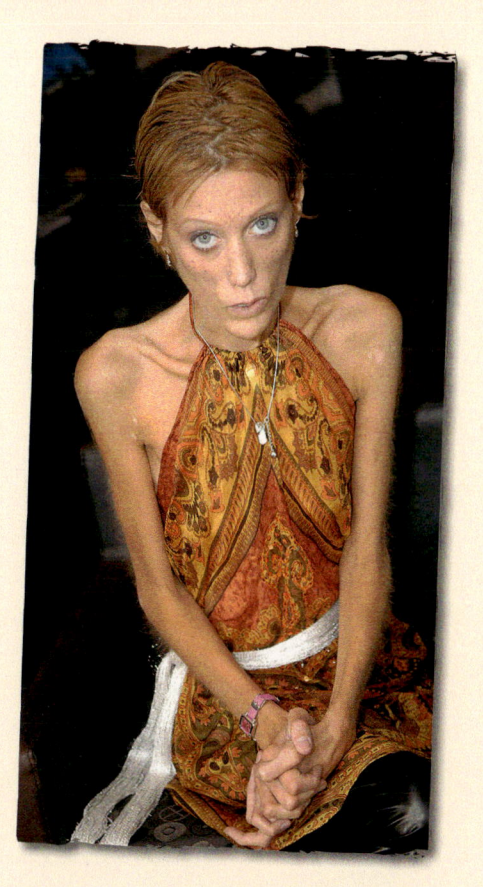

One day she collapsed at home and her parents rushed her to hospital. She was in a coma for
20 four days. She was 25 years old but she weighed only 25 kilos. She needed seven blood transfusions and doctors told her family that she would almost certainly die. "When I didn't die I surprised everyone, including myself. I know now what I want – I want to live." She is now writing a book about her life to try and help other people who suffer from anorexia.   *262 words*

Annotations

line 1   billboard – *Plakatwand*
line 4   weigh – *wiegen*
line 7   suffer from – *leiden an/unter*
line 15   forever – *(für) immer, ewig*
line 16   painful – *schmerzhaft*

❶ Questions on the text
Answer in **complete** English sentences, please.   Punkte

1.1 Why were the posters of Isabelle Caro so shocking?   2 P
1.2 What was the Nolita campaign about?   2 P
1.3 How did Isabelle try and stay thin?   2 P

Exam preparation

2 Aussagen über den Text 10 P

Kreuzen Sie (in einem Heft) an, ob folgende Aussagen richtig oder falsch sind. Kreuzen Sie nur an, wenn Sie sicher sind. Falsches Ankreuzen führt zu Punktabzug. Im Zweifel kreuzen Sie nichts an.

2.1 Isabelle Caro ist ein bekanntes italienisches Model.
2.2 Anorexia ist eine gefährliche Krankheit.
2.3 Die Nolita Werbekampagne richtete sich vor allem an junge Mädchen.
2.4 Das Ziel der Werbekampagne war, jungen Mädchen von einer Karriere als Model abzuraten.
2.5 Isabelle Caros Krankheit hat ihre Karriere als Model sogar gefördert.
2.6 The photos of Isabelle Caro were in fashion magazines.
2.7 The campaign against anorexia was organized by an Italian fashion magazine.
2.8 Thirteen-year-old girls who are tall and very thin are perfect 'size zero' models.
2.9 In the photos Isabelle was 32 and weighed only 27 kilos.
2.10 Isabelle was very lucky that she didn't die in hospital.

3 Finish the sentences 4 P

Use **only** information from the text, please.

3.1 Photos of Isabelle Caro shocked people because …
3.2 The campaign warned young girls about …
3.3 Anorexia helped Isabelle's career because …
3.4 The doctors at the hospital thought Isabelle would die because …

4 Matching 5 P

Match the beginnings 4.1–4.5 to five of the endings a)–g) according to the text. Two endings do not match.

4.1 The billboard posters showed a young woman
4.2 The photos of Isabelle Caro were
4.3 Nolita wanted to shock people and
4.4 Any young woman who tries to look like
4.5 Isabelle was in a coma for four days and

a) warn them about anorexia.
b) who looked like a living skeleton.
c) because nobody can stay thirteen forever.
d) her doctors thought she would die.
e) on billboards and in fashion magazines.
f) shocked everyone when she didn't die.
g) a 'size zero' model could die from anorexia.

Exam preparation

5 **Vocabulary work** 5 P
Find the word **in the text**:

5.1 A thin piece of wood from a tree
5.2 A very deep sleep that can happen to people who are seriously ill or badly hurt

Give the opposite:
5.3 living (line 3)
5.4 thin (line 4)
5.5 less (line 4)

6 **Grammar** 10 P

6.1 Fill in the correct forms of the verbs in brackets.

Millions of people … **(1 is seeing/saw/was seeing)** photos and posters of Isabelle Caro's body. Anorexia … **(2 turns/turned/will turn)** her body into a skeleton. The Italian clothes firm Nolita … **(3 were organizing/organized/organize)** this campaign against size zero, which … **(4 became/has become/will become)** a fashion ideal. They are worried that future models … **(5 wanted/are wanting/will want)** to be as thin as Isabelle, too.

6.2 Fill in the correct English words.

Isabelle Caro has been a model … **(1 seit)** she was 13. She has suffered … **(2 an/unter)** anorexia, a serious eating disorder, for … **(3 viele)** years. Hopefully she is getting … **(4 gesünder)** now. The Nolita campaign was very successful and it warned millions of … **(5 junger)** women about the illness.

Exam preparation

Text 2: Tattoo tips

Seventy-five percent of people who get tattoos regret it later. Alison Watts from Leeds had a tattoo when she was 16. "I really don't like my tattoo anymore. It's on my upper arm, so I can only wear clothes with long sleeves."

5   Louis Malloy is a professional tattoo artist. Louis has this advice for anyone who would like a tattoo:
- Do lots of research and find a design you really like because you'll have to live with it for the rest of your life.
- How big is it and where on your body do you want it? Will the tattoo fit into the routine of your life?
- Don't buy a cheap tattoo. Save up and get a good design.
- Always go to a professional tattoo artist. Look closely at the studio and the equipment. Is everything spotlessly clean?
- Ask to see previous examples of the tattooist's work.
- Follow aftercare instructions carefully.

157 words

Annotations

line 1   regret – *bedauern, bereuen*
line 7   research – *Forschung*
line 13   spotless(ly) – *makellos*
line 15   aftercare – *Nachbehandlung*

7 Mediation   14 P

Geben Sie die Hauptgesichtspunkte von Text 2 sinngemäß auf Deutsch wieder. Beachten Sie die folgenden Leitfragen. Schreiben Sie **ganze Sätze**.

- Wie viele Menschen wollen ihre Tattoos später entfernen lassen?
- Wer ist Louis Malloy?
- Welchen Rat gibt er Menschen, die sich ein Tattoo machen lassen wollen? Denken Sie an:

– Forschung   – Qualifikationen/Professionalität
– Größe   – Sauberkeit
– Stelle am Körper   – Erfahrung
– Qualität des Designs   – Nachbehandlung

8 Statement   6 P

"Tattoos are cool and fashionable."
Do you think this is true? Why? Why not? Give your opinion.
Write 30–40 words in **complete English sentences**, please.

Exam preparation

II Managing situations

9 Helping people

9.1 Giving directions — 3 P

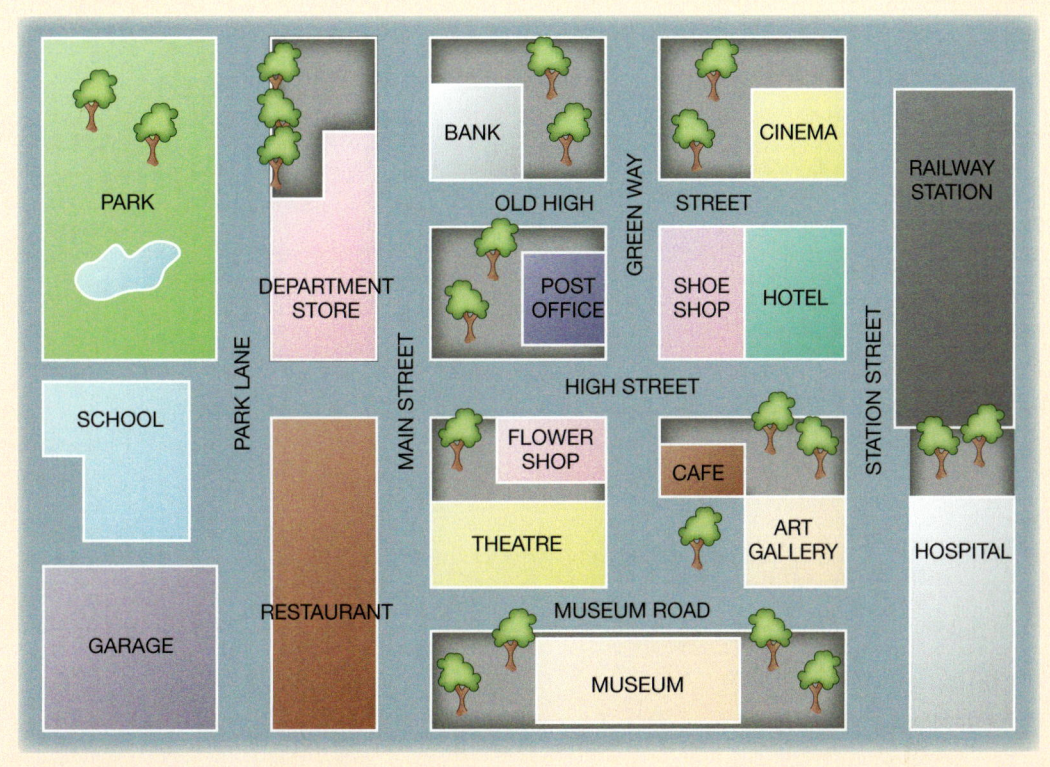

You are standing in front of the hospital on Station Street. A young man asks you, "Can you tell me the way to the bank on Old High Street, please?" Tell him how to get there.

9.2 Explaining signs — 3 P

Sie sind mit Ihren Eltern in einem britischen Supermarkt. Sie wollen bezahlen. Über der Kasse hängt ein Schild. Erklären Sie Ihren Eltern, was das Schild bedeutet.

**EXPRESS CASH DESK
NO MORE THAN 6 ITEMS**

Exam preparation

10 Telephoning 8 P

Mark Stiles is a receptionist at the Great Northern Hotel in Newcastle.
Find the phrases a)–h) of a caller that fit in to 10.1–10.8.

Mark	Good morning. This is the Great Northern Hotel. How can I help you?
Caller	(10.1) …
Mark	Can you spell your surname for me, please?
Caller	(10.2) …
Mark	Would you like a single or a double room, Mr Willoughby?
Caller	(10.3) …
Mark	When will you need the room?
Caller	(10.4) …
Mark	I'll just check. Yes, that's fine. Would you like a smoking or a non-smoking room?
Caller	(10.5) …
Mark	OK. How long will you be staying?
Caller	(10.6) …
Mark	That's no problem, Mr Willoughby. If you give me your email address or a telephone number, I will confirm your reservation.
Caller	(10.7) …
Mark	Thank you, Mr Willoughby. We will confirm your reservation by email as soon as possible.
Caller	(10.8) …

a) Next Tuesday.
b) I'm not sure. About four days. Perhaps longer.
c) Thank you. Goodbye.
d) Good morning. My name is Mike Willoughby. I'd like to book a room at your hotel, please.

e) A single room, please.
f) My email address is mike.willoughby@djinternet.com.
g) Certainly. It's W-i-l-l-o-u-g-h-b-y.
h) Non-smoking, please.

11 Guided composition 6 P

You are looking for a pen friend from an English-speaking country and you find this advert on the internet. Write an email to Rita. Write **complete English sentences**, please. The list will help you.

- Introduce yourself
- Tell her where you live
- Tell her about your family
- What are your favourite subjects at school?
- What are your favourite hobbies and leisure activities?

> **Wanted!**
> German pen friend (male or female)
> Hi! My name is Rita Maybury and I'm 16. I live in Dunedin. That's a town on the south coast of New Zealand. I have two younger brothers and a dog. I'm learning German at school. It's one of my favourite subjects. The others are sport and music. I like going for long walks. I often go sailing and fishing with my father. I love reading and I often get books from the library. I love listening to music, too. I've got 1,678 songs on my i-Pod! Interested? Please get in touch with me: rita@maybury.wicomnet.nz

Media stars

Unit 5

Springboard

In dieser Unit lerne ich, ...

- wie man das Datum schreibt;
- einen Text zusammenzufassen;
- Orts- und Zeitangaben zu machen.

What is a 'media star'? Basically, it's anyone who is famous. They can be film stars, singers, sports stars, writers, politicians or anyone who is often on television and is a 'celebrity'. People recognize them and admire them and this makes them useful for advertisers.

1 What can you say about the people in the photos?

I don't know who ... is.

... is/was a famous actor/ actress/model/...

He/She is advertising ... products.

2 Look through your old magazines and find an advert with a media star. Write 2 or 3 sentences about it.

The woman/man in the advert is ...
The product he/she is selling is ...
I would/wouldn't buy it because ...

Fun facts

- In most TV adverts for milk they use white paint!
- Without colouring, coca cola is green!

Text 1: James Dean – a media icon

21 Some media stars are still famous long after they have died or their careers have ended. They have become 'media icons'.

Although James Dean's acting career was very short, posters of him are still very popular with teenagers. In 1949 he was 18 and he left his uncle's farm in Indiana to go to New York and become an actor. He was very
5 good, but this did not help him in Hollywood. Film directors there thought he was too short and they only gave him work as an 'extra' in cheap films.

However, in February 1955 James got a role in the film 'East of Eden'. He played Caleb, an angry young man.
10 The film – and James – were a big success. Later that year he played the role of Jim Stark in the film 'Rebel Without a Cause'. Jim Stark is a young rebel and he is handsome, wild and dangerous. James played a similar role in 'Giant', his last film. These three films made James Dean into a teenage idol. Unfortunately, James didn't live to see 'Giant'. His love of fast cars killed him. On the 30th of September, 1955 his Porsche Spyder crashed into another car. James died in the crash.

1 Finish these sentences with a word from the text.

1 James Dean was an … .
2 He lived with his … .
3 They lived on a … .
4 Hollywood film directors said that James was too … .
5 They only gave him parts in … films.
6 In 1955 James Dean died in a car … .

2 Finish these sentences with information from the text.

1 James Dean was born …
2 He lived in Indiana until …
3 Although he was a good actor, he only …
4 His first big role …
5 In the same year he …
6 James died …

3 Find the opposites of these words in the text.

1 long (line 1)   4 expensive (line 7)   7 ugly (line 11)
2 bad (line 5)   5 west (line 9)   8 safe (line 11)
3 tall (line 6)   6 old (line 9)   9 hate (line 13)

4 Work in a group: Can you think of other 'media icons'? Collect information and talk about your 'media icon'.

Unit 5

Grammar

Remember: word order

- Eine Zeitangabe steht entweder am Satzanfang oder am Satzende.
  In 1949 James Dean was 18.   James Dean was 18 *in 1949*.
  Last week I was very busy.   I was very busy *last week*.

- Ortsangaben stehen meistens am Satzende (Reihenfolge: nah – weiter weg).
  James worked *in theatres in New York*. They lived *on a farm in Indiana*.

- Wenn beide Angaben zusammen am Satzende stehen, dann steht Ort vor Zeit.
  James went *to Hollywood a few years later*.

- Mehrere Angaben werden oft getrennt, Zeitangaben am Satzanfang und Ortsangaben am Satzende.
  On the 30th of September, 1955 James Dean died *in a hospital in Paso Robles*.

5 Put the parts into the right order to make sentences.

1. Ted / at 5.30 a.m. / yesterday / got up
2. my parents / a small apartment / in 1942 / in Skipper's Lane / moved into
3. on the south coast / a beach / we drove to / near Dover / yesterday afternoon
4. in Madrid / yesterday afternoon / our coach arrived / at 6.15 p.m. / at our hotel
5. afternoon / at 4.30 / our club meets / every Thursday

▶ Mehr Übungen zum Thema *word order* finden Sie auf Seite 97.

In Großbritannien schreibt man	entweder	11. June, 2001
	oder	11th (of) June, 2001
	oder	11.06.2001
In den USA schreibt man	entweder	June 11, 2001
	oder	6.11.2001

6 Copy this table into an exercise book. Then listen to the CD and fill in the missing information.

Name	Date of birth	Place of birth	Date of death	Place of death
…	…	Marion, …	…	Cholame, …
…	…	… , …	…	Vevey, …
…	…	Schöneberg, …	…	… , …
…	…	Tupelo, …	…	… , Tennessee

Text 2: The Beckhams Ltd

(23) David Beckham no longer plays as much football and his wife Victoria no longer sings a lot, but together, 'The Beckhams' are still powerful media icons. Firms pay millions to use them in their advertising. The Beckhams also use their media power to
5 earn money for charity.

For example, many parents of disabled children can not afford to buy expensive, special wheelchairs for their children, so the Beckhams' children's charity buys them. Ollie Rycraft, 13, was delighted with his new wheelchair because it meant that he
10 could be independent again.

But the Beckhams do not only work for their own charities. 'Malaria No More' has a very simple plan to fight malaria – the charity wants to give bed nets to every poor family in Africa. For $10, the charity can buy a bed net that will
15 protect a mother and child for five years. In a short video clip, David Beckham asked people to support them. When people saw this on television and on the internet, they donated millions of dollars. You can still see Beckham's clip on www.malarianomore.org/photovideo.php.

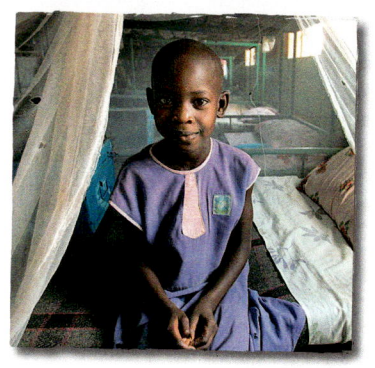

1 Match the beginnings 1–8 to the endings A–K. Three endings don't match.

1 The Beckhams are
2 They earn
3 One of their charities buys
4 The Beckhams helped
5 This charity wants to give
6 A bed net that costs
7 David Beckham made a video clip
8 The people who have seen this video clip

A expensive wheelchairs for disabled children.
B lives of luxury.
C the charity 'Malaria No More'.
D all over the southern part of Africa.
E have donated millions of dollars to the charity.
F bed nets to poor families in Africa.
G powerful media icons.
H ten dollars can protect a mother and child for five years.
I and asked people to give money to the charity.
J from multinational firms.
K millions of dollars for advertising products.

Unit 5

2 Geben Sie den Text ‚The Beckhams Ltd' sinngemäß auf Deutsch wieder. Schreiben Sie bitte einen zusammenhängenden Text. Die folgenden Leitfragen helfen Ihnen dabei.

- Warum sind die Beckhams begehrt bei Werbefirmen?
- Was machen die Beckhams für behinderte Kinder?
- Welches Ziel hat ‚Malaria No More'?
- Wie hilft ein Moskitonetz und was kostet es?
- Wie hat David Beckham ‚Malaria No More' unterstützt und welche Auswirkungen hatte das?

Grammar

Remember: word order

- Diese Wörter sind Bindewörter (*connectors*): **and, because, but, or, so, when**

- Sie verbinden ganze Sätze oder Teile von Sätzen miteinander.
  Many parents can't afford wheelchairs, **so** the Beckhams' children's charity pays for them.
  Advertising firms are interested in the Beckhams **because** they are media icons.

- Diese beiden Bindewörter (**mit Komma**) können auch am Anfang des Satzes stehen.
  Because they are media icons, advertising firms are interested in the Beckhams.
  When they saw the video clip, people donated money to the charity.

3 Join the sentences together with the connectors in brackets.

1 (but) Ollie Rycraft needed a special wheelchair. His parents couldn't afford it.
2 (or) People watched the video clip on TV. People watched it on the internet.
3 (so) Poor families in Africa can't afford bed nets. 'Malaria No More' buys the bed nets for them.
4 (and) David plays football. Victoria sings.
5 (when) The Beckhams support a charity. Millions of people will donate money to it.
6 (because) The Beckhams are media icons. Lots of people admire them.

▶ Mehr Übungen zum Thema *word order* finden Sie auf Seite 97.

4 In a group choose one of these two statements. Do you think the statement is true? Why? Why not?

1 "We need people that we can admire."   2 "Media icons earn too much money."

I agree with statement 1/2 because …
I agree with that.

I don't agree with statement 1/2 because …
I don't agree either.

I think the statement is fair / unfair / true / untrue / …

Job profile: Roadies

When they are on tour, a rock band or a pop group employ a lot of people. Because they travel around, they are all called 'roadies'. Their jobs are very different and are often very specialized.

① A tour manager is describing the jobs that different roadies do. Listen to the dialogue and match the job names with the photos.

beautician • cook • driver • lighting/sound technician • rigger • tour manager

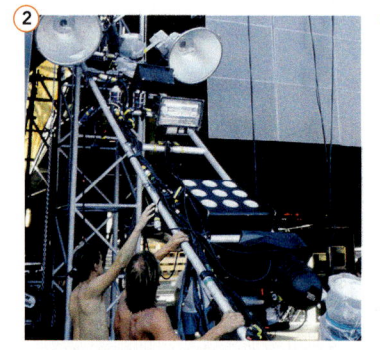

② Listen to the CD again and find two sentences about each job.

1 The tour manager organizes
  He deals with
2 The drivers drive
  They also help to
3 The riggers work
  They build
4 The lighting/sound technicians set up
  They also control
5 The beautician does
  She cuts
6 The cook does
  He cooks

A the stage.
B load and unload equipment.
C the microphones.
D everything on the tour.
E the stage lights.
F two hot meals every day.
G any problems during the tour.
H with steel scaffolding.
I their hair, too.
J the coach and the lorries.
K the catering.
L the make-up for the band.

Managing situations: Safety at work — Unit 5

You can see signs like these in factories, workshops, sport arenas, concert halls and cinemas.

1 2 3 4 5 6 7 8

1 Explain what these signs mean to an English visitor.

> **Here is some help:**
> - The square signs tell you where something is in an emergency.
>   *This is where you can find …*
>
>   > a first aid box • an emergency exit
>
> - The red and white signs tell you not to do something.
>   *Don't … !*
>
>   > smoke • enter this room
>
> - The black and yellow signs warn you about something.
>   *Be careful! The … here is/are … .*
>
>   > substances – toxic • floor – slippery
>
> - The round signs tell you what you must wear.
>   *You must wear … here.*
>
>   > a safety helmet • safety goggles

2 (25) An English apprentice has an accident in a German company while on work experience. Listen to him telling his supervisor what happened and then write an accident report in German. The questions below will help you.

- Wann und wo ist der Unfall passiert?
- Wo ist der Lehrling verletzt?
- Warum ist der Unfall passiert?

Ich kann jetzt …

- das Datum schreiben;
- einen Text zusammenfassen;
- Orts- und Zeitangaben machen.

Wie schätzen Sie sich ein? Können Sie das, oder möchten Sie weiter üben?

Extra material: Stars who care

Angelina Jolie

When she was filming 'Tomb Raider' in Cambodia, Angelina realized how horrible landmines are. Even after the wars they are used in, landmines kill and injure thousands of people every year – usually young children. Angelina now supports the campaign to ban land-
5 mines. She also supports charities that help refugees and she is an ambassador for the United Nations.

> **What you can do to help:**
> Organize a dinner party at your school. Send the money from tickets to the Adopt-A-Minefield Campaign. You can register your dinner at their website: www.1000dinners.com.

Chris Martin, lead singer of Coldplay

Chris thinks that fair trade will help fight poverty in Africa, not charity. Europe, Asia and the USA should pay a fair price for African products. Thousands of small farmers in Africa could then earn enough money to feed their families.

> **What you can do to help:**
> When you go shopping, only buy food with fair trade labels. Write to supermarkets that don't have fair trade products and complain.

1 Answer the following questions about the text.

1. Why are landmines so horrible?
2. How does Angelina Jolie support people affected by landmines?
3. Why should we pay a fair price for African products?
4. How can you help fair trade?

2 Now work in a group and choose one of your favourite media stars. What campaigns and charities do they support? Make a poster.

Shopping

Unit 6

Springboard

In dieser Unit lerne ich, …

- meine Vorlieben und Abneigungen auszudrücken;
- Personen und Sachen miteinander zu vergleichen;
- ein Verkaufsgespräch zu führen;
- eine Wegbeschreibung zu geben bzw. zu verstehen.

1 What are these products called?

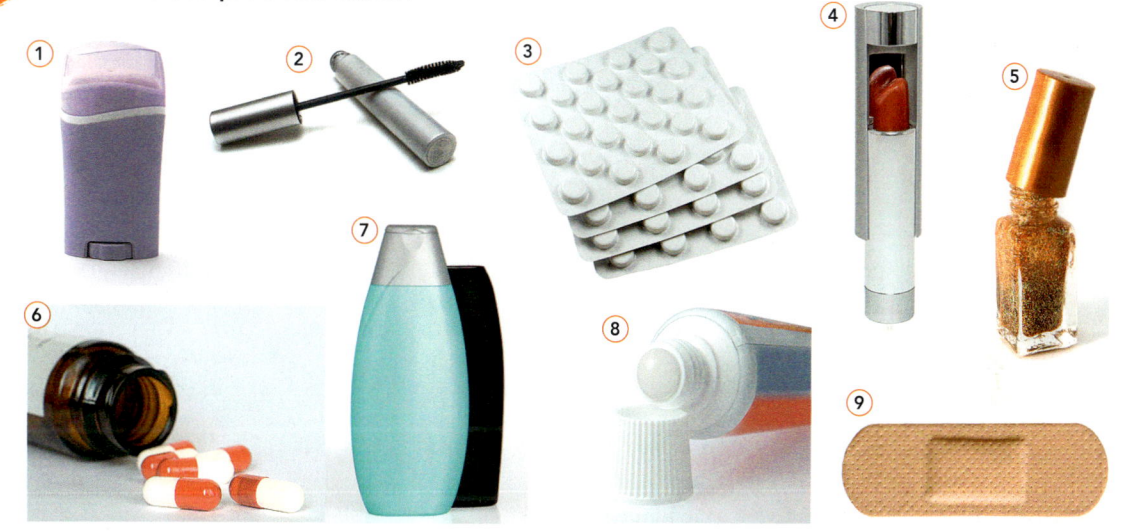

2 Organize the products above into the three categories below.

Bodycare	Cosmetics	Healthcare

3 Listen to the CD and write down all the prices you hear.

You hear:	You write:
sixty 'pea'	60 p
five pounds twenty-five	£ 5.25

Fun fact

The word 'shampoo' came to England from India in 1762. The Hindi word 'champo' means 'Wash your hair!'.

53

Text 1: Likes and dislikes

27 A group of college students are talking about what they like and dislike about clothes.

	Tessa	I enjoy shopping for clothes, especially with friends. It's not just about buying things. I like trying things on and finding the best prices. I hate looking around the shops with my boyfriend though. He's so impatient. He wants to go into a shop, find what he wants, buy it and leave.
5		
	Mark	Sounds sensible to me. I don't like shopping either. It's boring.
10	Brittany	I hate buying clothes because I can never find my size. I'm 1.85m tall and I'm not fat! So why do only special boutiques have clothes in my size?
	Tessa	I know what you mean. My shoe size is 44 and I sometimes have to buy men's shoes.
15		
	Jason	Jeans sizes are one of my problems. There are American sizes, French sizes, British sizes. And an 'L' in one store is often different to an 'L' in another store. So you have to try everything on before you buy it.
20	Harriet	Of course. But that's part of the fun, Jason. I like trying on different things. I haven't got much money to spend on clothes, so I have to choose carefully. But that means I'm also good at finding bargains.
	Pamela	I always buy clothes with a designer label. Then you know that it's top quality. They look better, too.
25	Brittany	Well, that's nice Pam, but we don't all have rich parents.
	Tessa	And we're not all worried about looking good.
	Mark	I don't think clothes with designer labels are worth the extra money.
	Brittany	Right. And is the designer label real or a copy?
30	Jason	Who cares? Buy the copy. It's cheaper and the quality is often just as good. And the girls will think you're cool because you're wearing expensive designer clothes. Isn't that right, Pamela?
	Pamela	No, of course it isn't. You have some really funny ideas, Jason!

Mission: Go to Gap, buy a pair of pants
Female   Male

Male
Time: 6 min
Cost: $33

Female
Time: 3 Hrs 26 min
Cost: $876

1 Are the following statements about the text true or false?

1. One of the girls is shorter than average.
2. One of the girls has problems buying shoes.
3. One of the boys thinks sizes are the same in every store.
4. One of the girls has rich parents.
5. One of the boys thinks girls only care about looking good.

Unit 6

2 Find words in the text that mean the same as these German words.

1 besonders, vor allem (line 1)
2 ungeduldig (line 6)
3 vernünftig (line 8)
4 Kleidergröße (line 11)
5 (nicht) viel (line 21)
6 Schnäppchen (line 22)

3 Make words from the text which translate the German terms below.

> have • look • spend • talk • try • walk

> about • around • into • on • on • to

1 umschauen
2 hineingehen
3 müssen
4 anprobieren
5 für etwas ausgeben
6 über etwas sprechen

Grammar

Remember: -ing form

- Die folgenden **Verben** drücken Vorlieben und Abneigungen aus. Bei den nachfolgenden Verben benutzt man die **-ing Form**.
  Tessa **enjoys** shopping. Mark **doesn't enjoy** looking at clothes.
  Harriet **likes** trying on different things. Mark **doesn't like** buying clothes.
  Harriet **loves** finding bargains. Tessa **hates** looking around the shops alone.

- Die **-ing Form** wird auch nach einer **Präposition** benutzt.
  It's not **about** buying things. I'm good **at** finding bargains.

4 Complete the text with the -ing forms of the verbs below.

> shop • carry • do • go • look • walk

I like … **(1)** out with my girlfriend, Monica. But I hate … **(2)** around a lot of different shops. Monica enjoys … **(3)** around stores and boutiques but I don't like … **(4)** all the things she buys! We believe in … **(5)** our own thing though. When I get tired of … **(6)** with Monica, I leave and go for a drink. Then we can't argue!

▶ Mehr Übungen zum Thema *-ing form* finden Sie auf Seite 93.

5 Group work: Talk about the things you like and dislike about clothes and shopping.

> I (don't) like shopping because …
>
> I enjoy going to …
>
> I hate buying …

Text 2: Is it an original or a copy?

(28) It is very easy to buy 'pirate' copies of designer products nowadays, and designers are not happy about it. Designer labels should be a guarantee of quality, they say. You pay more, but they are better than cheaper products. Cheap copies from Asia and China aren't as good as the original products. But this isn't always true. Some of these copies use the same materials and look exact-
5 ly the same. They are only cheaper because the people who make them work very hard. They work longer than the European workers who make the designer labels, but they earn less money.

Because they can earn more money if they pay their workers less, many designers buy these factories in Asia. The designers become business partners with the people who once made copies of their products. Nothing in the factories changes – the workers still work long hours and do not
10 earn a lot. The only difference is that the designer labels are now real. These designers then close many of their factories in Europe and the USA and thousands of workers lose their jobs. This is called 'outsourcing'.

However, not all designers do this. Many Italian workers have also lost their jobs, but factories in Rome, Turin and Milan are busier than ever. This is because some of the biggest Italian firms, like
15 Gucci, Dolce & Gabbana and Prada, have found another way of making a lot of money – they have replaced their Italian workers with cheaper workers from China. Handmade Italian shoes may cost €1,200 but they were probably made by Chinese immigrants and these immigrants work 12 hours each day and earn just €3 an hour.

1 Finish these sentences with information from the text.

1. Designers do not like copies because they …
2. There is sometimes no difference between designer products and the copies because …
3. Some designers close their factories in Europe because …
4. Some Italian designers use Chinese workers because …

2 Find the words in the text.

1. To get money for your work. (line 6)
2. The place where workers make products. (line 7)
3. When a business closes a factory because it can make things more cheaply elsewhere. (line 12)
4. Another word for business or company. (line 14)
5. Someone who lives in a foreign country. (line 17)

Unit 6

3 Complete this summary of the text with words from the box.

> cheaper • designers • factories • guarantee • immigrants • Italian • less • longer • pirate • workers

A designer label is no longer a … **(1)** of good quality. Some … **(2)** copies are just as good and they are … **(3)**, too. Some … **(4)** are now buying the … **(5)** that once made these copies. The workers in these factories work … **(6)** hours for … **(7)** money. Thousands of factory … **(8)** in the USA and Europe have lost their jobs. But many … **(9)** factories are still very busy. This is because the workers there are now … **(10)** from China.

4 Statement: Do you think pirate products are a problem? Why? Why not?
Write 30–40 words in complete English sentences.

> *I disagree with pirate copies because they …*
> *I think pirate copies are OK because they …*
> *We should/shouldn't buy … because …*

Grammar

Remember: Comparison of adjectives

- Englische Adjektive werden so gesteigert:
  - Einsilbige: *cheap* *cheaper (than)* *(the) cheapest*
  - Zweisilbige auf -y: *busy* *busier (than)* *(the) busiest*
  - Zwei- und Mehrsilbige: *expensive* *more expensive (than)* *(the) most expensive*

- Diese Adjektive werden unregelmäßig gesteigert:
  good – **better (than)** – **(the) best**   bad – **worse (than)** – **(the) worst**
  much/many – **more (than)** – **(the) most**   little – **less (than)** – **(the) least**

5 Use the correct form of the adjectives in brackets.

1. Pirate products are … **(cheap)** than designer products.
2. Designer labels are … **(expensive)** than normal clothes.
3. I think Louis Vuitton make the … **(pretty)** bags in the world.
4. European workers usually earn … **(much)** money than Asian workers.
5. Fashion models are usually … **(tall)** and … **(thin)** than normal women.
6. Rolex watches are … **(complicated)** than Japanese watches.
7. Heidi Klum is one of the world's … **(famous)** models.
8. Are Ray Ban sunglasses really the … **(good)** in the world?

▶ Mehr Übungen zum Thema *comparisons* finden Sie auf Seite 96.

Job profile: Sales assistant

John works in a boutique which sells women's clothing. Here he is helping a customer find a blouse.

1 Put the sentences from the box below in the right place to make a dialogue.

John	…
Customer	Yes, please. I'm looking for a blouse.
John	…
Customer	I'm usually an 'L'.
John	…
Customer	Yes, they're lovely. How much are they?
John	…
Customer	Oh, that's a bit too expensive for me.
John	…
Customer	They're really nice. I like the colours, too
John	…
Customer	Please. I'll try these two on: the blue one and the black one.
John	…
Customer	Thanks.

A That's fine. The changing rooms are opposite the cash desk.
B Hello. Can I help you?
C They're both £38.90.
D Well, these blouses here are cheaper. They're just £18.99 – a bargain.
E These are our latest blouses. What size are you?
F Would you like to try them on?
G OK. Here. This blouse is a lovely pink. And this one is light blue.

29 Now listen to the CD to check your dialogue. Then work with a partner and act it out.

2 Work with a partner and write and act a similar dialogue.

Here are some of the things you can change in your dialogue:
clothes: shirt, trousers, skirt, jacket, …
colours: dark green, sky blue, yellow, grey, white, …
sizes: S (small), M (medium), L (large), XL (extra large), XXL, …
prices: £23.90, $45.99, €64.50, …
places: behind, in front of, next to, near

Managing situations: Talking about jobs & directions   Unit 6

1 John's customer wants to know how to get to Shoe World. Fill in the gaps in John's directions.

> Look at this map. We're here on Baker Street. Go out and turn …**(1)**. Walk down …**(2)** and then turn right into …**(3)**. Now you turn right again into …**(4)**. Cross the street in front of the …**(5)** and Shoe World is there on the right.

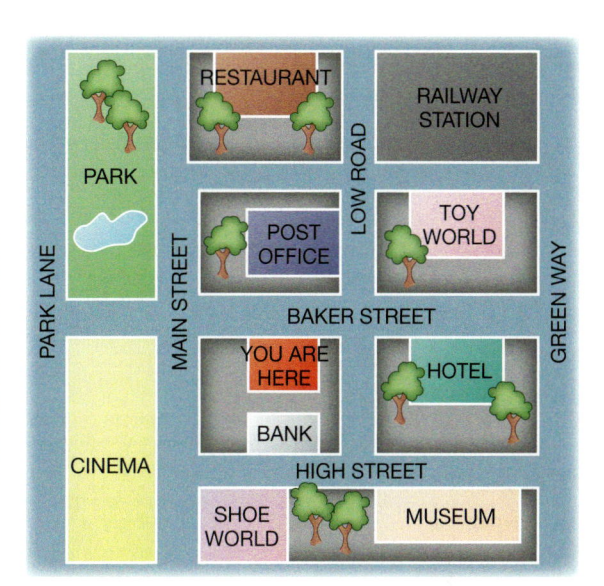

2 Work with a partner. Now give directions to different places on the map.

3 Read this part of an email where John talks about his job. Then answer the questions below.

> … I have just started a new job in a boutique in town. It's quite a good job really. We open at 9 and close at 5.30 every day Monday to Saturday and are also open on Sundays from 10 until 4. I only work five days a week though and luckily I only have to work every other Sunday. I arrive at 8.30 and sort out the clothes before we open. Then I help the customers throughout the day, with a lunch break from 12 until 1. At the end of the day, I count the money and clean the shop. I leave at about 6. It's hard work but fun. …

1 What are the opening times? Are they different to opening times here?
2 What are John's main jobs?

4 Write 30–40 words in English describing your last work placement.

Ich kann jetzt …

- meine Vorlieben und Abneigungen ausdrücken;
- Personen und Sachen miteinander vergleichen;
- ein Verkaufsgespräch führen;
- eine Wegbeschreibung geben bzw. verstehen.

Wie schätzen Sie sich ein? Können Sie das, oder möchten Sie weiter üben?

Extra material: The January sales

The January sales are very popular in Great Britain. Traditionally they start on 26 December. Even before the big stores open there are often long queues. The first people through the doors hope that they will find the best bargains.

1 The picture story shows Ted and Lucy's sales adventure. Write one or two sentences about each picture. There are some useful words and phrases in the box below.

> decide to – *sich entscheiden zu*
> join the queue – *sich hinten an einer Warteschlange anstellen*
> patient(ly) – *geduldig*
> unlock – *aufschließen, entsperren*
> a great rush – *ein großer Ansturm*
> purchases – *Anschaffungen*

We'll go early and get a good place.

JANUARY SALES AT HAMMONDS Doors open at 9.00 am

Good morning. Have you been here long?
About an hour or so.
Early the next morning ...

Brrr. It's cold!
Here, drink this. Only one hour more.

I'll meet you outside!

What did you buy?
A digital camera. It was a great bargain.

But you've already got a camera – and it's only a year old.
Yes, but it only has 6 megapixels. This camera has 10 megapixels.

I also got a jacket, shoes and T-shirts. They were all so cheap.

What have you got, Lucy?

Exam preparation

I Textarbeit

The Black Horse <u>reborn</u>!

People in Walcote were worried when Andy Clipston, a rich builder, bought the only pub in their village. They weren't surprised when he <u>knocked it down</u>. But they were surprised when he rebuilt
5 it seven months later. The pub was almost exactly the same, but it was better and further away from the very busy, noisy motorway.

The pub was Andy's local pub and he was worried that the motorway was slowly killing it. It was noisy and the glasses shook every time a big lorry drove past. There were <u>cracks</u> in the walls and
10 it was <u>shabby</u> and uncomfortable. But now The Black Horse is as peaceful and as <u>sturdy</u> as it was when it was new 200 years ago. It's now a low-energy building, too!

Andy didn't just rebuild the pub though; he also became the new landlord. He didn't know anything about beer, so he went on a special course for landlords. There Andy learned about traditional English beer and how to run a pub. He now works nights and weekends behind the bar.
15 Business is good and the pub is the centre of village life again. Local clubs meet there and there are darts and pool teams. Customers can enjoy live music on Fridays and weekends. Andy also employs two excellent cooks: a Thai and his British wife. So there is a choice between British and Thai cuisine.

Last week the Black Horse pub won a prize for being the best newly-built village pub.   *248 words*

Annotations

line 0   be reborn – *wiedergeboren sein, wieder aufleben*
line 3   knock sth down – *etwas abreißen*
line 9   crack – *Riss, Sprung*
line 10 shabby – *schäbig, verlottert, heruntergekommen*
line 10 sturdy – *robust, stabil*

1 Vocabulary work Punkte
Find the word **in the text**. 5 P

1.1 A word for somewhere that is quiet and is not hectic
1.2 The name for a man who owns and runs a pub

Give the opposite:
1.3 rich (line 2)
1.4 noisy (line 7)
1.5 new (line 11)

Exam preparation

2 Grammar 10P

2.1 Fill in the correct forms of the verbs in brackets.

1 The people of Walcote … (**1 is/are/were**) now very proud of their village pub.
2 The pub … (**2 looks/will look/is looking**) just like the old pub.
3 At the moment business … (**3 goes/went/is going**) well.
4 Last year, a pub in Lincolnshire … (**4 receives/received/was receiving**) the best pub award. Who … (**5 is getting/got/will get**) it next year?

2.2 Fill in the correct English words.

1 The new pub looks … (**1 *dasselbe***), but it is really much … (**2 *besser***).
2 It's now … (**3 *bequemer***) and it serves good food.
3 It attracts … (**4 *viele***) customers.
4 Andy is happy with … (**5 *seine***) new job.

3 Mediation 14P
Geben Sie die Hauptgesichtspunkte von Text 1 sinngemäß auf Deutsch wieder. Beachten Sie die folgenden Leitfragen. Schreiben Sie bitte **ganze Sätze**.

- Warum hat Andy Clipston die alte Dorfkneipe gekauft?
- Was machte er mit der Kneipe?
- Was musste Andy lernen?
- Wie hat er die neugebaute Kneipe belebt?
- Wie wurden seine Bemühungen belohnt?

4 Statement
"A disco is more important than a pub in a village."
Do you think this is true? Why? Why not? Give your opinion.
Write 30 – 40 words in **complete English sentences**, please.

Food and exercise Unit 7

Springboard

In dieser Unit lerne ich, …

- wie ich mich fit und gesund halten kann;
- Körperteile und Muskeln zu benennen;
- wie man telefoniert.

1 There are many different types of food. Find pictures of food and make a poster for these nine categories.

DRINKS BAKERY PRODUCTS DAIRY PRODUCTS SWEETS FRUIT

VEGETABLES NUTS MEAT FISH

2 Copy the following table into an exercise book and put in the food items from your project. (Some food items will go in more than one category.)

PROTEIN	CARBOHYDRATES	VITAMINS	FAT
sausage	*bread*	*cucumber*	*sausage*

3 What do you enjoy eating? Mark these food items in your table with a plus sign (+).

Fun facts

- People in France eat about 500,000,000 snails per year.
- Lemons contain more sugar than strawberries!

Text 1: A healthy lifestyle

Harry Waterman has been a fitness trainer for ten years. Carol Patterson, his partner, has taught food and nutrition at a local technical college for five years. They have just opened their own fitness studio and offer special fitness courses for teenagers.

Harry: I have worked in three fitness studios since I left school. I have trained lots of teenagers and I know what their problems are. Most of them are overweight. They want to lose
5 weight and look better. But overweight teenagers need more than just an hour on a fitness machine. They are overweight because their lifestyle is wrong. They don't get enough exercise in their daily lives.
10 They sit for hours in lessons at school, they travel by car, bus and train and then they sit at home in front of the TV or the computer.

That's why Carol and I have introduced a special fitness course for teenagers.
15 I show them how to put more physical activity into their daily lives. For example, they can use the stairs instead of lifts, walk to school, take the dog for a walk or do more housework. And they can also do things with their friends to get fit: go on a bike tour, play Frisbee, look around the shops, etc. All these little things add up. When they have done that, an hour or two with
20 a fitness machine can improve their muscles.

Carol: More physical activity helps but healthy food is really important too. Most teenagers eat the wrong things. They eat food that contains too much fat, sugar and salt. Also, they don't get enough vitamins or fibre. I show them that they can lose weight, be healthier and look better by eating more lean
25 meat, fish, cereals and fresh fruit and vegetables. After a few weeks, you can see the difference and the teenagers even start to enjoy it.

1 Find words or expressions in the text that complete the definitions below.

1 … is the science of food.
2 A person who is heavier than normal for his or her age and size is …
3 People with different … live in different ways and do and eat different things.
4 … is any physical activity that improves a person's health.
5 … meat is meat with no fat (or very little fat).

Unit 7

2 Finish the sentences with information from the text.

1. Overweight teenagers need to …
2. In a special course teenagers learn about …
3. Healthy food contains less … and more …

Grammar

Remember: present perfect

- Wenn wir die Dauer einer Situation oder Handlung betonen wollen, können wir das **present perfect** mit **for** (Zeitdauer) oder **since** (Zeitpunkt) benutzen.
  Harry Waterman **has been** a fitness trainer **for** ten years.
  I **have worked** in three fitness studios **since** I left school.

- Situationen/Ereignisse, die **noch andauern**, werden ganz ohne Zeitangabe oder mit **just** benutzt.
  Harry **has trained** lots of teenagers. They **have just opened** their own fitness studio.

- Das *present perfect* wird mit *have/has* + Partizip Perfekt (3. Form des Verbs) gebildet.

- Signalwörter sind: *already, before, so far, ever, never, just, recently, not yet,* usw.

3 Complete the sentences with the present perfect forms of the verbs in brackets.

1. Harry Waterman … **(help)** a lot of people to lose weight since he left school.
2. He … **(work)** with teenagers for many years.
3. They … **(start)** their own business – a fitness studio.
4. They … **(just move)** into a new building.
5. A local newspaper … **(write)** about Harry and Carol's special course for teenagers already.
6. Harry … **(just see)** his first client.

> Mehr Übungen zum Thema *present perfect* finden Sie auf Seite 90.

4 A healthy diet contains protein, carbohydrates, some fat and vitamins. Work with a partner and plan three healthy meals for one day that you both like.

I like … for breakfast. What about you?

We could have … for lunch / dinner / tea.

I don't really like … I'd prefer …

- In the UK **breakfast** during the week is a quick meal, usually just cereal or toast. Some people still eat a traditional fried breakfast (eggs, sausages, tomatoes, bacon) at the weekend.
- **Lunch** can be either a sandwich or a hot meal. Some people, especially in the North of England and in Scotland, call their midday meal **dinner**. The evening meal is called **dinner** or **tea**.

Text 2: Captain Cook and a space flight to Mars

(31) What has Captain Cook, who died in 1779, got to do with a space flight to Mars? The simple answer is: 'healthy food'. We all need the vitamins that come from the fresh food
5 that we eat. This was a big problem for people who sailed on very long voyages because food loses vitamins when it isn't fresh. Many sailors became very ill after months at sea with no fresh food and not
10 enough Vitamin C. Their skin turned black and their hair and teeth fell out. A lot of them died. They called this terrible illness 'scurvy'.

Captain Cook went on three long voyages to Australia and New Zealand. On his first voyage
15 there were five sailors who became ill with scurvy, but they didn't die. On his next two voyages nobody became ill and nobody died from scurvy. So how did Captain Cook do it? This was a very important question for the British Royal Navy.

The answer isn't simple. It was partly the kind of food that he took with him and how he stored it. His sailors had fresh eggs for breakfast. They kept the eggs in barrels of oil and they stayed
20 fresh for many months. Captain Cook also took barrels of 'sauerkraut', which contains calcium, magnesium, Vitamin C and lots of fibre. This was an idea from one of his sailors, who was German. The crew also drank grog, which was a mixture of strong rum and water. The rum disinfected the water, which was usually bad on a long voyage.

Captain Cook also believed that a happy crew was a healthy crew. He looked after his sailors
25 well, who loved him for this. They had more space below decks, good food and warm, clean clothes. They also had regular hours of work, leisure and sleep. Captain Cook and his officers organized leisure-time activities: concerts, dancing, fishing and deck games.

Fun fact
- When the water on his ship became bad, Admiral Vernon (1684–1757) mixed it with rum and lemon juice so that his crew could drink it. This became a tradition in the British Royal Navy. Sailors got two grog rations daily. This tradition ended in 1970.

1 Geben Sie den Text sinngemäß auf Deutsch wieder. Schreiben Sie bitte einen zusammenhängenden Text. Die folgenden Punkte helfen Ihnen dabei.

- die Parallelen zwischen einer langen Reise in einem Raumschiff und einer Reise in einem alten Segelschiff
- die Folgen von Vitaminmangel bei der Ernährung
- wie Captain Cook diese Krankheit besiegt hat

Unit 7

2 Look at the text and find the opposite of these words.

1. lived (line 1)
2. complicated (line 3)
3. small (line 5)
4. short (line 6)
5. infected (line 23)
6. less (line 25)

3 Which words from the text do these definitions describe?

1. A long journey in a ship or spaceship
2. Someone who works on a ship
3. The time when you are not working

Grammar

Remember: Relative pronouns *who*, *which*, *that*

- Bei Personen benutzt man **who** oder **that**.
  On his first voyage there were **five sailors** **who/that** *became ill with scurvy.*

- Bei Tieren und Sachen benutzt man **which** oder **that**.
  We all need the **vitamins** **that/which** *come from the fresh food* **that/which** *we eat.*

  Ein Tipp: Wenn Sie unsicher sind, **that** ist immer richtig!

4 Complete the sentences with the correct relative pronouns.

1. On a long voyage the water … the sailors drank was usually bad.
2. One of the sailors … sailed with Captain Cook was German.
3. The rum … disinfected the water was strong.
4. All the men … sailed with Captain Cook liked him.
5. The ship … Captain Cook sailed in was called the Endeavour.
6. The eggs … the sailors ate were kept in barrels of oil.

▶ Mehr Übungen zum Thema *relative pronouns* finden Sie auf Seite 94.

5 Listen to the CD and make notes in an exercise book. Then listen again and answer the questions.

1. When and where was James Cook born?
2. What were his first two jobs after leaving school?
3. Where was his next job and what was it?
4. What was a 'cat'?
5. How old was James when he left Whitby?

Job profile: Fitness trainer

Harry Waterman knows that it is important to do 'warm up' exercises before people use the machines. Here he describes some exercises that he uses.

1 Look at the pictures of the exercises.
Fill in the missing body parts.

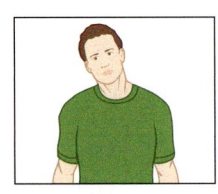

This exercise is good for people who work at a desk or a computer. Move the …(1) in a full circle. This stretches the …(2) muscles.

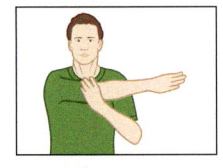

Exercise relieves stress, which can cause headaches.
In this exercise you stretch your right …(3) across your …(4).

We call this exercise the cat stretch. It relaxes the muscles in the …(5).

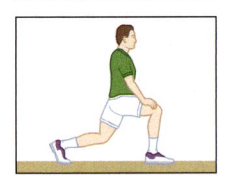

This stretches the muscles in the upper …(6).
It's a good exercise to do before any physical activity.

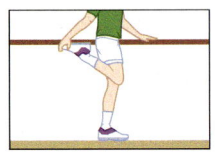

For this exercise you must stand on one …(7).
Then you lift the other one behind you.
It stretches the muscles around the …(8).

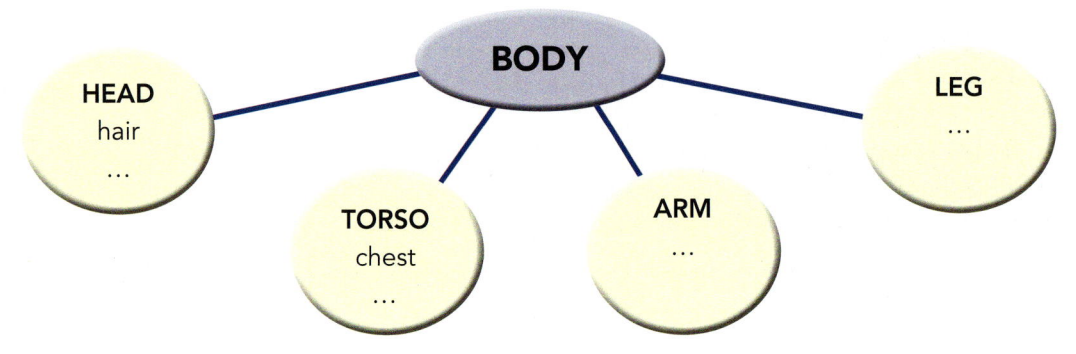

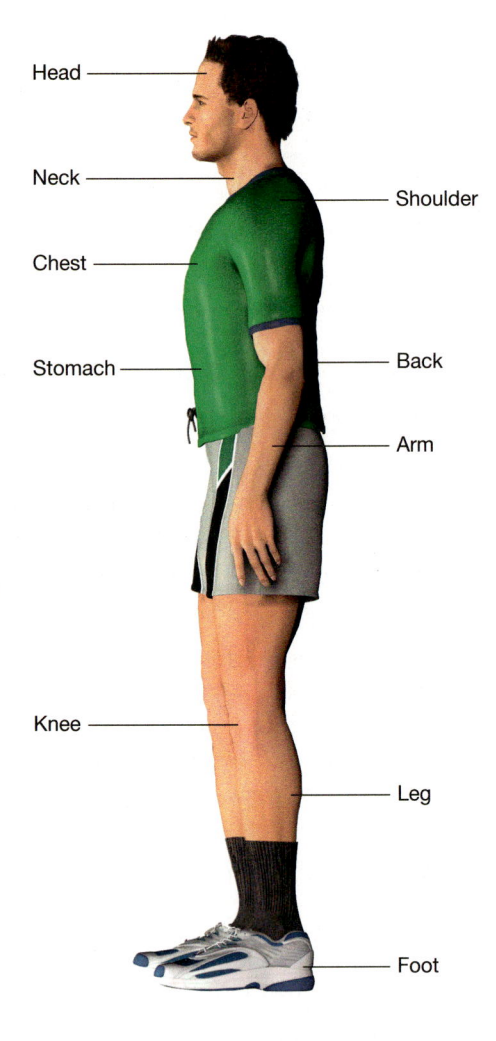

Head
Neck
Chest
Stomach
Shoulder
Back
Arm
Knee
Leg
Foot

2 Copy this diagram into an exercise book and then collect more words.

BODY

HEAD
hair
…

TORSO
chest
…

ARM
…

LEG
…

Managing situations: Telephoning   Unit 7

A Can you put me through to …, please?
B Could you ask him/her to call me back?
C Please hold the line while I connect you.
D Could you take a message for me, please?
E Sorry, I must have dialled the wrong number.
F I'll pass the message on to him/her.
G Who's speaking, please?
H I'm afraid he/she isn't available.
I I'm sorry his/her line's busy.
J Thanks for calling.
K Can I take a message?
L Would you like to leave a message?

1 Match the phrases in the box above with the following situations. Sometimes more than one phrase is possible.

1 You want to talk to somebody.
2 You want to ask somebody to call you back later.
3 You want to know who is calling / who you are talking to.
4 You want to tell the caller that you can put him/her through now.
5 You want to tell the caller why you cannot put him/her through.
6 You want to ask if you can leave a message.
7 You want to ask if you can take a message.
8 You want to apologize for dialling the wrong number.
9 You promise to pass the message on to somebody.
10 You want to end the telephone call.

2 Work with a partner. Complete this telephone dialogue using the phrases above.

A: **Pep Fitness Studio**

Melden Sie sich mit dem Firmennamen.

Nennen Sie Ihren eigenen Namen. Fragen Sie, wie Sie behilflich sein können.

Mr/Mrs … ist nicht da. Er/Sie ist … Sie fragen, ob Sie etwas ausrichten können.

B: **Salesperson for fitness machines**

Grüßen Sie und nennen Sie Ihren Namen.

Bitten Sie darum, mit Mr/Mrs/… verbunden zu werden.

Sie bedanken sich. Ja, Sie möchten eine Nachricht hinterlassen. Mr/Mrs … soll zurückrufen. Sie sind unter der Nummer … zu erreichen.

Ich kann jetzt …

- mich fit und gesund halten;
- Körperteile und Muskeln benennen;
- telefonieren.

Wie schätzen Sie sich ein? Können Sie das, oder möchten Sie weiter üben?

Extra material: A new TV programme

Fat children to face 'bush tucker' TV trial

The BBC is planning a new reality show where overweight teenagers have to hunt for food to survive.

The programme, which is called Fat Teens Can't
5 Hunt, will send 10 British teenagers, aged 16 to 19, to live with an Aboriginal tribe in the Australian outback. Cameras will follow the group's attempt to live on a "bush tucker" diet for a month. During this time they will have to catch,
10 kill and cook any animals or insects they want to eat.

Britain has the fattest teenagers in Europe – one in three are overweight or obese. Producers of the programme hope that the experiment will help the teenagers to think about their relationship with food before they reach adulthood.

15 The BBC3 series will be filmed during the summer and producers are now looking for teenagers. It follows Channel 4's plans for a similar show where participants have to find food in a rubbish dump.

- In Britain there are now four times (4x) more overweight teenagers than in 1980.
- In 2028 half of all adults in Britain will be overweight.

1 Do you think schools should make their pupils do more physical activity?

> I think it is a good/bad/terrible idea.

> Yes, young people need rules. Their schools should ...

> No, young people must want to do this. Their schools shouldn't ...

> You can/can't make people change their lifestyles. Trying to make people do things is ...

Adventures in Australia

Unit 8

Springboard

In dieser Unit lerne ich, ...

- wie man um Information bittet;
- wie man Personen und Sachen beschreibt;
- wie man ‚small talk' macht.

A quiz about Australia

1 How much do you know about Australia? Try and answer the questions with a partner then listen to the CD to see if you were right.

1. Who landed in Australia on the 19th of April, 1770?
2. What did the first settlers call the people who were already in Australia when they arrived?
3. What is this?
4. What is the name of this musical instrument?
5. What do Australians call the hot, dry part of their country?
6. What is the name of this Australian tourist attraction?
7. What is the name of this famous underwater attraction?
8. What animal is this?

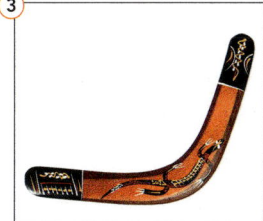

2 With a partner find more interesting photos and facts about Australia. Make question cards and organize a quiz.

How many sheep are there in Australia?

There are one hundred and twenty million sheep in Australia. (But only twenty million people!)

71

Text 1: German girls find lost boy

(34) 'Live Australia' is a travel agency that arranges for young people from the EU to spend time working and travelling around Australia. This article is from the agency's magazine.

German girls find lost boy

Karin Neumunster, 18 and Brigitte Rossmann, 19 are both from Stuttgart in Germany. They spent last year on our work programme travelling and working their way across Australia. They worked in bars, restaurants and offices in Sydney, Cairns
5   and small towns all other the country. Here they tell us about how they helped an autistic boy in Wemmis Creek.

"We were working as waitresses in Wemmis Creek when we heard about Glen. One morning he took the school bus to the school for disabled children, but he didn't go into his class. He walked into the outback. The school soon noticed that he wasn't in his class and they called
10   the police. Two police officers arrived quickly and they immediately called for more help. The police organized a carefully planned search for Glen. Ten police officers and thirty volunteers searched the area with cars, motorbikes and tracker dogs. They had to stop when it became dark though.

When we heard about Glen, we jumped on our motorbikes and joined the search. We camped
15   in the outback so that we could start early. But we needed water first, so we rode to a sheep farm that was marked on our map. On the way to the farm we saw a water pump and decided to get water there. When we got there, we saw this young boy. He looked fine. He was playing quite happily with his portable playstation and he completely ignored us. We called the police and took him back to Wemmis Creek. We were just so glad that we could help."

1 Look at the photos and find the English names in the text.

Unit 8

2 Finish the sentences with information from the text.

1 Glen wasn't in his class, so the school …
2 Two police officers arrived and …
3 On the first day they searched until …
4 Two German waitresses camped in the outback because …
5 They rode to the sheep farm first because …
6 Glen ignored the two girls because …

Grammar

Remember: Adjectives and adverbs

- **Adjektive** beschreiben meistens Nomen.
  *a school for **disabled** children • the **coolest** place • a **careful** search • a **hot** day*

- **Adverbien** beschreiben meistens Verben, aber auch Adjektive. Viele enden auf -ly.
  *they **soon** noticed • they arrived **quickly** • they **immediately** called • a **carefully** planned search*

- Wichtige unregelmäßigen Adverbien sind:
  good** – **well** • **hard** – **hard** • **fast** – **fast** • **early** – **early

- Bei diesen Verben benutzt man immer **Adjektive**: be, become, feel, look, smell (riechen, duften), sound (klingen), taste (schmecken).
  *It became **dark**. • The outback is very **hot**. • Glen looked **fine**. • The girls felt **good**.*

3 Complete the sentences with either the adjective or the adverb.

1 The police organized a *careful/carefully* search for the autistic boy.
2 The police and the volunteers *careful/carefully* searched the area.
3 Glen's mother was *angry/angrily* with the driver of the school bus.
4 She shouted at him *angry/angrily*.
5 The police organized the search *quick/quickly*.
6 Two police officers made a *quick/quickly* search of the school.
7 Glen can play his portable playstation *good/well*.
8 The two German girls who found Glen felt really *good/well*.

▶ Mehr Übungen zum Thema *adjectives and adverbs* finden Sie auf Seite 95.

Text 2: Solo around the world

Reporter (35) With me in our Melbourne studio today is Jesse Martin. Last year, Jesse sailed solo around the world. He was only seventeen and was the youngest person to make the trip. Did you grow up with boats, Jesse?

Jesse No, not really. My family had a house near the beach but I didn't learn to sail until I was fourteen.

Reporter You lived in Cow Bay – that's in northern Australia, near Cairns, right?

Jesse Yes. My parents moved there when I was little. They lived in Germany for a while before that because my dad is German. I was born in Munich actually.

Reporter Jesse began and ended his solo voyage around the world here in Melbourne. He was alone at sea for eleven months. That was a dangerous voyage for a 17-year old teenager, Jesse. Why did your parents allow you to do it?

Jesse I think it was because they knew I could do it. It actually wasn't all that difficult or dangerous really. I'm not the world's best sailor, but I'm very careful. I checked my position every day. I checked my sails and equipment. I didn't take any risks or do anything stupid.

Reporter But there must have been times when you were frightened?

Jesse Oh, yes. For example, my boat nearly hit a whale in the South Atlantic and I ran into giant waves near the Cape of Good Hope. But the most dangerous moment was near the end. I nearly ran into a big tanker during the night. I just didn't see it.

Reporter How exciting. But you did it. What was the first thing you did after you landed in Melbourne after almost a year?

Jesse It sounds silly but I missed real food and I was really hungry. So I ate a hamburger.

Reporter Right. And then you wrote a book about your voyage.

Jesse Yes, it's called 'Lionheart'. That was the name of my boat.

1 Complete these statements with information from the text.

1 Jesse Martin is famous because …
2 Jesse's voyage, which took eleven months, started …
3 Jesse nearly ran into a big tanker because …
4 After he returned home from his voyage, Jesse …
5 'Lionheart' is the name of …

2 Put these sentences into the correct order.

A His parents came to Australia from Germany.
B Jesse was very careful and he checked his position and his equipment every day.
C Jesse wrote a book about his voyage.
D Jesse's voyage began in Melbourne and it took eleven months.
E When he was 17, Jesse Martin sailed solo around the world.
F Although Jesse's family lived near the beach, he didn't learn to sail until he was fourteen.

Grammar

Remember: Questions and short answers

- Im *simple present* und im *simple past* brauchen **modale Hilfsverben** und das Verb **be** keine weiteren Verben (Hilfsverben), um Fragen zu bilden. Das Verb stellt man vor das Subjekt.
  You **can** sail.   **Can** you sail?   Yes, I **can**./No, I **can't**.
  He **is** hungry.   **Is** he hungry?   Yes, he **is**./No, he **isn't**.

- **Vollverben** in einer *progressive*-Form benutzen eine Form von **be**, um Fragen zu bilden:
  wait   **Is** your dad **waiting** for you?   Yes, he **is**./No, he **isn't**.

- Alle anderen **Vollverben** brauchen bei der Fragebildung **do/did** oder ein **Hilfsverb** in der entsprechenden Zeitform.
  run   **Did** you **run** into a tanker?   Yes, I **did**./No, I **didn't**.
  do   **Have** you **done** this before?   Yes, I **have**./No, I **haven't**.

3 Complete the questions.

1 … Jesse and the reporter in a studio in Melbourne?   – Yes, they are.
2 … Jesse the youngest person to sail solo around the world?   – Yes, he was.
3 … his voyage take eleven months?   – Yes, it did.
4 … his parents live near Cairns?   – Yes, they do.
5 … they lived there since Jesse was two years old?   – Yes, they have.

4 Complete the short answers.

1 Did Jesse finish his voyage in Sydney?   – …
2 Was his brother with him for part of the voyage?   – …
3 Have his parents got a house in Cow Bay?   – …
4 Was Jesse's voyage dangerous?   – …
5 Has Jesse written a book about whales?   – …

▶ Mehr Übungen zum Thema *questions and answers* finden Sie auf Seite 91.

Job profile: A woodworker

Desmond Antonov's parents came from Kiev in the Ukraine but Desmond was born in Sydney. He is an apprentice at Oyster Bay Boatbuilders.

I really enjoy my job here. It's a small firm – just the boss, his secretary, four woodworkers and me. We all use our first names. I call the boss Tommy and he calls me Des – and then he tells me what he wants me to do. That's the Australian way. The work here is interest-
5 ing because we build boats with wood in the old traditional way. I enjoy building boats and I love sailing them, too. I learn a lot on the job because the other woodworkers are very experienced. At the moment I'm learning about old hand tools and how to use them. At work we use power tools, of course. But the boss says that a good
10 woodworker should also know how to use the old hand tools.
On Thursdays and Fridays I also go to a woodworking course at a local technical college. I already have Certificate 1 and 2, and I'm now studying for Certificate 3. I like the course because it's practical and hands-on. I hope to start the Certificate 4 course next year.

1 Answer the following questions on the text.

1. How many people work at Oyster Bay Boatbuilders?
2. Why does Desmond enjoy his job?
3. What qualifications does Desmond have?

2 Desmond is working on a new ship. What tools does he need?

chisel   drill   hammer   nail   saw   tape measure

He needs a …
- to cut the timber.
- to make holes in the wood.
- to hold pieces of timber together.
- to carve the wood.
- to measure the timber.
- to put the nails in the wood.

Managing situations: Small talk at a party — Unit 8

Tommy Sheridan, the general manager at Oyster Bay Boatbuilders, has invited all the woodworkers and their wives and girlfriends to a barbecue party on the beach.

1 What does Desmond say? Put the sentences from the box below in the right place to complete the dialogue.

Tommy	G'day, Des! I'm glad you could make it.
Desmond	(1) …
Tommy	And is this your girlfriend?
Desmond	(2) …
Tommy	Nice to meet you. That's my wife over there. I think you know Jenny already, Des.
Desmond	(3) …
Tommy	Hey, Jenny. Look who's here. I'm serving the drinks and she's grilling hamburgers.
Desmond	(4) …
Tommy	They certainly do! I haven't had one yet. Here. Would you like a drink?
Desmond	(5) …
Tommy	What do you fancy? We've got everything. Juice? Soda?
Desmond	(6) …
Tommy	OK. Two cans of ice cold orange soda. Here you are.
Desmond	(7) …
Tommy	Sounds good. I haven't eaten anything yet. Could you bring me a hamburger too?
Desmond	(8) …

- **A** Mmh! Those hamburgers smell really good.
- **B** Thanks, Tommy. We'll go and say hello to your wife. And I'll try the hamburgers.
- **C** That's right, Tommy. This is Rachel. Rachel, this is Tommy Sheridan, my boss.
- **D** Hi, Tommy. Thanks for inviting us.
- **E** Sure, Tommy. We'll be back in a minute or two.
- **F** That's right. We met at the Christmas party.
- **G** Orange soda would be great if you have it.
- **H** Yes, please. Something cold would be great, Tommy. It's really hot today.

36 Now listen to the CD to check your dialogue. Practise the dialogue with a partner and then write a similar party conversation.

> **Ich kann jetzt …**
> - um Information bitten;
> - Personen und Sachen beschreiben;
> - ‚small talk' machen.
>
> Wie schätzen Sie sich ein? Können Sie das, oder möchten Sie weiter üben?

Extra material: A job abroad

Live Australia – Working Holidays

Our working holidays programme gives you the chance to get to know Australia. You can travel around for up to twelve months and we will help you find jobs while you are there. So there will be no money problems. There's no fixed plan – you can travel where you want, when you want. It's a great way to get experience of both work and another culture. So what are you waiting for?

"I loved my time in Australia. I spent six months working in Sydney, Melbourne and Cairns. The Live Australia people were really helpful. They helped me find a room and some really interesting jobs. And I got to spend time relaxing too, even at Bondi Beach! I might come back again next year!"
Daniel Carter, 19

Live Australia offers you:

- Help arranging a working holiday visa
- Someone to meet you at the airport when you arrive and a week's free accommodation
- Help finding jobs through our agency which has links across the whole country
- Travel and accommodation discounts
- A 24-hour emergency phone number

Applicants must:

- Be at least 18
- Be US or EU citizens
- Have quite a good level of English
- Pay for flights to and from their home country
- Pay a programme fee of €400

1 Are the statements about the text true or false?

1 The 'Live Australia' programme lasts 12 months.
2 You don't have to pay for accommodation when you first arrive.
3 There is someone available 24 hours a day if you have a problem.
4 German citizens can not take part in the programme.
5 The programme costs nothing.

2 Imagine you would like to go on the Live Australia programme. Write a letter telling the company about yourself. The list will help you.

- What is your name?
- How good is your English?
- Why do you want to go on the programme?
- What work would you like to do?

Exam preparation

I Textarbeit

Text 1: Just one of the team

Stephanie Morris, 27, is the only female firefighter in Carrboro, North Carolina. She has been a firefighter for almost seven years.

Although she is the only woman, Stephanie is
5 treated like any other member of the team. She enjoys working with her <u>fellow firefighters</u> and they have all become close friends. This is important when they have to deal with horrible scenes, because they understand each other and
10 can talk about things afterwards.

Stephanie's husband Brian is also a firefighter. He works in Durham, a nearby town so her kids (aged 1, 4 and 5) think everyone must have a firefighter in their family.

15 As a female firefighter, Stephanie is an important role model for her two daughters. But there are some disadvantages for women. Firefighters often have to lift and carry heavy things so they must be very fit and strong. This can be more difficult for women but all firefighters get free <u>gym</u> membership to help with this. Most of the equipment is still made for men, so things like helmets, gloves, boots, jackets and <u>breathing apparatus</u> can be too big for a woman.

20 But there are also some advantages. Most firefighters only work ten days a month, which is great for a working mother with small children. Women are also often smaller and lighter than men and can fit into small spaces more easily. This can be crucial when the firefighters are searching ruins for <u>survivors</u>.

238 words

Annotations

line 6 fellow firefighter – *Feuerwehrkamerad(in)*
line 17 gym – *Turnhalle; Fitnessstudio*
line 19 breathing apparatus – *Atemschutzgerät*
line 23 survivor – *Überlebende(r)*

① Questions on the text   Punkte
Answer in complete English sentences, please.

    1.1 How long has Stephanie worked for the Carrboro Fire Department? **2 P**
    1.2 What does Stephanie's husband do? **2 P**
    1.3 How often does Stephanie work in a month? **2 P**

Exam preparation

2 **Aussagen über den Text**   10 P

Kreuzen Sie (in einem Heft) an, ob folgende Aussagen richtig oder falsch sind.
Kreuzen Sie nur an, wenn Sie sicher sind. Falsches Ankreuzen führt zu Punktabzug.
Im Zweifel kreuzen Sie nichts an.

2.1 Es gibt auch andere Feuerwehrfrauen in Carrboro.
2.2 Carrboro ist eine Kleinstadt in Nord Carolina.
2.3 Stephanies männliche Kollegen machen ihr das Leben schwer.
2.4 Stephanie arbeitet mit ihrem Mann zusammen.
2.5 Stephanie hat einen Sohn.
2.6 Carrboro is the only town in the area.
2.7 Firefighters must be healthy and very fit.
2.8 Firefighting has both advantages and disadvantages for women.
2.9 Women are usually just as big and as strong as men.
2.10 Female firefighters may have problems with their firefighting equipment.

3 **Finish the sentences**   4 P

Use **only** information from the text, please.

3.1 Stephanie's fellow firefighters treat …
3.2 Stephanie is an important role model for her daughters because …
3.3 Being a firefighter is a good job for working mothers because …
3.4 Firefighters must be fit and strong …

4 **Matching**   5 P

Match the beginnings 4.1–4.5 to five of the endings a)–g) according to the text.
Two endings do not match.

4.1 Stephanie has been a firefighter
4.2 Stephanie and her male colleagues
4.3 Firefighters sometimes see
4.4 All firefighters must be fit and strong
4.5 The firefighting equipment can

a) since 2000.
b) because their job is very hard.
c) for seven years.
d) be too big for women.
e) have problems.
f) are all good friends.
g) some horrible things.

Exam preparation

5 **Vocabulary work**   5P

Find the word **in the text**.

   5.1 A person you admire and would like to be like
   5.2 Somebody who lives through a dangerous situation or a catastrophic event

   Give the opposite:
   5.3 heavy (line 16)
   5.4 strong (line 17)
   5.5 difficult (line 17)

6 **Grammar**   10P

   6.1 Fill in the correct forms of the verbs in brackets.

Stephanie … **(1 start/started/was starting)** work as a firefighter seven years ago. Firefighters have to be very fit so she … **(2 trains/trained/train)** in the gym a lot, even though she normally … **(3 will work/worked/works)** only ten days a month. Although she … **(4 will be/is/was)** friends with her fellow firefighters, she hopes another woman … **(5 will arrive/arrive/arrived)** at the fire station soon.

   6.2 Fill in the correct English words.

Stephanie enjoys … **(1 *ihre*)** work because she can help … **(2 *viele*)** people. The working hours are also … **(3 *besser*)** than her last job. This is important … **(4 *weil*)** she wants to spend … **(5 *mehr*)** time with her children.

Exam preparation

Text 2: A rooftop rescue

When his ball landed on a rooftop, Jason Machin, 9, went after it. Showing no fear he climbed up a 12 m plastic drainpipe and pulled himself onto the roof of the building. Unfortunately he didn't have the courage to climb down. He
5 called his friends and they brought his father. Mr Machin borrowed a ladder from a neighbour, but it wasn't long enough. Mr Machin says, "The ladder was too short but I climbed up anyway because I could see how frightened Jason was. I talked to him and he calmed down."

10 Mr Machin then called the fire brigade and a firefighter helped Jason down from the roof. It isn't the first time that Jason has got himself into a dangerous situation. His father once had to rescue him from the edge of a high bridge near their home. "Jason often doesn't realize how dangerous
15 some situations are," said Mr Machin. *152 words*

Annotations

line 1 rooftop – *Dach, Außendach*
line 3 drainpipe – *Abflussrohr, Fallrohr*
line 9 calm down – *abregen, sich berühigen*
line 13 edge – *Rand, Kante*

7 Mediation 14 P

Geben Sie die Hauptgesichtspunkte von Text 2 sinngemäß auf Deutsch wieder. Beachten Sie die folgenden Leitfragen. Schreiben Sie bitte **ganze Sätze**.

- Warum kletterte Jason auf das Dach?
- Wie kam er nach oben?
- Warum konnte er nicht wieder hinunterklettern?
- Wer kam ihm zu Hilfe?
- Woran scheiterte diesen Rettungsversuch?
- Wie wurde Jason schließlich gerettet?
- Was sagt Jasons Vater über ihn?

8 Statement 6 P

"Jason didn't climb onto the roof because he was brave, but because he was stupid."
Do you think this is true? Why? Why not? Give your opinion.
Write 30–40 words in **complete English sentences**, please.

Exam preparation

II Managing situations

9 Helping people

9.1 Giving directions 3P

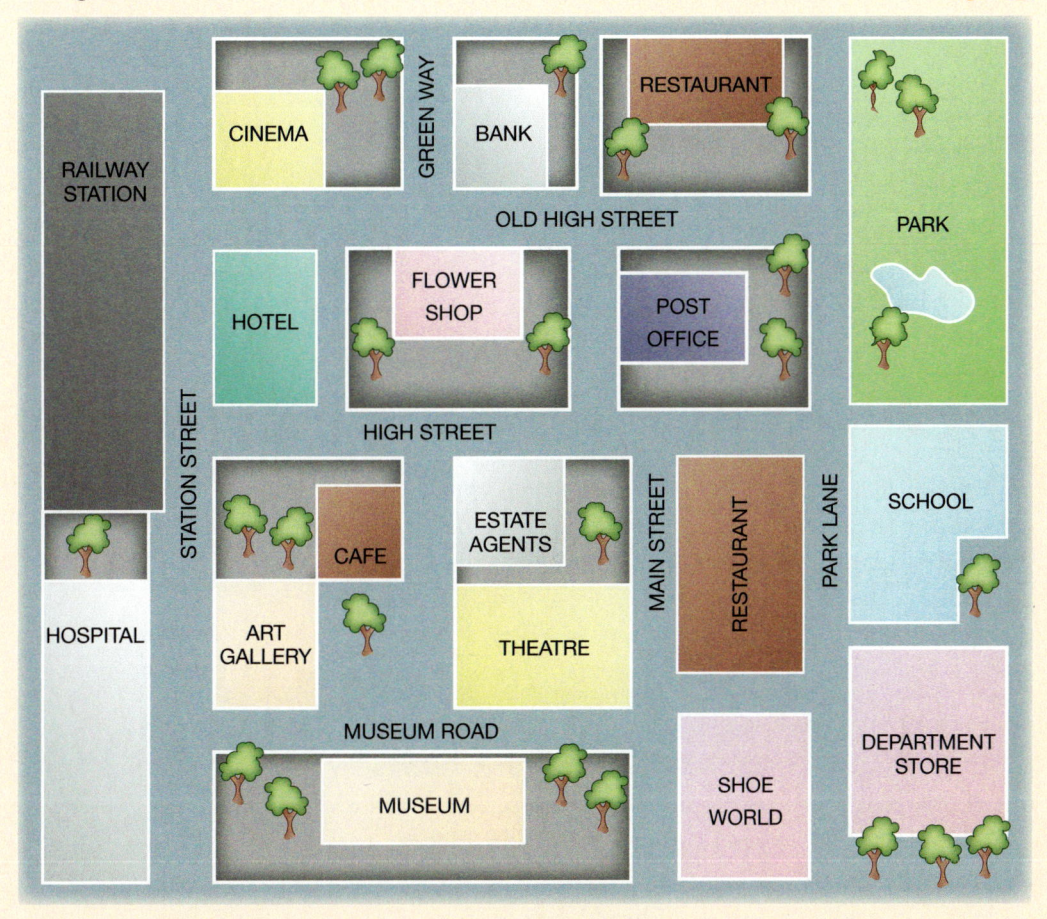

You are standing in front of the theatre on Main Street when your mobile phone rings. It's a friend and he/she wants to meet you. He/She is at the railway station. Tell your friend where he/she can meet you and give directions.

9.2 Explaining signs 3P
Where could you see this notice: A, B or C?

PLEASE TURN OFF YOUR MOBILE PHONE

A At a supermarket
B In a cinema
C On a bus

Exam preparation

10 Telephoning   8 P

Sally Billings is a telephone receptionist in a hotel in Edinburgh.
Find the phrases a)–h) of a caller that fit in to 10.1–10.8.

Sally	Good afternoon. Sally Billings speaking. How can I help you?
Caller	(10.1) …
Sally	And who's calling, please?
Caller	(10.2) …
Sally	Okay. Could you spell that for me, please?
Caller	(10.3) …
Sally	Thank you. And may I ask why you are calling?
Caller	(10.4) …
Sally	Okay, Mr Pommerjee. One moment, please. I'm afraid he's not in the office at the moment. Can he ring you back?
Caller	(10.5) …
Sally	That's 01316 754 830.
Caller	(10.6) …
Sally	And when are you available for him to call?
Caller	(10.7) …
Sally	Great. I'll give him the message when he arrives.
Caller	(10.8) …
Sally	You're welcome. Goodbye.

a) Thank you very much.
b) This is Patil Pommerjee speaking.
c) Certainly. I have an appointment with Jeff on Thursday but I have to cancel it.
d) Yes, that would be great. The number is 01316 754 830.
e) Hello. I'd like to speak to Mr Jeff Watson, please.
f) I'm at home until 3 p.m. today.
g) Of course. It's P-A-T-I-L P-O-M-M-E-R-J-E-E.
h) Yes. That's right.

11 Guided composition   6 P

You want to work as a receptionist in a hotel in Edinburgh. In a letter, tell the company about yourself. Write **complete English sentences**, please. The list will help you.

- What is your name?
- How old are you?
- Where do you live?
- How good is your English?
- Why do you want to work for the company?

Dear Sir or Madam
My name is …
Yours faithfully

Lerntipps

1 Textarbeit

A Vor dem Lesen/Hören

- Lesen Sie die Anweisungen zu jeder Aufgabe ganz genau – und dann noch einmal! Wenn Sie die Aufgabe nicht richtig verstanden haben, machen Sie unnötige Fehler.
- Bevor Sie den Text lesen/hören, sehen Sie das Foto und die Überschrift an. Sie sagen Ihnen etwas über das Thema des Textes.

B Texte lesen/hören

- Sie sollten den Text erst einmal überfliegen oder anhören, ohne Notizen zu machen. Suchen Sie die Hauptpunkte: Um was geht es? Texte beginnen häufig mit einer kurzen Zusammenfassung des Inhalts.
- Jetzt lesen/hören Sie den Text noch einmal, aber langsam und genau. Danach sollten Sie diese vier Fragen beantworten können: Wer ist dabei? Was geschieht? Wo geschieht es? Wann geschieht es?

C Die Bedeutung unbekannter Wörter erschließen

- Kennen Sie ein ähnliches englisches Wort? Z. B. wenn das unbekannte Wort ein Substantiv ist, kennen Sie ein ähnliches Verb? (*product – produce*)
- Kennen Sie ein ähnliches deutsches Wort? (*crime* – Krimi)
- Lesen Sie den ganzen Satz. Der Kontext kann Ihnen helfen.
- Listen Sie die unbekannten Wörter aus dem Text auf. Vergleichen Sie Ihre Liste mit den Listen von anderen Klassenkameraden. Vielleicht können Sie sich gegenseitig helfen?
- Erst wenn das alles nicht hilft, sehen Sie in der Wortliste hinten im Buch nach.

Lerntipps

2 Vokabeln lernen

- Schreiben Sie neue Vokabeln immer in ein Vokabelheft und wiederholen Sie diese regelmäßig.

- Es ist wichtig, nicht zu viele neue Vokabeln an einem Tag zu lernen. Mehr als zehn Wörter pro Tag sollten Sie nicht lernen, sonst werden Sie diese schnell wieder vergessen.

- Hier ein Paar Tipps, wie Sie sich neue Vokabeln einprägen können:
  - Schreiben Sie neue Wörter auf kleine Zettel und heften Sie sie zu Hause sichtbar an.
  - Verbinden Sie Wörter und Wendungen mit Bildern.
  - Gruppieren Sie neue Wörter, die thematisch zusammengehören. Sie können Listen erstellen oder *word spiders* anfertigen. Diese *word spiders* können einzelne Wörter sowie Redewendungen erhalten.
  - Gruppieren Sie Wörter mit gegensätzlichen Bedeutungen (*good – bad*) oder Wörter mit graduellen Unterschieden (*morning – afternoon – night*).

- Um neue Wörter richtig anzuwenden, müssen Sie wissen, wie sie gebraucht werden. Deshalb ist es sinnvoll, Redewendungen statt einzelner Wörter zu lernen (*go by bike*, *have a shower*).

3 Texte verfassen

- Bevor Sie beginnen zu schreiben, überlegen Sie, was Sie schreiben möchten und in welcher Reihenfolge. Es kann dabei helfen, zunächst Stichworte zu schreiben.

- Fragewörter (*who*, *where*, *why*) helfen Ihnen, sich über das Thema Klarheit zu verschaffen.

- Lesen Sie abschließend immer Ihren Text durch. Erst konzentrieren Sie sich auf den Inhalt. Danach verbessern Sie Ihren Text nach sprachlichen Gesichtspunkten – z. B. gibt es Rechtschreib- oder Grammatikfehler?

4 Sprechen

- Haben Sie keine Angst, Fehler zu machen. Sie lernen nicht sprechen, wenn Sie nichts sagen.

- Oft hilft es, mit sich selbst Englisch zu sprechen. Sie verlieren damit Ihre Scheu und gewöhnen Sie sich an die englische Aussprache.

Extra grammar

Inhalt

1. Simple present .... S. 87
2. Present progressive .... S. 88
3. Simple past .... S. 89
4. Present perfect .... S. 90
5. Questions and short answers .... S. 91
6. Modal verbs .... S. 92
7. -ing form .... S. 93
8. Relative pronouns .... S. 94
9. Adjectives and adverbs .... S. 95
10. Comparison of adjectives .... S. 96
11. Word order .... S. 97
12. Prepositions .... S. 98

1 Simple present

▶ Unit 1, Seite 7

Grammar

Remember: simple present

- Wir benutzten das *simple present*, um regelmäßige Handlungen zu beschreiben.
  *I **work** in an animal clinic.*
- Die drei Stolpersteine sind:
  ▶ die 3. Person Singular (*he/she/it*):   Brad **works** in a film studio.
  ▶ die Bildung von Fragen: **Do** James and Lucy **work** with Brad? – Yes, they **do**.
                           Does Brad **enjoy** his work? – Yes, he **does**.
  ▶ Verneinungen: Brad and Lucy **don't like** reporters.
                           Brad **doesn't travel** to the studio by bus.

a) **You are interviewing Brad James, an actor. Use the present simple to write about him.**

1. "I usually get up at 8.00."   *Brad usually **gets up** at 8.00.*
2. "I travel to the film studio by car everyday."
3. "I do most of my work in America."
4. "But sometimes I fly to other countries."
5. "Most days I work 8 or 9 hours."
6. "I like my job but I don't like being famous."
7. "I don't talk to journalists very often."
8. "I don't give many interviews."

b) **Fill in the gaps with the simple present form of the verbs in brackets.**

1. She … **(have)** two brothers and a sister.
2. I always … **(play)** football on Saturdays.
3. We … **(not work)** together anymore.
4. … you … **(enjoy)** your job?
5. It normally … **(rain)** a lot where I live.
6. They … **(not go)** to school on Saturday in Britain.

Extra grammar

2 **Present progressive** ▶ Unit 3, Seite 27

> **Grammar**
>
> **Remember: present progressive**
>
> - Diese Zeitform (Verlaufsform) gibt es nicht im Deutschen. Sie beschreibt, was gerade geschieht: What **are** you **doing**? – I **am watching** TV.
>   (Was machst du gerade? – Ich sehe gerade fern.)
>
> - Die Verlaufsform der Gegenwart wird so gebildet:
>   **am/is/are** + **-ing** Form des Verbs
>   (z. B.: *try – trying, happen – happening, look – looking*)
>   Verneinung: **am not/isn't/aren't** + **-ing** Form

a) **You are at a party. Use the present progressive to describe what you and the other guests are doing.**

1. Joshua und seine Schwester kochen gerade.   *Joshua and his sister* **are cooking**.
2. Fatima redet gerade mit Paul.
3. Cecelia trinkt gerade ein Cola.
4. Matthew zieht gerade seinen Mantel aus.
5. David sucht gerade nach einer CD.
6. Amelia und ihr Freund streiten sich gerade.
7. Leah isst gerade ein Stück Kuchen.
8. Ich sitze gerade auf dem Sofa.

> **Grammar**
>
> **Remember: simple present vs. present progressive**
>
> - Wir benutzten das *simple present*, um regelmäßige Handlungen zu beschreiben. Signalwörter: *always, often, at six o'clock, on Monday,* usw.
>
> - Wir benutzen das *present progressive*, um zu beschreiben, was gerade geschieht. Signalwörter: *at the moment, now, just, at present,* usw.

b) **Complete the sentences with either the simple present or the present progressive of the verb in brackets.**

1. Samantha … **(work)** in a supermarket at present.
2. At weekends Phillip … **(help)** in an old people's home.
3. What … **(George/do)** now?
4. Caitlin … **(like)** school. She … **(learn)** about the environment at the moment.
5. Loretta … **(talk)** to Mark right now. They … **(be)** good friends.

Extra grammar

3 Simple past

▶ Unit 2, Seite 15

Grammar

Remember: simple past

- Die Vergangenheitsform ist bei allen Personen (*I, he, she, you,* usw.) gleich.
  *Jane **wanted** to go on holiday. Ben and Lily **wanted** to go with her.*

- Es gibt regelmäßige und unregelmäßige Vergangenheitsformen.
  *They **travelled** together. They **went** by car.*

- Fragen und Verneinungen werden mit ***did*** gebildet.
  ***Did** Jane **enjoy** her holiday? – Yes, she **did**. She **had** a lot of fun.*

- Signalwörter sind: *yesterday, last week/month/year, two hours ago, in 2007,* usw.

▶ Eine Liste der unregelmäßigen Verben finden Sie auf Seite 99.

a) Complete this story about an unlucky criminal using the simple past of the verbs in brackets.

Fred *arrived* (arrive) at the house at 10.00 p.m. He …**(1 use)** a ladder to get to a window on the first floor. The window …**(2 be)** broken, so he …**(3 open)** it easily. Just then, a dog …**(4 bark)**. The noise …**(5 scare)** Fred and he …**(6 fall)** through the window. Then the dog …**(7 start)** to bark more loudly. Fred …**(8 try)** to get away but the dog … **(9 appear)** at the door. Fred …**(10 be)** in a lot of trouble.

b) Fill in the gaps using the simple past of the irregular verbs in brackets.

1 I … **(buy)** a new blouse last week.
2 He … **(eat)** a lot at the party last weekend.
3 It … **(take)** a long time to get to school yesterday.
4 We … **(see)** Lucy last night. We … **(go)** to the cinema together.
5 He … **(find)** a new job last week. I … **(know)** he would.

c) Complete the sentences using the simple past of the verbs in brackets.

1 I don't work at the bakery anymore. I … **(not like)** it there.
2 We … **(not go)** to the cinema last night. We … **(not have)** enough money.
3 He … **(not like)** his birthday present last year.
4 They … **(not come)** to the party last week.
5 I … **(not finish)** my homework on time.

Extra grammar

4 Present perfect

➤ Unit 7, Seite 65

Grammar

Remember: present perfect

- Wenn wir die Dauer einer Situation oder Handlung betonen wollen, können wir das **present perfect** mit **for** (Zeitdauer) oder **since** (Zeitpunkt) benutzen.
  Dan **has been** a mechanic **for** two years.
  I **have lived** here **since** July.

- Situationen/Ereignisse, die **noch andauern**, werden ganz ohne Zeitangabe oder mit **just** benutzt.
  Jenny **has read** a lot of books.
  She **has just finished** the last Harry Potter book.

- Das *present perfect* wird mit *have/has* + Partizip Perfekt (3. Form des Verbs) gebildet.

- Signalwörter sind: *already, before, so far, ever, never, just, recently, not yet,* usw.

a) **Complete the sentences with *for* or *since*.**

1. Georg has worked in the shop … three years.
2. Amy has lived in London … she was 12.
3. I have bought 3 DVDs … September.
4. Alex has been much happier … he finished his exams.
5. Tim and Liz have lived in America … a long time.
6. I haven't seen Peter and Jane … months!

b) **Fill in the gaps with the present perfect form of the verb in brackets.**

1. Gary … **(work)** as a mechanic since he left school.
2. I … **(be)** a trainee hairdresser for six weeks.
3. We … **(eat)** the whole cake already.
4. She … **(see)** the film before.
5. They … **(move)** house recently.

c) **Translate these sentences into English using the present perfect.**

1. Hast du schon gegessen heute?
2. Nein, ich habe noch nicht gegessen.
3. Hat Michaela dieses Buch schon gelesen?
4. Haben Jan und Oskar diesen Film schon gesehen?
5. Ich kenne Susan seit Jahren.

Extra grammar

5 Questions and short answers
> Unit 8, Seite 75

Grammar

Remember: Questions and short answers

- Im *simple present* und im *simple past* brauchen **modale Hilfsverben** und das Verb **be** keine weiteren Verben (Hilfsverben) um Fragen zu bilden. Das Verb stellt man vor das Subjekt.
  You **can** swim.   **Can** you swim?   Yes, I **can**. / No, I **can't**.
  He **is** tired.   **Is** he tired?   Yes, he **is**. / No, he **isn't**.

- **Vollverben** in einer *progressive*-Form benutzen eine Form von **be** um Fragen zu bilden:
  go   **Are** you **going** home now?   Yes, I **am**. / No, I **am not**.

- Alle anderen **Vollverben** brauchen bei der Fragebildung **do**/**did** oder ein **Hilfsverb** in der entsprechenden Zeitform.
  watch   **Did** you **watch** TV last night?   Yes, I **did**. / No, I **didn't**.
  do   **Have** you **done** this before?   Yes, I **have**. / No, I **haven't**.

a) Translate these questions into English.

1. Gehst du oft ins Kino?   *Do you go to the cinema often?*
2. Hast du viele DVDs?
3. Warst du bei der Party gestern?
4. Hat sie lange hier gewohnt?
5. Kannst du gut singen?
6. Was machst du gerade?
7. War er schon in England?
8. Geht ihr jetzt in den Supermarkt?

b) Fill in the correct short answers.

1. Have you ever been to the US?   No, …
2. Did you like the new Bond film?   Yes, …
3. Is Brian coming to the cinema with us?   Yes, …
4. Can you play the piano?   No, …
5. Do you go to the gym?   No, …
6. Can you go to the football match tomorrow? Yes, …
7. Are you enjoying the book?   No, …
8. Have you seen Amy recently?   Yes, …

Extra grammar

6 Modal verbs
▶ Unit 4, Seite 33

Grammar

Remember: modal verbs

- Im Englischen benutzen wir modale Hilfsverben nur in Verbindung mit einem Vollverb.

	simple past form
We **can** go shopping on Saturday if you want.	**could**
We **will** visit you next week. It **won't** be until Friday though.	**would – wouldn't**
It **may** look old, but it **must** be warm and comfortable!	**might – had to**

- Die beiden Formen **must** und **have to** sind austauschbar. Da **must** keine *past*- oder *future*-Form hat, benutzen wir **had to**, **didn't have to** (*past*) oder **will have to, won't have to** (*future*):
  I **had to** learn for the test last week.
  I **won't have to** do another test until next year now.

a) Choose the best modal verb in brackets to complete each sentence.

1. You … **(must / may)** turn off your mobile phone in the library.
2. Mike wears glasses because he … **(cannot / must not)** see very well.
3. Emily … **(has to / may)** take her dog for a walk every day.
4. Please … **(will / can)** I go to the party?
5. Olivia and Caroline … **(could / will)** help you but they don't have time.
6. I … **(could / had to)** learn for the test last week.

b) Match the sentences.

1. Lee has hurt his leg.
2. James is studying maths.
3. Chris is very fat.
4. Matt's parents are rich.
5. Alex doesn't have a mobile.
6. Ian smokes too much.
7. Leo has lost his shoe.
8. Erik has lots of work to do.

A He can't afford one.
B He must try to stop.
C He doesn't have to find a job.
D He can't play football.
E He has to find it quickly.
F He wants to work in a bank.
G He mustn't go out with Fiona.
H He should lose weight.

Extra grammar

7 -ing form
▶ Unit 6, Seite 55

Grammar

Remember: -ing form

- Die folgenden **Verben** drücken Vorlieben und Abneigungen aus.
  Bei den nachfolgenden Verben benutzt man die **-ing Form**.
  Janet **enjoys shopping**.   Mark **doesn't enjoy reading** books.
  Laura **likes going** to the cinema.   James **doesn't like watching** films on TV.
  Ross **loves travelling**.   Rebecca **hates staying** at home at the weekend.

- Die **-ing Form** wird auch nach einer **Präposition** benutzt.
  I'm interested **in going** to London.   I'm good **at writing** stories.

a) Complete the sentences using the -ing form of the verb in brackets.

1 Chris enjoys … **(listen)** to pop music.
2 Rebecca is good at … **(organise)** parties.
3 David doesn't like … **(write)** essays.
4 Jane loves … **(make)** cakes.
5 Ruth doesn't enjoy … **(study)** French.
6 Phil is interested in … **(build)** robots.

b) Match the beginnings (1–5) with the endings (A–E).

1 I'm good   A in playing football.
2 He's interested   B to meeting us.
3 I'm sorry   C at singing.
4 They're looking forward D about working part time.
5 She's thinking   E for being late.

c) Translate these sentences into English using the -ing form.

1 Meine Schwester kann gut schwimmen.   *My sister is good at **swimming**.*
2 Tony spielt sehr gerne Gitarre.
3 Spielst du gerne Fußball?
4 Mein Vater liest nicht gern.
5 Geht ihr gerne ins Kino?
6 Wir gehen nicht gerne zum Zahnarzt.
7 Meine Mutter kauft gerne Schuhe.
8 Matthew kann gut kochen.

Extra grammar

8 Relative pronouns

▶ Unit 7, Seite 67

Grammar

Remember: Relative pronouns *who*, *which*, *that*

- Bei Personen benutzt man **who** oder **that**.
  *I spoke to **the people** who/that have moved in next door.*

- Bei Tieren und Sachen benutzt man **which** oder **that**.
  *We went to the **cinema** that/which opened last week.*

Ein Tipp: Wenn Sie unsicher sind, **that** ist immer richtig!

a) Say which sentence is wrong, A or B.

1. A There are many restaurants which serve Indian food in Britain.
   B There are many restaurants who serve Indian food in Britain.

2. A She's the girl which went to Spain last year.
   B She's the girl who went to Spain last year.

3. A Do you know which book we need for our English lesson?
   B Do you know who book we need for our English lesson?

4. A I need someone which can help me with my homework.
   B I need someone who can help me with my homework.

5. A I need a car which is safe.
   B I need a car who is safe.

b) Complete these sentences using *that*, *which* or *who*.
There may be more than one possible answer.

1. The police spoke to Mrs Lyster … wanted to report a crime.
2. She said a man took her bag … had all her money in it.
3. She gave the police information … could help to find the man.
4. The police are talking to people … were there when it happened.
5. Anyone … helps find the man will get a reward.

Extra grammar

9 Adjectives and adverbs
▶ Unit 8, Seite 73

> **Grammar**
>
> **Remember: Adjectives and adverbs**
>
> - **Adjektive** beschreiben meistens Nomen.
>   a **blue** coat • a **new** car • a **beautiful** day
>
> - **Adverbien** beschreiben meistens Verben, aber auch Adjektive. Viele enden auf *-ly*.
>   he moved **quickly** • they left **immediately** • a **beautifully** painted vase
>
> - Wichtige unregelmäßigen Adverbien sind:
>   *good* – *well* • *hard* – *hard* • *fast* – *fast* • *early* – *early*
>
> - Bei diesen Verben benutzt man immer **Adjektive**: *be, become, feel, look, smell* (riechen, duften), *sound* (klingen), *taste* (schmecken).
>   It is **cold**. • The cake looked **nice**. • He felt **tired**.

a) Complete the sentences with one of the words in brackets.

1. Liam plays tennis very … **(good / well)**.
2. Sheila bought an … **(expensive / expensively)** dress for the party.
3. The food last night tasted … **(good / well)**.
4. It was a … **(great / greatly)** holiday. We had a … **(wonderful / wonderfully)** time.
5. You don't sound very … **(happy / happily)**.
6. I worked really … **(hard / hardly)** last night.
7. You look … **(beautiful / beautifully)** in that dress.
8. He always eats very … **(slow / slowly)**.

b) Fill in the gaps with the right form of the word in brackets.

1. You look … **(tired)**. Did you sleep … **(bad)** last night?
2. Do you have to drive so … **(fast)**? It's very … **(dangerous)**.
3. The music is too … **(loud)**. I can't concentrate … **(proper)**.
4. Your project was … **(good)** researched. … **(good)** done!
5. I worked … **(hard)** on the project. It was a … **(difficult)** topic.
6. Our … **(new)** dog is … **(real)** … **(friendly)**.
7. It's an … **(extreme)** … **(nice)** place to go.
8. I've never seen anyone run so … **(quick)**.

Extra grammar

10 Comparison of adjectives ▶ Unit 6, Seite 57

Grammar

Remember: Comparison of adjectives

- Englische Adjektive werden so gesteigert:
  - Einsilbige: cheap — cheap**er (than)** — **(the)** cheap**est**
  - Zweisilbige auf -y: busy — bus**ier (than)** — **(the)** bus**iest**
  - Zwei- und Mehrsilbige: expensive — **more** expensive **(than)** — **(the) most** expensive

- Diese Adjektive werden unregelmäßig gesteigert:
  good – **better (than)** – **(the) best**   bad – **worse (than)** – **(the) worst**
  much/many – **more (than)** – **(the) most**   little – **less (than)** – **(the) least**

a) Make comparisons using the adjectives in brackets.

1. England / Germany **(big)**   *Germany is bigger than England.*
2. Madonna / Britney Spears **(old)**
3. the Nile / the Thames **(long)**
4. plastic / gold **(expensive)**
5. paper / metal **(heavy)**
6. France / Scotland **(small)**

b) Complete the sentences.

1. Finn is younger than Leah and Ben, so Finn is *the youngest.*
2. Ali is thinner than Aneeq and Ted, so Ali is …
3. Phil is taller than Ed and Will, so Phil is …
4. David is nicer than Mike and Paul, so David is …
5. Craig is more intelligent than Zoe and Jenny, so Craig is …
6. Adam is more annoying than Marcus or Joe, so Adam is …
7. Naomi is shorter than Daisy and Clare, so Naomi is …
8. Ian is richer than Felix and James, so Ian is …

c) Complete the sentences with the right form of the adjectives in brackets.

1. It's the … **(expensive)** book I have ever bought.
2. I'll use this bag. It's … **(big)** than the other one.
3. I think Janine is the … **(pretty)** girl in our class.
4. The film was … **(good)** than I expected.
5. Our new house is … **(small)** than the old one.
6. She got the … **(bad)** mark in the test last week.

Extra grammar

11 Word order

▶ Unit 5, Seiten 47 & 49

Grammar

Remember: word order

- Eine Zeitangabe steht entweder am Satzanfang oder am Satzende.
  Last week I was very busy.   I was very busy **last week**.

- Ortsangaben stehen meistens am Satzende (Reihenfolge: nah – weiter weg).
  We went **to the cinema in London**.

- Wenn beide Angaben zusammen am Satzende stehen, dann steht Ort vor Zeit.
  We went **to Florida last year**.

- Diese Wörter sind Bindewörter (*connectors*): **and**, **because**, **but**, **or**, **so**, **when**
  Sie verbinden ganze Sätze oder Teile von Sätzen miteinander.
  It was cold, **so** I put a jacket on.

- **Because** und **when** (**mit Komma**) können auch am Anfang des Satzes stehen.
  Because I was late, I missed the beginning of the film.

a) **Decide which sentence (A or B) is correct.**

1. A I'm going to the doctor's today.
   B I'm going today to the doctor's.
2. A I have an appointment at 3 o'clock there.
   B I have an appointment there at 3 o'clock.
3. A I need to go afterwards to the supermarket.
   B I need to go to the supermarket afterwards.
4. A My friends and I have booked a table in a restaurant for 7 o'clock.
   B My friends and I have booked a table for 7 o'clock in a restaurant.
5. A My parents want me to be at home by 10 o'clock.
   B My parents want me to be by 10 o'clock at home.

b) **Complete each sentence with a suitable connector from the box.**

because • but • or • so • when

1. I can't afford an MP3 player, … I should earn some money.
2. I will have enough money … I find a part-time job.
3. I want to work at weekends … my parents don't want me to.
4. I could work in a supermarket … I could work in a shop.
5. I don't want to be a waitress … it can be very tiring.

Extra grammar

12 Prepositions

> Unit 3, Seite 25

Grammar

Remember: Prepositions

- Präpositionen sind Verhältniswörter. Sie sagen etwas aus über räumliche Beziehungen:
  *Jane works **at** the new hospital.*
- oder über zeitliche Beziehungen:
  *We have to do homework **after** school.*

a) Choose the correct ending (A or B) for each sentence.

1. Thomas leaves the house
   A on 9 o'clock.
   B at 9 o'clock.
2. He usually walks
   A to school.
   B at school.
3. But sometimes he goes
   A with bus.
   B by bus.
4. Thomas likes to play football
   A over school.
   B after school.
5. He often plays
   A with his friends.
   B under his friends.
6. Then Thomas does his homework
   A at his room.
   B in his room.

b) Complete the text using the prepositions from the box below.

> at • before • behind • for • from • on • on • to • up • with

…(1) Saturday Ben wanted to see a film. He went …(2) the cinema. He bought a ticket …(3) an action film. Ben looked …(4) the ticket to see where his seat was. Ben sat down just …(5) the film started. Ben watched the adverts …(6) the big screen. But the girls …(7) him were still talking. Another man was eating popcorn …(8) a big tub. He made a lot of noise. Then the man's mobile phone rang and he started a conversation …(9) his girlfriend. Ben got …(10) and left the cinema. He was very angry.

Irregular verbs

be	was/were	been	sein
become	became	become	werden
begin	began	begun	anfangen, beginnen
break	broke	broken	brechen
bring	brought	brought	bringen
build	built	built	bauen
buy	bought	bought	kaufen
catch	caught	caught	fangen
choose	chose	chosen	wählen
come	came	come	kommen
cost	cost	cost	kosten
cut	cut	cut	schneiden
do	did	done	tun, machen
draw	drew	drawn	zeichnen
dream	dreamt	dreamt	träumen
drink	drank	drunk	trinken
drive	drove	driven	fahren
eat	ate	eaten	essen
fall	fell	fallen	fallen
feed	fed	fed	füttern, ernähren
feel	felt	felt	(sich) fühlen, empfinden
find	found	found	finden
fly	flew	flown	fliegen
forget	forgot	forgotten	vergessen
get	got	got	bekommen
give	gave	given	geben
go	went	gone	gehen, fahren
grow	grew	grown	wachsen
hang	hung	hung	hängen
have	had	had	haben
hear	heard	heard	hören
hide	hid	hidden	(sich) verstecken
hit	hit	hit	schlagen
hold	held	held	halten, festhalten
keep	kept	kept	behalten
know	knew	known	kennen, wissen
lay	laid	laid	legen
learn	learnt/learned	learnt/learned	lernen
leave	left	left	abfahren, verlassen
let	let	let	lassen
lie	lay	lain	liegen
lose	lost	lost	verlieren
make	made	made	machen
mean	meant	meant	meinen, bedeuten
meet	met	met	treffen
pay	paid	paid	bezahlen
put	put	put	setzen, stellen, legen
read	read	read	lesen
ride	rode	ridden	reiten, fahren
run	ran	run	laufen, rennen
say	said	said	sagen
see	saw	seen	sehen
sell	sold	sold	verkaufen
send	sent	sent	senden, schicken
set	set	set	setzen, stellen
show	showed	shown	zeigen
shut	shut	shut	schließen
sing	sang	sung	singen
sit	sat	sat	sitzen
sleep	slept	slept	schlafen
smell	smelt/smelled	smelt/smelled	riechen
speak	spoke	spoken	sprechen
spell	spelt/spelled	spelt/spelled	buchstabieren
spend	spent	spent	ausgeben, verbringen
stand	stood	stood	stehen
steal	stole	stolen	stehlen
swim	swam	swum	schwimmen
take	took	taken	nehmen
teach	taught	taught	unterrichten, beibringen
tell	told	told	sagen, erzählen
think	thought	thought	denken
throw	threw	thrown	werfen
understand	understood	understood	verstehen
wear	wore	worn	tragen
win	won	won	gewinnen
write	wrote	written	schreiben

Grundwortschatz

Diese Liste enthält ca. 600 Grundwörter, die in Job fit Englisch als bekannt vorausgesetzt werden.

A

a, an	ein/e
about	über, etwa
above	über, oben
across	(quer) über
address	Adresse
adult	Erwachsene/r
after	nach
afternoon	Nachmittag
again	wieder
age	Zeitalter, Alter
ago	vor
to agree	zustimmen, vereinbaren
alcohol	Alkohol
all	alle(s)
to allow	erlauben, (zu)lassen
almost	fast, beinahe
alone	allein(e)
along	entlang
already	schon, bereits
also	auch, außerdem
although	obwohl
always	immer
and	und
another	noch eine
answer; to answer	Antwort, Lösung; (be)antworten
any	irgendetwas, -welche, jede
anyone	jemand, jede/r
anything	etwas, alles
April	April
area	Gebiet, Bereich
arm	Arm
around	herum
to arrive	ankommen
article	Artikel
as	wie, als, da
to ask	fragen, bitten
at	an, bei, auf
away	weg, entfernt

B

back	zurück
bad	schlecht, schlimm
bag	Tasche
ball	Ball, Kugel
bank	Bank
bar	Bar
to be	sein
to be able to	können
to be born	geboren werden
because	weil
to become	werden
bed	Bett
beer	Bier
to begin	anfangen, beginnen
behind	hinter, hinten
to believe	glauben
to belong	gehören
below	unter, unten
best	beste/r/s, am besten
better	besser
between	zwischen
big	groß
bit, a bit of	ein bisschen, etwas
black	schwarz
blue	blau
body	Körper
book; to book	Buch; buchen, bestellen
boring	langweilig
both	beide
boy	Junge
boyfriend	Freund
bread	Brot
breakfast	Frühstück
to bring	bringen, holen
Britain	Großbritannien
British	britisch
brother	Bruder
brown	braun
to build	(auf)bauen
bus	(Linien-)Bus
but	aber, sondern
to buy	kaufen
by	durch, mit, bei
bye	tschüs

C

café	Café
cake	Kuchen, Torte
call; to call	Anruf; (an)rufen
camera	Fotoapparat, Kamera
can	dürfen, können
car	Auto
card	Karte
to carry	tragen
centre	Zentrum
change; to change	(Ver-)Änderung; (aus)wechseln, (sich) ändern
cheap	billig, günstig
child	Kind
chocolate	Schokolade
to choose	(aus)wählen
Christmas	Weihnachten
cinema	Kino
city	(Groß-)Stadt
class	Klasse
to climb	klettern, steigen
clock	Uhr
close; to close	nahe; schließen
clothes	Kleidung, Kleider
club	Klub
coffee	Kaffee
cold	kalt
to collect	sammeln
college	Fachhochschule
colour	Farbe
to come	kommen, geliefert werden
company	Firma, Unternehmen
computer	Computer
concert	Konzert
cool	kühl, cool
cost; to cost	Kosten; kosten
country	Land, Staat
to cross	kreuzen
culture	Kultur
to cut	schneiden

D

date	Datum, Termin
daughter	Tochter
day	Tag
December	Dezember
to decide	(sich) entscheiden, beschließen
to describe	beschreiben
to die	sterben
difference	Unterschied
different	anders, verschieden
difficult	schwer, schwierig
to do	tun, machen
doctor	Arzt, Ärztin
dog	Hund
door	Tür
down	unten
drink; to drink	Getränk; trinken
during	während

E

each	jede/r/s
early	früh
easy	leicht, einfach
to eat	essen
eight	acht
eleven	elf
email	E-Mail
end; to end	Ende, Schluss; (be)enden
energy	Energie
England	England
English	englisch
enough	ausreichend, genug
to enter	eintreten, eingeben
even	sogar (noch)
evening	Abend

Grundwortschatz

ever	je(mals)	to go	gehen, fahren	it	es
every	jede/r/s	good	gut	its	sein/e
everybody	jede/r	goodbye	auf Wiedersehen		
everyone	jede/r/s, alle	green	grün	**J**	
everything	alles	grey	grau	January	Januar
expensive	teuer	group	Gruppe	job	Arbeit, Stelle
eye	Auge	to grow	wachsen, anbauen	to join	beitreten, verbinden
				July	Juli
F		**H**		June	Juni
face	Gesicht	hair	Haar(e)	just	einfach, nur, genau
fair	fair	hand	Hand		
to fall	fallen	to happen	passieren, geschehen	**K**	
family	Familie	happy	glücklich, froh, zufrieden	to keep	(be)halten
fast	schnell	hard	schwer	kind	nett; Art, Sorte
fat	fett, dick	to have	haben	to know	kennen, wissen
father	Vater	he	er		
favourite	Liebling, Lieblings-	head	Kopf	**L**	
February	Februar	healthy	gesund	lady	Dame
to feel	(sich) fühlen	to hear	hören	large	groß, umfangreich
few, a few	ein paar, wenig/e	hello	Hallo	last	letzte/r/s, zuletzt
fewer	weniger	help; to help	Hilfe; helfen	later	später
fifth	fünfte/r/s	her	ihr	to lead	führen
fight; to fight	Kampf; kämpfen	here	hier	to learn	lernen, erfahren
film	Film	here's	hier ist	least	wenigstens
to find	finden, suchen	hey	he	to leave	(ver)lassen
to finish	(be)enden	hi	hallo	left	linke/r/s, links; übrig
first	erste/r/s, zuerst	high	hoch	less	weniger, abzüglich
fish	Fisch	him	ihn, ihm	lesson	Lektion, (Unterrichts-)Stunde
five	fünf	his	sein/e	letter	Brief, Buchstabe
flat	flach; Wohnung	hit; to hit	Schlager; schlagen	life	Leben
to fly	fliegen	to hold	(ab)halten	light	Licht, Leuchte; hell, leicht
food	Essen, Nahrung	hole	Loch	like; to like	wie; mögen, gern tun
foot, feet	Fuß, Füße	holiday	Ferien, Urlaub, Feiertag	line	Linie, Zeile
football	Fußball	home	Zuhause, Heim; nach Hause	list	Liste
for	für	hope; to hope	Hoffnung; hoffen	to listen	zuhören
forever	für immer, ewig	hot	heiß, warm	little	klein, wenig
four	vier	hour	Stunde	to live	wohnen, leben
fourteen	vierzehn	house	Haus	long	lang
fourth	vierte/r/s	how	wie	to look	(aus)sehen, blicken
free	kostenlos, frei	however	doch, jedoch	to lose	verlieren
Friday	Freitag	hundred	hundert	lot, a lot of	viel, viele
friend	Freund/in			loud	laut
friendly	freund(schaft)lich	**I**		to love	lieben, sehr gern mögen
from	von	I	ich	low	niedrig
fun	Spaß	ice	Eis		
funny	komisch, merkwürdig	idea	Idee, Gedanke	**M**	
future	Zukunft; (zu)künftig	if	wenn, falls, ob	main	hauptsächlich, wichtigste
		ill	krank	to make	machen
G		important	wichtig	man	Mann, Mensch
game	Spiel	in	in	many	viele
garden	Garten	inside	innerhalb, drinnen	map	Karte
German	deutsch	instead	stattdessen, anstatt	mark; to mark	Note, Zensur; markieren, kennzeichnen
Germany	Deutschland	interest; to interest	Interesse, Zins(en); interessieren	may	dürfen, können, mögen
to get	holen, bekommen, werden	interesting	interessant	me	mir, mich
girl	Mädchen	internet	Internet	meat	Fleisch
girlfriend	Freundin	into	in … hinein	medium	mittlere; Medium, Mittel
to give	geben				

Grundwortschatz

to meet	(zusammen)treffen, begegnen
message	Mitteilung, Nachricht
middle	Mitte
might	könnte(n) (vielleicht)
milk	Milch
minute	Minute
to mix	mischen
mobile phone	Mobiltelefon, Handy
modern	modern
moment, at the moment	Moment, augenblicklich
Monday	Montag
money	Geld
month	Monat
more	mehr
morning	Morgen
most	meist
mother	Mutter
to move	(sich) bewegen, umziehen
much	viel
music	Musik
must	müssen
my	mein/e
myself	selbst

N

name	Name
near	nahe
nearly	beinahe, nahezu
to need	brauchen, benötigen
never	nie(mals)
new	neu
newspaper	Zeitung
next	nächst; danach
nice	schön, nett
night	Nacht
nine	neun
no	nein, kein/e
nobody	niemand
normal	normal
not	nicht
note	Notiz
nothing	nichts
now	nun, jetzt
number	Nummer, Zahl

O

October	Oktober
of	von
office	Büro, Amt
often	oft, häufig
old	alt
on	auf, an, am
once	einmal, einst, sobald
one	eins, man
online	online

only	nur, einzig
open; to open	offen; öffnen, beginnen
opinion	Meinung, Einschätzung
or	oder
orange	Orange
other	andere/r/s
our	unser/e
out	aus
outside	außer(halb)
over	(vor)über

P

page	Seite
pair	Paar
paper	Papier, Zeitung
parents	Eltern
part	Teil, Rolle
partner	Partner/in
party	Party, Partei
past	vorbei, nach; Vergangenheit
to pay	(be)zahlen
pen	Füller, Kugelschreiber
percent	Prozent
perfect	vollkommen, perfekt
perhaps	vielleicht, eventuell
person	Mensch, Person
photo	Foto
phrase	(Rede-)Wendung, Ausdruck
picture	Bild
piece	Stück, Teil
pink	rosa
place; to place	Stelle, Platz; setzen, stellen
plan; to plan	Plan; planen
to play	spielen
please	bitte
point	Punkt; Komma
police	Polizei
poor	arm, schlecht, mangelhaft
position	Stellung
possible	möglich, denkbar
poster	Poster, Plakat
pound	Pfund
price	(Kauf-)Preis
probably	wahrscheinlich
problem	Problem
project	Projekt
to pull	ziehen
put	setzen, stellen, legen

Q

question	Frage
quick	schnell, rasch
quickly	schnell, rasch
quiet	still, ruhig
quite	ziemlich, ganz

R

rain; to rain	Regen; regnen
to read	lesen
really	wirklich, eigentlich, tatsächlich
reason	Vernunft, Grund
red	rot
restaurant	Restaurant
return; to return	Rückfahrkarte; zurückkehren, -gehen
ride; to ride	Fahrt; fahren
right	rechts, rechte/r/s, richtig; Recht
to ring	klingeln, läuten
road	(Land-)Straße
role	Rolle
room	Zimmer, Raum
round	Runde; rund
to run	laufen (lassen)

S

sad	traurig
same	gleiche/r/s, der-, die-, dasselbe
Saturday	Sonnabend, Samstag
to say	sagen
school	Schule
sea	See
second	zweite/r/s; Sekunde
to see	sehen
to seem	(er)scheinen
to sell	(sich) verkaufen
to send	senden, schicken
September	September
seven	sieben
seventeen	siebzehn
seventy	siebzig
she	sie
shoe	Schuh
shop; to shop	Laden, Geschäft; einkaufen
should	solle/n, sollte/n
shout; to shout	Schrei; schreien
show; to show	Show; zeigen
side	Seite, Rand
sign	(An-)Zeichen
simple	einfach
since	da, weil, seit
to sing	singen
to sit	sitzen, sich hinsetzen
situation	Situation, Lage
six	sechs
sixteen	sechzehn
sixty	sechzig
sleep; to sleep	Schlaf; schlafen
small	klein
so	also, damit, deshalb, so (dass)
some	einige, etwas
somebody	jemand
someone	jemand

Grundwortschatz

something	etwas	to think	denken, meinen, finden, glauben	warm	warm
sometimes	manchmal	third	dritte/r/s	to wash	waschen
somewhere	irgendwo(hin)	thirteen	dreizehn	to watch	beobachten
son	Sohn	thirty	dreißig	water	Wasser
song	Lied	this, these	dies, diese/r/s; diese	way	Weg, Methode, Art (und Weise)
soon	bald	thought	Gedanke	we	wir
sorry	traurig; Verzeihung	three	drei	to wear	tragen, anhaben
sort	Sorte, Art	through	durch	week	Woche
to speak	sprechen, reden	Thursday	Donnerstag	weekend	Wochenende
sport	Sport	ticket	Karte, Fahrschein	welcome	Willkommen; willkommen
to stand	stehen, aushalten	time	Zeit, Mal	well	gesund, gut, also
start; to start	Beginn; anfangen, starten, beginnen	to	zu, nach	what	was, welche/r/s
stay; to stay	Aufenthalt; bleiben	today	heute	when	wenn, als, wann
still	still, trotzdem, (immer) noch	together	zusammen	where	wo(hin)
to stop	(an) halten, aufhören (mit)	tomorrow	morgen	which	welche/r/s
story	Erzählung, Geschichte	too	zu, auch	white	weiß
street	Straße	top	Spitze, Gipfel; Spitzen-	who	wer, der/die/das, welche(r/s)
student	Student/in, Lernende/r	tourist	Tourist/in	whole	ganz
stupid	dumm	towards	auf … zu	whose	wessen, dessen
summer	Sommer	town	Stadt	why	warum
Sunday	Sonntag	train; to train	Zug; trainieren	will	Wille; werde(n), wollen
supermarket	Supermarkt	travel; to travel	Reisen; reisen, fahren	to win	gewinnen, siegen
sure	freilich, sicher(lich)	tree	Baum	wind	Wind
sweet	süß	to try	versuchen, probieren	wine	Wein
to swim	schwimmen	Tuesday	Dienstag	winter	Winter
		turn; to turn	Wendung; (sich) drehen	with	mit, bei
T		TV	Fernsehen	without	ohne
to take	nehmen, bringen, dauern	twelve	zwölf	woman	Frau
talk; to talk	Gespräch, Unterhaltung, Vortrag ; sprechen, reden	twenty	zwanzig	word	Wort
tall	groß	two	zwei	work; to work	Arbeit, Werk; funktionieren, arbeiten
tea	Tee			worker	Arbeiter/in
to teach	unterrichten, lehren	**U**		world	Welt
team	Mannschaft	UK	Vereinigtes Königreich	would	würde/n
teenager	Teenager	under	unter	to write	schreiben
telephone; to telephone	Telefon; telefonieren	to understand	verstehen, begreifen	wrong	falsch
television	Fernsehen, Fernseher	unfair	unfair		
to tell	sagen, erzählen	United Kingdom	Vereinigtes Königreich	**Y**	
ten	zehn	until	bis	yeah	ja
test; to test	Test, Prüfung; untersuchen, prüfen	up	auf	year	Jahr
text	Text	us	uns	yellow	gelb
than	als	to use	benutzen, verwenden	yes	ja
thank you	danke			yesterday	gestern
thanks	Dank; danke	**V**		you	du, Sie, ihr, dich, dir, Ihnen, euch, man
that, those	das, dass; jene	very	sehr	young	jung
the	der/die/das	video	Video	your	dein/e, Ihr/e, euer/e
theatre	Theater	village	Dorf	yourself	du/Sie selbst, (Sie) sich
their	ihr/e	visit; to visit	Besuch; besuchen, besichtigen		
them	ihnen, sie				
then	dann	**W**			
there	da, dort(hin)	to wait	warten		
there's	es gibt	walk; to walk	Spaziergang; (zu Fuß) gehen		
they	sie	wall	Wand, Mauer		
thing	Sache, Ding, Gegenstand	to want	wollen		

Chronologisches Wörterverzeichnis

Dieses Wörterverzeichnis enthält alle Wörter, die nicht in der Liste des Grundwortschatzes enthalten sind, d. h. die nicht als bekannt vorausgesetzt werden.

5

springboard	['sprɪŋbɔːd]	Sprungbrett
present	['preznt]	Gegenwart
mountain bike	['maʊntən baɪk]	Mountainbike
moped	['məʊped]	Moped, Mofa

6

extra	['ekstrə]	zusätzlich
useful	['juːsfl]	nützlich
animal	['ænɪml]	Tier
clinic	['klɪnɪk]	Klinik
attendant	[ə'tendənt]	Pfleger/in
veterinary	['vetnri]	tierärztlich, Veterinär-
assistant	[ə'sɪstənt]	Assistent/in, Helfer/in
to clean	[kliːn]	reinigen, säubern
cage	[keɪdʒ]	Käfig
pocket money	['pɒkɪt mʌni]	Taschengeld
to deliver	[dɪ'lɪvə]	austragen, zustellen
to spend on	['spend ɒn]	ausgeben für
to save	[seɪv]	(auf)sparen
rest	[rest]	Rest
neighbour	['neɪbə]	Nachbar/in
for example	[fər ɪɡ'zɑːmpl]	zum Beispiel
to clear	[klɪə]	räumen
snow	[snəʊ]	Schnee
statement	['steɪtmənt]	Aussage
true	[truː]	richtig, zutreffend
false	[fɔːls]	falsch
mokick	['məʊkɪk]	Kleinmotorrad (mit Kickstarter)
shopping	['ʃɒpɪŋ]	Einkäufe

7

opposite	['ɒpəzɪt]	Gegenteil
unfriendly	[ʌn'frendli]	unfreundlich
to hate	[heɪt]	hassen
useless	['juːsləs]	nutzlos, sinnlos
grammar	['ɡræmə]	Grammatik
to remember	[rɪ'membə]	sich erinnern (an), daran denken
to enjoy	[ɪn'dʒɔɪ]	gefallen, gern haben/tun
to complete	[kəm'pliːt]	vervollständigen, ergänzen
sentence	['sentəns]	Satz, Strafe
correct	[kə'rekt]	richtig
form	[fɔːm]	Form
verb	[vɜːb]	Verb
in brackets	[ɪn 'brækɪts]	in Klammern
Mr	['mɪstə]	Herr
Mrs	['mɪsɪz]	Frau
to copy	['kɒpi]	abschreiben, kopieren, übertragen
table	['teɪbl]	Tabelle
exercise book	['eksəsaɪz bʊk]	(Schul-)Heft

uncle	['ʌŋkl]	Onkel
to exchange	[ɪks'tʃeɪndʒ]	(aus)tauschen
to check	[tʃek]	(über)prüfen, kontrollieren
spelling	['spelɪŋ]	Rechtschreibung
mistake	[mɪ'steɪk]	Fehler, Irrtum
missing	['mɪsɪŋ]	fehlend
information	[ˌɪnfə'meɪʃn]	Information(en), Angaben
final	['faɪnl]	letzte/r/s, End-

8

to prepare	[prɪ'peə]	vorbereiten
lunch	[lʌntʃ]	Mittagessen
waste of time	[ˌweɪst əf 'taɪm]	Zeitverschwendung
qualification	[ˌkwɒlɪfɪ'keɪʃn]	Abschluss (einer Ausbildung)
algebra	['ældʒɪbrə]	Algebra
geometry	[dʒi'ɒmətri]	Geometrie
exam	[ɪɡ'zæm]	Prüfung, Examen
to pass (an exam)	[pɑːs ən ɪɡ'zæm]	(ein Examen) bestehen
subject	['sʌbdʒɪkt]	(Schul-)Fach
Spanish	['spænɪʃ]	Spanisch
to mean	[miːn]	bedeuten
Spain	[speɪn]	Spanien
practical	['præktɪkl]	praktisch
let's	[lets]	lass/t uns
topic	['tɒpɪk]	Thema
to be interested in	[bi 'ɪntrəstɪd ɪn]	sich interessieren für
odd	[ɒd]	nicht passend
to fit	[fɪt]	passen (zu)
Africa	['afrɪkə]	Afrika
USA	[juː es 'eɪ]	die Vereinigten Staaten von Amerika

9

pupil	['pjuːpl]	Schüler/in
to match	[mætʃ]	zuordnen
beginning	[bɪ'ɡɪnɪŋ]	Anfang, Beginn
ending	['endɪŋ]	Endung, (Satz-)Ende
woodwork	['wʊdwɜːk]	Werken mit Holz, Holzarbeit
metalwork	['metlwɜːk]	Werken mit Metall, Metallarbeit
domestic science	[dəˌmestɪk 'saɪəns]	Hauswirtschaft
technical drawing	[ˌteknɪkl 'drɔːɪŋ]	technisches Zeichnen
information technology	[ɪnfəˌmeɪʃn tek'nɒlədʒi]	Computertechnik
religious education	[rɪˌlɪdʒəs edʒʊ'keɪʃn]	Religion(sunterricht)
scale	[skeɪl]	Skala, Maßstab
to add	[æd]	addieren, zusammenzählen

Chronologisches Wörterverzeichnis

total	['təʊtl]	(End-)Summe
mostly	['məʊstli]	meistens
to compare	[kəm'peə]	vergleichen

10

profile	['prəʊfaɪl]	Profil, Porträt, (Berufs-)Bild
farm	[fɑːm]	Bauernhof
zoo	[zuː]	Zoo, Tierpark
nurse	[nɜːs]	Krankenpfleger/in
hospital	['hɒspɪtl]	Hospital, Krankenhaus
pet	[pet]	Heim-, Haustier
owner	['əʊnə]	Besitzer/in
to file	[faɪl]	eingeben, ablegen
vet	[vet]	Tierarzt, -ärztin
to examine	[ɪg'zæmɪn]	untersuchen
tiger	['taɪgə]	Tiger
real	[rɪəl]	echt, richtig
to feed	[fiːd]	füttern
bottle	['bɒtl]	Flasche
clean	[kliːn]	sauber
typical	['tɪpɪkl]	typisch
cow	[kaʊ]	Kuh
horse	[hɔːs]	Pferd
fresh	[freʃ]	frisch
air	[eə]	Luft

11

to manage	['mænɪdʒ]	bewältigen, fertig werden mit
to rewrite	[ˌriː'raɪt]	umschreiben, neu schreiben
order	['ɔːdə]	Reihenfolge
to look forward to	[ˌlʊk 'fɔːwəd tə]	sich freuen auf
dear	[dɪə]	liebe/r
Dr	['dɒktə]	Dr.
of one's own	[əv wʌnz 'əʊn]	eigen
cat	[kæt]	Katze
Yours sincerely	[jɔːz sɪn'sɪəli]	Mit freundlichen Grüßen
instruction	[ɪn'strʌkʃn]	Anweisung
rabbit	['ræbɪt]	Kaninchen
p.m.	[ˌpiː 'em]	nachmittags
oh	[əʊ]	Null
double	['dʌbl]	doppelt, zweimal
to pick up	[ˌpɪk 'ʌp]	abholen
fine	[faɪn]	gut, in Ordnung

12

material	[mə'tɪəriəl]	Material, Stoff
to wake up	[ˌweɪk 'ʌp]	aufwachen
snake	[sneɪk]	Schlange
to be asleep	[bi ə'sliːp]	schlafen
operation	[ˌɒpə'reɪʃn]	Operation, Eingriff
to be afraid of	[bi ə'freɪd əv]	Angst haben vor, sich fürchten vor
careful	['keəfl]	vorsichtig
poisonous	['pɔɪzənəs]	giftig
to measure	['meʒə]	messen
centimetre	['sentɪmiːtə]	Zentimeter
type	[taɪp]	Art
fact	[fækt]	Tatsache, Fakt
patient	['peɪʃnt]	Patient/in
o'clock	[ə'klɒk]	um ... Uhr
straw	[strɔː]	Stroh
transport box	['trænspɔːt bɒks]	Transportbox
to lift	[lɪft]	(an-, hoch)heben
carefully	['keəfəli]	vorsichtig
waiting room	['weɪtɪŋ ruːm]	Wartezimmer
busy	['bɪzi]	beschäftigt
desk	[desk]	(Schreib-)Tisch, Schalter
slowly	['sləʊli]	langsam
to hiss	[hɪs]	zischen
fear	[fɪə]	Angst, Furcht
doorbell	['dɔːbel]	Türklingel
summary	['sʌməri]	Zusammenfassung
following	['fɒləʊɪŋ]	folgende/r/s
to draw	[drɔː]	zeichnen
garter snake	['gɑːtə sneɪk]	Strumpfbandnatter
stripe	[straɪp]	Streifen
broad	[brɔːd]	breit
spot	[spɒt]	Fleck(en), Punkt
rat	[ræt]	Ratte
worm	[wɜːm]	Wurm

14

teenage	['tiːneɪdʒ]	für Teenager, Teenage-
magazine	[ˌmægə'ziːn]	Zeitschrift, Magazin
to print	[prɪnt]	(ab)drucken
reader	['riːdə]	Leser/in
expert	['ekspɜːt]	Fachmann/frau, Experte/Expertin
advice	[əd'vaɪs]	Rat(schlag), Ratschläge
to smoke	[sməʊk]	rauchen
to smell	[smel]	riechen
ashtray	['æʃtreɪ]	Aschenbecher
to laugh	[lɑːf]	lachen
to hang out	[ˌhæŋ 'aʊt]	rumhängen, sich rumtreiben
to sneak	[sniːk]	klauen, stibitzen
treat	[triːt]	etw Besonderes
to steal	[stiːl]	stehlen
packet	['pækɪt]	Packung, Päckchen
chewing gum	['tʃuːɪŋ gʌm]	Kaugummi
make-up	['meɪkʌp]	Make-up, Schminke
silly	['sɪli]	töricht, albern
paper clip	['peɪpə klɪp]	Büroklammer
to get into trouble	[ˌget ɪntə 'trʌbl]	Probleme bekommen
dad	[dæd]	Papa, Vater
vodka	['vɒdkə]	Wodka
angry	['æŋgri]	böse, wütend
to be worried	[bi 'wʌrid]	Angst haben
old-fashioned	[ˌəʊld 'fæʃnd]	altmodisch
sensible	['sensəbl]	vernünftig

Chronologisches Wörterverzeichnis

curfew	[ˈkɜːfjuː]	Ausgangssperre, Zapfenstreich
to disagree	[ˌdɪsəˈgriː]	anderer Meinung sein, nicht zustimmen
to trust	[trʌst]	vertrauen
to link	[lɪŋk]	verbinden

15

meaning	[ˈmiːnɪŋ]	Bedeutung
helpful	[ˈhelpfl]	hilfreich, nützlich
warning	[ˈwɔːnɪŋ]	Warnung
tip	[tɪp]	Hinweis, Tipp
wink	[wɪŋk]	Zwinkern, Blinzeln
husband	[ˈhʌzbənd]	(Ehe-)Mann
wife	[waɪf]	(Ehe-)Frau
ear	[ɪə]	Ohr
Irish	[ˈaɪrɪʃ]	irisch
dance	[dɑːns]	Tanz
limit	[ˈlɪmɪt]	Grenze, Frist
dialogue	[ˈdaɪəlɒg]	Dialog
to act	[ækt]	(nach)spielen, aufführen
argument	[ˈɑːgjumənt]	Streit, Auseinandersetzung
to lie	[laɪ]	lügen
truth	[truːθ]	Wahrheit

16

unexpected	[ˌʌnɪkˈspektɪd]	unerwartet
to groan	[grəʊn]	stöhnen
pain	[peɪn]	Schmerz(en)
stomach ache	[ˈstʌmək eɪk]	Magenschmerzen
local	[ˈləʊkl]	hiesig, einheimisch
winner	[ˈwɪnə]	Gewinner/in, Sieger/in
standard	[ˈstændəd]	Standard
to miss	[mɪs]	fehlen
single	[ˈsɪŋgl]	einzig
marketing	[ˈmɑːkɪtɪŋ]	Vertrieb, Vertriebs-
manager	[ˈmænɪdʒə]	Leiter/in
prize	[praɪz]	Preis, Gewinn
sick	[sɪk]	krank
Tenerife	[ˌtenəˈriːf]	Teneriffa
bitter	[ˈbɪtə]	verbittert
sunny	[ˈsʌni]	sonnig
wonderful	[ˈwʌndəfl]	wunderbar, wundervoll
reporter	[rɪˈpɔːtə]	Reporter/in
before	[bɪˈfɔː]	bevor

17

hurt	[hɜːt]	verletzt
firm	[fɜːm]	Firma
loser	[ˈluːzə]	Verlierer/in
terrible	[ˈterəbl]	schrecklich, furchtbar
worst	[wɜːst]	schlechteste, schlimmste
surprise	[səˈpraɪz]	Überraschung
to surprise	[səˈpraɪz]	überraschen
serious	[ˈsɪəriəs]	ernst(haft)
sickness	[ˈsɪknəs]	Krankheit
accident	[ˈæksɪdənt]	Unfall
fire	[ˈfaɪə]	Feuer, Brand
death	[deθ]	Tod

18

airport	[ˈeəpɔːt]	Flughafen
personnel	[ˌpɜːsəˈnel]	Personal, Mitarbeiter
Europe	[ˈjʊərəp]	Europa
to employ	[ɪmˈplɔɪ]	beschäftigen
description	[dɪˈskrɪpʃn]	Beschreibung
to unload	[ˌʌnˈləʊd]	entladen, ausladen
plane	[pleɪn]	Flugzeug
terminal	[ˈtɜːmɪnl]	Abfertigung(sgebäude)
suitcase	[ˈsuːtkeɪs]	Koffer
to load	[ləʊd]	(ver)laden
passenger	[ˈpæsɪndʒə]	Passagier/in, Fluggast
announcement	[əˈnaʊnsmənt]	Durchsage
to deal with	[ˈdiːl wɪð]	sich befassen mit, bearbeiten
complaint	[kəmˈpleɪnt]	Beschwerde, Beanstandung, Reklamation
to guard	[gɑːd]	bewachen
building	[ˈbɪldɪŋ]	Gebäude
runway	[ˈrʌnweɪ]	Start-, Landebahn
to search	[sɜːtʃ]	(durch)suchen
aircraft	[ˈeəkrɑːft]	Flugzeug(e)
luggage	[ˈlʌgɪdʒ]	Gepäck
floor	[flɔː]	(Fuß-)Boden, Flur
machine	[məˈʃiːn]	Maschine, Gerät
to remove	[rɪˈmuːv]	entfernen, beseitigen
graffiti	[grəˈfiːti]	Wandschmierereien, Graffiti
security	[sɪˈkjʊərəti]	Sicherheit
officer	[ˈɒfɪsə]	(Polizei-)Beamter/Beamtin
handler	[ˈhændlə]	Transporteur
general	[ˈdʒenrəl]	allgemein, normal
cleaner	[ˈkliːnə]	Reinigungskraft

19

mediation	[ˌmiːdiˈeɪʃn]	Vermittlung, Dolmetschen
haircut	[ˈheəkʌt]	Haarschnitt, Frisur
flight	[flaɪt]	Flug
step	[step]	Schritt

20

sand	[sænd]	Sand
beach	[biːtʃ]	Strand

21

preparation	[ˌprepəˈreɪʃn]	Vorbereitung
crocodile	[ˈkrɒkədaɪl]	Krokodil
hunter	[ˈhʌntə]	Jäger/in
to catch	[kætʃ]	fangen
wild	[waɪld]	wild
lizard	[ˈlɪzəd]	Eidechse
well known	[ˌwel ˈnəʊn]	sehr bekannt, berühmt

Chronologisches Wörterverzeichnis

to relocate	[ˌriːləʊˈkeɪt]	umsiedeln		**24**		
river	[ˈrɪvə]	Fluss		bean	[biːn]	Bohne
to take over	[ˌteɪk ˈəʊvə]	übernehmen		finalist	[ˈfaɪnəlɪst]	Endspielteilnehmer/in
popular	[ˈpɒpjələ]	beliebt, populär		championship	[ˈtʃæmpiənʃɪp]	Meisterschaft
Australia	[ɒˈstreɪliə]	Australien		branch	[brɑːntʃ]	Filiale, Zweigstelle
visitor	[ˈvɪzɪtə]	Besucher/in		dustman	[ˈdʌstmən]	Müllwerker
Australian	[ɒˈstreɪliən]	australisch		rubbish	[ˈrʌbɪʃ]	Abfall, Müll
reptile	[ˈreptaɪl]	Reptil		dirt	[dɜːt]	Schmutz, Dreck
nature	[ˈneɪtʃə]	Natur		bath	[bɑːθ]	Bad
to protect	[prəˈtekt]	schützen		dinner	[ˈdɪnə]	Abendessen
wildlife	[ˈwaɪldlaɪf]	Tierwelt		dirty	[ˈdɜːti]	schmutzig
especially	[ɪˈspeʃəli]	besonders, insbesondere		dream	[driːm]	Traum
to be frightened of	[bi ˈfraɪtnd əv]	Angst haben vor		handbook	[ˈhændbʊk]	Bedienungsanleitung, Handbuch
to campaign	[kæmˈpeɪn]	kämpfen, sich einsetzen (für)		customer	[ˈkʌstəmə]	Kunde/Kundin
programme	[ˈprəʊɡræm]	Sendung, Programm		to complain	[kəmˈpleɪn]	(sich) beschweren
warrior	[ˈwɒriə]	Krieger/in, Aktivist/in		training	[ˈtreɪnɪŋ]	Schulung, Training
unusual	[ʌnˈjuːʒʊəl]	ungewöhnlich, unüblich		course	[kɔːs]	Kurs, Lehrgang
honeymoon	[ˈhʌnimuːn]	Flitterwochen, Hochzeitsreise		**25**		
hunt	[hʌnt]	Jagd		to marry	[ˈmæri]	heiraten
to wrestle	[ˈresl]	ringen		preposition	[ˌprepəˈzɪʃn]	Präposition, Verhältniswort
series	[ˈsɪəriːz]	Serie, Sendereihe		biscuit	[ˈbɪskɪt]	Keks
deadly	[ˈdedli]	tödlich		usually	[ˈjuːʒəli]	gewöhnlich, meistens
success	[səkˈses]	Erfolg		window	[ˈwɪndəʊ]	Fenster
famous	[ˈfeɪməs]	berühmt		**26**		
rich	[rɪtʃ]	reich		advert	[ˈædvɜːt]	Inserat, Anzeige
naturalist	[ˈnætʃrəlɪst]	Naturforscher/in		sqm	[ˈskweə miːtə]	Quadratmeter
dangerous	[ˈdeɪndʒərəs]	gefährlich		bedroom	[ˈbedrʊm]	Schlafzimmer
in front of	[ɪn ˈfrʌnt əv]	vor		living room	[ˈlɪvɪŋ rʊm]	Wohnzimmer
stingray	[ˈstɪŋreɪ]	Stachelrochen		dining room	[ˈdaɪnɪŋ rʊm]	Esszimmer
to stab	[stæb]	stechen		station	[ˈsteɪʃn]	Bahnhof
heart	[hɑːt]	Herz		rent	[rent]	Miete
to kill	[kɪl]	töten		per	[pə]	pro
annotation	[ˌænəˈteɪʃn]	Anmerkung		heating	[ˈhiːtɪŋ]	Heizung
22				deposit	[dɪˈpɒzɪt]	Anzahlung, Kaution
earn	[ɜːn]	verdienen		to contact	[ˈkɒntækt]	Kontakt aufnehmen zu, sich wenden an
according to	[əˈkɔːdɪŋ tə]	zufolge, laut, nach		appointment	[əˈpɔɪntmənt]	Termin, Verabredung
to attack	[əˈtæk]	angreifen		couple	[ˈkʌpl]	Paar, Ehepaar
23				bathroom	[ˈbɑːθrʊm]	Bad(ezimmer)
barista	[bəˈriːstə]	Barmann		empty	[ˈempti]	leer
waiter	[ˈweɪtə]	Kellner, Ober		to include	[ɪnˈkluːd]	umfassen, einschließen
waitress	[ˈweɪtrɪs]	Kellnerin, Serviererin		plus	[plʌs]	außerdem
bakery	[ˈbeɪkəri]	Bäckerei		afterwards	[ˈɑːftəwədz]	danach, hinterher
caterer	[ˈkeɪtərə]	Lieferant von Fertiggerichten und Getränken		pub	[pʌb]	Gaststätte, Lokal
cook	[kʊk]	Koch, Köchin		dark	[dɑːk]	dunkel, düster
barman	[ˈbɑːmən]	Barkeeper		to afford	[əˈfɔːd]	(es) sich leisten (können)
kitchen	[ˈkɪtʃɪn]	Küche		to forget	[fəˈget]	vergessen
baker's shop	[ˌbeɪkəz ˈʃɒp]	Bäckerei		no way	[ˌnəʊ ˈweɪ]	auf keinen Fall, kommt überhaupt nicht in Frage
private	[ˈpraɪvət]	privat		tired	[ˈtaɪəd]	müde
meal	[miːl]	Essen, Mahlzeit		hungry	[ˈhʌŋɡri]	hungrig
guest	[gest]	Gast		chicken	[ˈtʃɪkɪn]	Huhn, Hähnchen
cocktail	[ˈkɒkteɪl]	Cocktail		sandwich	[ˈsænwɪdʒ]	Sandwich, belegtes Brot

Chronologisches Wörterverzeichnis

27
progressive	[prəˈgresɪv]	Verlaufsform
estate agent	[ɪˈsteɪt eɪdʒənt]	Immobilienmakler/in
certainly	[ˈsɜːtnli]	sicherlich, bestimmt
to prefer	[prɪˈfɜː]	bevorzugen
particular	[pəˈtɪkjələ]	bestimmt
square metre	[ˈskweə miːtə]	Quadratmeter

28
chef	[ʃef]	Chefkoch/köchin, Küchenchef/in
properly	[ˈprɒpəli]	richtig, korrekt
plate	[pleɪt]	Teller, Platte
key	[kiː]	Schlüssel
fruit	[fruːt]	Obst
vegetable	[ˈvedʒtəbl]	Gemüse
reservation	[ˌrezəˈveɪʃn]	Reservierung, (Tisch-)Bestellung

29
direction	[dəˈrekʃn]	Wegbeschreibung
caller	[ˈkɔːlə]	Anrufer/in
to follow	[ˈfɒləʊ]	folgen
route	[ruːt]	Strecke, Weg
straight ahead	[ˌstreɪt əˈhed]	geradeaus
crossroads	[ˈkrɒsrəʊdz]	Kreuzung
junction	[ˈdʒʌŋkʃn]	(Straßen-)Kreuzung
similar	[ˈsɪmələ]	ähnlich

30
date	[deɪt]	Verabredung, Rendezvous
to organize	[ˈɔːgənaɪz]	organisieren
treasure hunt	[ˈtreʒə hʌnt]	Schatzsuche, Schnitzeljagd
to suggest	[səˈdʒest]	vorschlagen
canal	[kəˈnæl]	Kanal
stress	[stres]	Stress
comfortable	[ˈkʌmftəbl]	bequem, wohl
whether	[ˈweðə]	ob
lake	[leɪk]	(Binnen-)See
boat	[bəʊt]	Boot
fishing	[ˈfɪʃɪŋ]	Angeln
hamburger	[ˈhæmbɜːgə]	Hamburger
anyway	[ˈeniweɪ]	jedenfalls, wie dem auch sei
minced beef	[ˌmɪnst ˈbiːf]	Rinderhack(fleisch)
salad	[ˈsæləd]	Salat
onion	[ˈʌnjən]	Zwiebel
tomato	[təˈmɑːtəʊ]	Tomate
roll	[rəʊl]	Brötchen
recipe	[ˈresəpi]	(Koch-)Rezept
sailing	[ˈseɪlɪŋ]	Segeln
to avoid	[əˈvɔɪd]	(ver)meiden
to invite	[ɪnˈvaɪt]	einladen

31
heritage	[ˈherɪtɪdʒ]	Erbe
history	[ˈhɪstri]	Geschichte
multi-cultural	[ˌmʌlti ˈkʌltʃərəl]	multikulturell
Scouser	[ˈskaʊsə]	Liverpooler/in
guide	[gaɪd]	(Reise-)Führer
band	[bænd]	(Musik-)Kapelle
arena	[əˈriːnə]	Arena, Stadion
historic	[hɪˈstɒrɪk]	historisch
dock	[dɒk]	Pier, Kai
attraction	[əˈtrækʃn]	Anziehung(spunkt), Attraktion
port	[pɔːt]	Hafen(stadt)
maritime	[ˈmærɪtaɪm]	Schiffahrts-
museum	[mjuˈziːəm]	Museum
ship	[ʃɪp]	Schiff
captain	[ˈkæptɪn]	Kapitän
voyage	[ˈvɔɪɪdʒ]	(See-)Reise

32
radio	[ˈreɪdiəʊ]	Radio, Rundfunk
to introduce oneself	[ˌɪntrəˈdjuːs wʌnself]	sich vorstellen
professional	[prəˈfeʃnl]	professionell, berufstätig
woodworker	[ˈwʊdwɜːkə]	Tischler/in
wood	[wʊd]	Holz
Munich	[ˈmjuːnɪk]	München
bricklayer	[ˈbrɪkleɪə]	Maurer/in
stonemason	[ˈstəʊnmeɪsn]	Steinmetz
plasterer	[ˈplɑːstərə]	Gipser/in
painter	[ˈpeɪntə]	Maler/in, Anstreicher/in
unlimited	[ʌnˈlɪmɪtɪd]	unbegrenzt
reputation	[ˌrepjuˈteɪʃn]	Ruf
master certificate	[ˌmɑːstə səˈtɪfɪkət]	Meisterdiplom
to respect	[rɪˈspekt]	respektieren
actually	[ˈæktʃuəli]	tatsächlich
to renovate	[ˈrenəveɪt]	renovieren
prince	[prɪns]	Prinz
synagogue	[ˈsɪnəgɒg]	Synagoge
beautiful	[ˈbjuːtɪfl]	schön
repair	[rɪˈpeə]	Reparatur
frame	[freɪm]	Rahmen
seat	[siːt]	(Sitz-)Platz, Stuhl
furniture	[ˈfɜːnɪtʃə]	Möbel(stücke), Möblierung
paint	[peɪnt]	Farbe
ceiling	[ˈsiːlɪŋ]	(Zimmer-)Decke
complicated	[ˈkɒmplɪkeɪtɪd]	kompliziert
design	[dɪˈzaɪn]	Entwurf, Konstruktion
brick	[brɪk]	Ziegel(stein), Backstein
stone	[stəʊn]	Stein
church	[tʃɜːtʃ]	Kirche
pump	[pʌmp]	Pumpe
pump house	[ˈpʌmp haʊs]	Pumpenhaus
school-leaver	[ˌskuːlˈliːvə]	Schulabgänger/in
vocational	[vəʊˈkeɪʃnl]	beruflich

Chronologisches Wörterverzeichnis

33

renovation	[ˌrenəˈveɪʃn]	Renovierung
modal	[ˈməʊdl]	Modal(verb)
brewery	[ˈbruːəri]	Brauerei
tap	[tæp]	Zapfhahn
skilled	[skɪld]	gelernt, ausgebildet, Fach-
restoration	[ˌrestəˈreɪʃn]	Wiederherstellung, Restaurierung
specialized	[ˈspeʃəlaɪzd]	spezialisiert

34

business	[ˈbɪznəs]	Geschäft, Firma
coast	[kəʊst]	Küste
outback	[ˈaʊtbæk]	australischer Busch
dry	[draɪ]	trocken
to drive	[draɪv]	(mit dem Auto) fahren
equipment	[ɪˈkwɪpmənt]	Ausrüstung
fuel	[ˈfjuːəl]	Treibstoff
mechanic	[mɪˈkænɪk]	Mechaniker/in
garage	[ˈgærɑːʒ]	(Auto-)Werkstatt
exactly	[ɪgˈzæktli]	exakt, genau
trip	[trɪp]	Ausflug, Reise
tour	[tʊə]	Tour, Rundreise
safety	[ˈseɪfti]	Sicherheit
heat	[hiːt]	Hitze
fly	[flaɪ]	Fliege
dust	[dʌst]	Staub
four-wheel drive	[ˌfɔː wiːl ˈdraɪv]	Vierradantrieb
to get stuck	[get ˈstʌk]	stecken bleiben
to dig	[dɪg]	graben
driver	[ˈdraɪvə]	Fahrer/in
air filter	[ˈeə fɪltə]	Luftfilter
trailer	[ˈtreɪlə]	Wohnwagen
to fit	[fɪt]	installieren, einbauen
satellite	[ˈsætəlaɪt]	Satellit
air conditioning	[ˈeə kəndɪʃnɪŋ]	Klimaanlage
spare	[speə]	Ersatz-
battery	[ˈbætəri]	Batterie
special	[ˈspeʃl]	speziell
tank	[tæŋk]	Tank, (Benzin-)Kanister
etc.	[ˌet ˈsetərə]	usw.
though	[ðəʊ]	allerdings, jedoch
profit	[ˈprɒfɪt]	Profit, Gewinn
Polish	[ˈpəʊlɪʃ]	polnisch
to produce	[prəˈdjuːs]	produzieren
SUV	[ˌes juː ˈviː]	Geländewagen (mit Vierradantrieb)
camping	[ˈkæmpɪŋ]	Camping
gas cooker	[ˈgæs kʊkə]	Gasherd
flashlight	[ˈflæʃlaɪt]	Arbeitsleuchte, Taschenlampe
tent	[tent]	Zelt
sleeping bag	[ˈsliːpɪŋbæg]	Schlafsack
workshop	[ˈwɜːkʃɒp]	Werkstatt

35

illustration	[ˌɪləˈstreɪʃn]	Abbildung
leisure	[ˈleʒə]	Freizeit

36

accelerator	[əkˈseləreɪtə]	Gaspedal
brake	[breɪk]	Bremse
clutch	[klʌtʃ]	Kupplung
engine	[ˈendʒɪn]	Motor
exhaust	[ɪgˈzɔːst]	Auspuff(rohr)
steering wheel	[ˈstɪərɪŋ wiːl]	Lenkrad
tyre	[ˈtaɪə]	Reifen
wheel	[wiːl]	Rad
windscreen	[ˈwɪndskriːn]	Windschutzscheibe
item	[ˈaɪtəm]	Artikel, Gegenstand
glasses	[ˈglɑːsɪz]	Brille
protective	[prəˈtektɪv]	Schutz-
glove	[glʌv]	Handschuh
boot	[buːt]	Stiefel
helmet	[ˈhelmɪt]	(Schutz-)Helm
ear protectors	[ɪə prəˈtektəz]	Ohrenschützer
cup mask	[ˈkʌp mɑːsk]	Schutzmaske
lung	[lʌŋ]	Lunge

37

cordless	[ˈkɔːdləs]	schnur-, kabellos
drill	[drɪl]	Bohrer
operating	[ˈɒpəreɪtɪŋ]	Bedienungs-
screwdriver	[ˈskruːdraɪvə]	Schraubenzieher, Schrauber
screw	[skruː]	Schraube
to apply	[əˈplaɪ]	anwenden
pressure	[ˈpreʃə]	Druck
to increase	[ɪnˈkriːs]	steigern, erhöhen
speed	[spiːd]	Geschwindigkeit
gradually	[ˈgrædʒuəli]	allmählich, nach und nach
to damage	[ˈdæmɪdʒ]	beschädigen
to drill	[drɪl]	bohren
to split	[splɪt]	spalten, platzen
adjusting ring	[əˈdʒʌstɪŋ rɪŋ]	Stellring
to proceed	[prəˈsiːd]	(weiter-, fort)fahren
as follows	[əz ˈfɒləʊz]	wie folgt
metal	[ˈmetl]	Metall
to slip	[slɪp]	verrutschen
indentation	[ˌɪndenˈteɪʃn]	Vertiefung, Delle
centre-punch	[ˈsentə pʌntʃ]	(An-)Körner
hammer	[ˈhæmə]	Hammer
lubricant	[ˈluːbrɪkənt]	Gleit-, Schmiermittel
apart from	[əˈpɑːt frəm]	außer, abgesehen von
iron	[ˈaɪən]	Eisen
brass	[brɑːs]	Messing

38

rule	[ruːl]	Vorschrift, Regel
to concentrate on	[ˈkɒnsntreɪt ɒn]	sich konzentrieren auf
loose	[luːs]	weit (geschnitten), lose

Chronologisches Wörterverzeichnis

purpose	['pɜːpəs]	Zweck, Ziel
power cord	['paʊə kɔːd]	Netz-, Stromkabel
power source	['paʊə sɔːs]	Energiequelle
goggles	['gɒglz]	Schutzbrille
wet	[wet]	nass, feucht
condition	[kən'dɪʃn]	Bedingung
tool	[tuːl]	Werkzeug, Gerät
failure to follow	[ˌfeɪljə tə 'fɒləʊ]	Nichtbeachtung
to result in	[rɪ'zʌlt ɪn]	führen zu, zur Folge haben
electric shock	[ɪˌlektrɪk 'ʃɒk]	Stromschlag
injury	['ɪndʒəri]	Verletzung
safe	[seɪf]	sicher
distance	['dɪstəns]	Entfernung, Abstand
distraction	[dɪ'strækʃn]	Ablenkung
to cause	[kɔːz]	verursachen
untidy	[ʌn'taɪdi]	unordentlich, unaufgeräumt
risk	[rɪsk]	Risiko
thick	[θɪk]	dick
to dress	[dres]	(sich) anziehen, kleiden
jewellery	['dʒuːəlri]	Schmuck
to disconnect	[ˌdɪskə'nekt]	trennen, herausziehen
damaged	['dæmɪdʒd]	beschädigt
while	[waɪl]	während
appropriate	[ə'prəʊpriət]	geeignet, passend

39

size	[saɪz]	Größe
zero	['zɪərəʊ]	Null
giant	['dʒaɪənt]	riesig
billboard	['bɪlbɔːd]	Reklametafel, Werbeplakat
French	[frentʃ]	französisch
model	['mɒdl]	Model
to shock	[ʃɒk]	schockieren
to horrify	['hɒrɪfaɪ]	entsetzen
million	['mɪljən]	Million
skeleton	['skelɪtn]	Skelett
leg	[leg]	Bein
thin	[θɪn]	dünn
stick	[stɪk]	Stock, Stecken
to weigh	[weɪ]	wiegen
kilo	['kiːləʊ]	Kilo
fashion	['fæʃn]	Mode
Italian	[ɪ'tæljən]	italienisch
against	[ə'genst]	gegen
to suffer from	['sʌfə frəm]	leiden an
anorexia	[ˌænə'reksɪə]	Magersucht
career	[kə'rɪə]	Karriere, Laufbahn
ideal	[aɪ'diːəl]	ideal
cup	[kʌp]	Tasse
sugar	['ʃʊgə]	Zucker
painful	['peɪnfl]	schmerzhaft
cramp	[kræmp]	Krampf
modelling job	['mɒdlɪŋ dʒɒb]	Auftrag als (Foto-)Modell
to collapse	[kə'læps]	zusammenbrechen
to rush	[rʌʃ]	schnell bringen
coma	['kəʊmə]	Koma
blood	[blʌd]	Blut
transfusion	[træns'fjuːʒn]	Transfusion
including	[ɪn'kluːdɪŋ]	einschließlich, inbegriffen
shocking	['ʃɒkɪŋ]	schrecklich, schockierend

40

to be lucky	[bi 'lʌki]	Glück haben
to warn	[wɔːn]	warnen, darauf hinweisen
illness	['ɪlnəs]	Krankheit

41

vocabulary	[və'kæbjələri]	Wortschatz
deep	[diːp]	tief
seriously	['sɪərɪəsli]	ernst(haft)
badly	['bædli]	schwer, schlimm
to fill in	[ˌfɪl 'ɪn]	eintragen, -setzen
eating disorder	[ˌiːtɪŋ dɪs'ɔːdə]	Essstörung
hopefully	['həʊpfli]	hoffentlich
successful	[sək'sesfl]	erfolgreich

42

tattoo	[tə'tuː]	Tätowierung
to regret	[rɪ'gret]	bedauern, bereuen
not ... anymore	[eni'mɔː]	nicht ... mehr
upper	['ʌpə]	Ober-
sleeve	[sliːv]	Ärmel
artist	['ɑːtɪst]	Künstler/in
research	[rɪ'sɜːtʃ]	Nachforschung(en)
routine	[ruː'tiːn]	routinemäßige Tätigkeit
closely	['kləʊsli]	genau
studio	['stjuːdiəʊ]	Studio
spotlessly	['spɒtləsli]	makellos
previous	['priːviəs]	vorhergehend, früher
tattooist	[tə'tuːɪst]	Tätowierer/in
aftercare	['ɑːftəkeə]	Nachsorge, -behandlung
spotless	['spɒtləs]	sauber, makellos
fashionable	['fæʃnəbl]	modisch, schick

43

king	[kɪŋ]	König
to explain	[ɪk'spleɪn]	erklären, erläutern
express	[ɪk'spres]	Schnell-
cash desk	['kæʃ desk]	Kasse

44

receptionist	[rɪ'sepʃənɪst]	Empfang(smitarbeiter/in)
great	[greɪt]	groß
northern	['nɔːðən]	nördlich
to spell	[spel]	buchstabieren
surname	['sɜːneɪm]	Nach-, Familienname
smoking	['sməʊkɪŋ]	Raucher-
non-smoking	[ˌnɒn 'sməʊkɪŋ]	Nichtraucher-
either	['aɪðə]	entweder
to confirm	[kən'fɜːm]	bestätigen
composition	[ˌkɒmpə'zɪʃn]	Aufsatz
hobby	['hɒbi]	Hobby
activity	[æk'tɪvəti]	Aktivität, Beschäftigung

Chronologisches Wörterverzeichnis

male	[meɪl]	männlich
female	['fiːmeɪl]	weiblich
south	[saʊθ]	Süd-
New Zealand	[ˌnjuː 'ziːlənd]	Neuseeland
library	['laɪbrəri]	Bücherei, Bibliothek
to get in touch with	[get ɪn 'tʌtʃ wɪð]	(sich) in Verbindung setzen mit

45

media	['miːdiə]	Medien
star	[stɑː]	Star, Stern
basically	['beɪsɪkli]	im Grunde, grundsätzlich
singer	['sɪŋə]	Sänger/in
writer	['raɪtə]	Schriftsteller/in, Autor/in
politician	[ˌpɒlə'tɪʃn]	Politiker/in
celebrity	[sə'lebrəti]	Prominente/r, Berühmtheit
to recognize	['rekəgnaɪz]	(wieder) erkennen
to admire	[əd'maɪə]	bewundern
advertiser	['ædvətaɪzə]	Inserent/in, Werbefirma
product	['prɒdʌkt]	Produkt, Erzeugnis
actor	['æktə]	Schauspieler
actress	['æktrəs]	Schauspielerin
colouring	['kʌlərɪŋ]	Einfärbung

46

icon	['aɪkɒn]	Ikone, Symbol
acting	['æktɪŋ]	schauspielerisch
short	[ʃɔːt]	kurz
director	[də'rektə]	Regisseur/in
east	[iːst]	östlich
rebel	['rebl]	Rebell
cause	[kɔːz]	Grund, Anlass
handsome	['hænsəm]	gut aussehend
idol	['aɪdl]	Idol, Vorbild
unfortunately	[ʌn'fɔːtʃənətli]	unglücklicherweise, leider
crash	[kræʃ]	Unfall
west	[west]	westlich
ugly	['ʌgli]	hässlich

47

apartment	[ə'pɑːtmənt]	Wohnung, Apartment
skipper	['skɪpə]	Kapitän
lane	[leɪn]	Gasse, Weg
coach	[kəʊtʃ]	Reisebus
birth	[bɜːθ]	Geburt

48

powerful	['paʊəfl]	mächtig, einflussreich
advertising	['ædvətaɪzɪŋ]	Werbung, Reklame
charity	['tʃærəti]	Wohltätigkeit
disabled	[dɪs'eɪbld]	(körper)behindert
wheelchair	['wiːltʃeə]	Rollstuhl
delighted	[dɪ'laɪtɪd]	(sehr) erfreut
independent	[ˌɪndɪ'pendənt]	unabhängig
malaria	[mə'leəriə]	Malaria
net	[net]	(Moskito-)Netz
to support	[sə'pɔːt]	unterstützen
to donate	[dəʊ'neɪt]	spenden
dollar	['dɒlə]	Dollar
clip	[klɪp]	(Video-)Clip, kurzer (Werbe-)Film
luxury	['lʌkʃəri]	Luxus
southern	['sʌðən]	südlich
multinational	[ˌmʌlti'næʃnəl]	multinational

49

connector	[kə'nektə]	Bindewort
untrue	[ʌn'truː]	unwahr

50

roadie	['rəʊdi]	Roadie
beautician	[ˌbjuː'tɪʃn]	Kosmetiker/in
lighting	['laɪtɪŋ]	Beleuchtung, Licht
sound	[saʊnd]	Ton
technician	[tek'nɪʃn]	Techniker/in
rigger	['rɪgə]	Bühnenarbeiter/in
to set up	[ˌset 'ʌp]	aufbauen
to control	[kən'trəʊl]	kontrollieren, regeln
stage	[steɪdʒ]	Bühne
microphone	['maɪkrəfəʊn]	Mikrophon
steel	[stiːl]	Stahl
scaffolding	['skæfəldɪŋ]	(Bau-)Gerüst
catering	['keɪtərɪŋ]	Versorgung mit Speisen und Getränken

51

factory	['fæktəri]	Fabrik
emergency	[ɪ'mɜːdʒənsi]	Notfall
first aid	[ˌfɜːst 'eɪd]	erste Hilfe
exit	['eksɪt]	Ausgang
substance	['sʌbstəns]	Substanz, Stoff
toxic	['tɒksɪk]	giftig, toxisch
slippery	['slɪpəri]	glatt, rutschig
apprentice	[ə'prentɪs]	Lehrling, Auszubildende/r
work experience	['wɜːk ɪkspɪəriəns]	Praktikum
supervisor	['suːpəvaɪzə]	Ausbilder/in
report	[rɪ'pɔːt]	Bericht

52

to care	[keə]	sich kümmern
tomb	[tuːm]	Grab
raider	['reɪdə]	Plünderer, Schänder
Cambodia	[kæm'bəʊdiə]	Kambodscha
to realize	['rɪəlaɪz]	(sich) bewusst werden
horrible	['hɒrəbl]	schrecklich, furchtbar
landmine	['lændmaɪn]	Landmine
war	[wɔː]	Krieg
to injure	['ɪndʒə]	verletzen
thousand	['θaʊznd]	tausend
to ban	[bæn]	verbieten
refugee	[ˌrefjuˈdʒiː]	Flüchtling
ambassador	[æm'bæsədə]	Botschafter/in

Chronologisches Wörterverzeichnis

United Nations	[juˌnaɪtɪd ˈneɪʃnz]	Vereinte Nationen		immigrant	[ˈɪmɪɡrənt]	Einwanderer, Einwanderin
to adopt	[əˈdɒpt]	adoptieren, (die Patenschaft) übernehmen		cheaply	[ˈtʃiːpli]	billig
				elsewhere	[ˌelsˈweə]	anderswo, woanders
minefield	[ˈmaɪnfiːld]	Minenfeld		foreign	[ˈfɒrən]	ausländisch, fremd
to register	[ˈredʒɪstə]	eintragen lassen				
trade	[treɪd]	Handel		**57**		
poverty	[ˈpɒvəti]	Armut		production	[prəˈdʌkʃn]	Produktion, Herstellung
Asia	[ˈeɪʃə]	Asien		comparison	[kəmˈpærɪsn]	Vergleich, Steigerung
African	[ˈæfrɪkən]	afrikanisch		worse	[wɜːs]	schlechter, schlimmer
farmer	[ˈfɑːmə]	Bauer, Bäuerin		adjective	[ˈædʒɪktɪv]	Adjektiv, Eigenschaftswort
				pretty	[ˈprɪti]	hübsch
53				Asian	[ˈeɪʃn]	asiatisch
label	[ˈleɪbl]	Aufkleber, Etikett		Japanese	[ˌdʒæpəˈniːz]	japanisch
category	[ˈkætəɡəri]	Kategorie, Klasse		sunglasses	[ˈsʌnɡlɑːsɪz]	Sonnenbrille
bodycare	[ˈbɒdikeə]	Körperpflege				
cosmetics	[kɒzˈmetɪks]	Kosmetik(a)		**58**		
healthcare	[ˈhelθkeə]	Gesundheit(sfürsorge)		sales assistant	[ˈseɪlz əsɪstənt]	Verkäufer/in
pea	[piː]	Erbse		clothing	[ˈkləʊðɪŋ]	Bekleidung, Kleidung
shampoo	[ʃæmˈpuː]	Shampoo		blouse	[blaʊz]	Bluse
India	[ˈɪndiə]	Indien		lovely	[ˈlʌvli]	schön, hübsch
Hindi	[ˈhɪndi]	Hindi		latest	[ˈleɪtɪst]	neueste
				shirt	[ʃɜːt]	Hemd
54				trousers	[ˈtraʊzəz]	Hose(n)
dislike	[dɪsˈlaɪk]	Abneigung		skirt	[skɜːt]	Rock
impatient	[ɪmˈpeɪʃnt]	ungeduldig		jacket	[ˈdʒækɪt]	Jacke, Jackett
boutique	[buːˈtiːk]	Boutique		sky	[skaɪ]	Himmel
jeans	[dʒiːnz]	Jeans				
American	[əˈmerɪkən]	amerikanisch		**59**		
store	[stɔː]	Laden, Geschäft		gap	[ɡæp]	Lücke
bargain	[ˈbɑːɡɪn]	(günstiges) Angebot, Schnäppchen		baker	[ˈbeɪkə]	Bäcker/in
				luckily	[ˈlʌkɪli]	glücklicherweise, zum Glück
designer	[dɪˈzaɪnə]	Designer/in		throughout	[θruːˈaʊt]	die ganze Zeit hindurch, während
quality	[ˈkwɒləti]	Qualität				
to be worth	[bi ˈwɜːθ]	wert sein		break	[breɪk]	Pause
average	[ˈævərɪdʒ]	Durchschnitt, durchschnittlich		to count	[kaʊnt]	zählen
				opening times	[ˈəʊpnɪŋ taɪmz]	Öffnungszeiten
55				placement	[ˈpleɪsmənt]	Praktikum
to translate	[trænsˈleɪt]	übersetzen, übertragen				
term	[tɜːm]	Bezeichnung, Ausdruck		**60**		
to argue	[ˈɑːɡjuː]	(sich) streiten		sales	[seɪlz]	Schluss-, Ausverkauf
				traditionally	[trəˈdɪʃənəli]	traditionell
56				queue	[kjuː]	(Warte-)Schlange
original	[əˈrɪdʒənl]	Original		adventure	[ədˈventʃə]	Abenteuer
pirate	[ˈpaɪrət]	Pirat		to unlock	[ˌʌnˈlɒk]	aufschließen
nowadays	[ˈnaʊədeɪz]	heutzutage		purchase	[ˈpɜːtʃəs]	(Ein-)Kauf
guarantee	[ˌɡærənˈtiː]	Garantie		super	[ˈsuːpə]	super, großartig
China	[ˈtʃaɪnə]	China		digital	[ˈdɪdʒɪtl]	digital
European	[ˌjʊərəˈpiːən]	europäisch		megapixel	[ˈmeɡəpɪksl]	Megapixel
outsourcing	[ˈaʊtsɔːsɪŋ]	Auslagern (von Arbeitsprozessen)		guilty	[ˈɡɪlti]	schuldbewusst
				61		
Rome	[rəʊm]	Rom		reborn	[ˌriːˈbɔːn]	wiedergeboren
Turin	[ˌtjʊəˈrɪn]	Turin		builder	[ˈbɪldə]	Bauunternehmer/in
Milan	[mɪˈlæn]	Mailand		to knock down	[ˌnɒk ˈdaʊn]	abreißen
to replace	[rɪˈpleɪs]	ersetzen, austauschen		to rebuild	[ˌriːˈbɪld]	wieder aufbauen
handmade	[ˌhændˈmeɪd]	handgemacht, -gefertigt		further	[ˈfɜːðə]	weiter
Chinese	[tʃaɪˈniːz]	chinesisch				

Chronologisches Wörterverzeichnis

noisy	[ˈnɔɪzi]	laut, lärmend
motorway	[ˈməʊtəweɪ]	Autobahn
to shake	[ʃeɪk]	klirren, zittern
lorry	[ˈlɒri]	Lastwagen, Lkw
crack	[kræk]	Riss, Sprung, Spalt(e)
shabby	[ˈʃæbi]	schäbig
uncomfortable	[ʌnˈkʌmftəbl]	unbequem, ungemütlich
peaceful	[ˈpiːsfl]	friedlich, ruhig
sturdy	[ˈstɜːdi]	massiv, fest
landlord	[ˈlændlɔːd]	Wirt
traditional	[trəˈdɪʃənl]	traditionell
darts	[dɑːts]	Darts, Pfeilwurfspiel
pool	[puːl]	(Pool-)Billard
live	[laɪv]	live
excellent	[ˈeksələnt]	ausgezeichnet, hervorragend
Thai	[taɪ]	Thai(länder/in)
choice	[tʃɔɪs]	Auswahl
cuisine	[kwɪˈziːn]	Küche, Kochkunst
newly	[ˈnjuːli]	neu
hectic	[ˈhektɪk]	hektisch

62

proud	[praʊd]	stolz
to receive	[rɪˈsiːv]	erhalten, bekommen
award	[əˈwɔːd]	Auszeichnung, Preis
to serve	[sɜːv]	servieren, anbieten
to attract	[əˈtrækt]	anziehen, anlocken

63

dairy	[ˈdeəri]	Milch-
nut	[nʌt]	Nuss
protein	[ˈprəʊtiːn]	Protein
sausage	[ˈsɒsɪdʒ]	(Brat-)Wurst, Würstchen
carbohydrate	[ˌkɑːbəʊˈhaɪdreɪt]	Kohle(n)hydrat
vitamin	[ˈvɪtəmɪn]	Vitamin
cucumber	[ˈkjuːkʌmbə]	Gurke
France	[frɑːns]	Frankreich
snail	[sneɪl]	Schnecke
lemon	[ˈlemən]	Zitrone
to contain	[kənˈteɪn]	enthalten
strawberry	[ˈstrɔːbəri]	Erdbeere

64

lifestyle	[ˈlaɪfstaɪl]	Lebensstil, Lifestyle
fitness	[ˈfɪtnəs]	Fitness, Kondition
trainer	[ˈtreɪnə]	Trainer/in
nutrition	[njuˈtrɪʃn]	Ernährung
to offer	[ˈɒfə]	(an)bieten
overweight	[ˌəʊvəˈweɪt]	übergewichtig
to lose weight	[luːz ˈweɪt]	abnehmen
daily	[ˈdeɪli]	täglich
physical	[ˈfɪzɪkl]	körperlich
stairs	[steəz]	Treppe(n)
housework	[ˈhaʊswɜːk]	Hausarbeit(en)
Frisbee	[ˈfrɪzbi]	Wurfscheibe
to improve	[ɪmˈpruːv]	verbessern
muscle	[ˈmʌsl]	Muskel
salt	[sɔːlt]	Salz
fibre	[ˈfaɪbə]	Faser, Ballaststoff
lean	[liːn]	mager
cereal	[ˈsɪəriəl]	Getreideflocken, Müsli
expression	[ɪkˈspreʃn]	Ausdruck
definition	[ˌdefɪˈnɪʃn]	Definition
heavy	[ˈhevi]	schwer
health	[helθ]	Gesundheit(szustand)

65

client	[ˈklaɪənt]	Kunde/Kundin
diet	[ˈdaɪət]	Ernährung, Diät(kost)
to mind	[maɪnd]	etw dagegen haben
toast	[təʊst]	Toast
fried	[fraɪd]	gebraten
egg	[eg]	Ei
bacon	[ˈbeɪkən]	Schinkenspeck
North	[nɔːθ]	Norden
Scotland	[ˈskɒtlənd]	Schottland
midday	[ˌmɪdˈdeɪ]	Mittag, Mittags-

66

space	[speɪs]	Raum
to sail	[seɪl]	segeln
sailor	[ˈseɪlə]	Seemann, Matrose
skin	[skɪn]	Haut
tooth, teeth	[tuːθ, tiːθ]	Zahn, Zähne
scurvy	[ˈskɜːvi]	Skorbut
Royal Navy	[ˌrɔɪəl ˈneɪvi]	Königliche Marine
partly	[ˈpɑːtli]	teilweise, zum Teil
barrel	[ˈbærəl]	Fass, Tonne
oil	[ɔɪl]	Öl
calcium	[ˈkælsiəm]	Kalzium
magnesium	[mægˈniːziəm]	Magnesium
crew	[kruː]	Besatzung, Mannschaft
grog	[grɒg]	Grog
mixture	[ˈmɪkstʃə]	Mischung
strong	[strɒŋ]	stark, kräftig
rum	[rʌm]	Rum
to disinfect	[ˌdɪsɪnˈfekt]	desinfizieren
deck	[dek]	Deck
regular	[ˈregjələ]	regelmäßig
Admiral	[ˈædmərəl]	Admiral
juice	[dʒuːs]	Saft
tradition	[trəˈdɪʃn]	Tradition, Brauch
ration	[ˈræʃn]	Ration, Zuteilung

67

to infect	[ɪnˈfekt]	infizieren, anstecken
journey	[ˈdʒɜːni]	Reise, Fahrt
spaceship	[ˈspeɪsʃɪp]	Raumschiff
wooden	[ˈwʊdn]	aus Holz, Holz-
container	[kənˈteɪnə]	Behälter, Gefäß
relative pronoun	[ˌrelətɪv ˈprəʊnaʊn]	Relativpronomen

Chronologisches Wörterverzeichnis

68

full	[fʊl]	voll, vollständig
circle	[ˈsɜːkl]	Kreis
to stretch	[stretʃ]	strecken, dehnen
to relax	[rɪˈlæks]	entspannen
to relieve	[rɪˈliːv]	lindern, erleichtern
headache	[ˈhedeɪk]	Kopfschmerzen
diagram	[ˈdaɪəgræm]	grafische Darstellung, Grafik

69

to connect	[kəˈnekt]	verbinden
to dial	[ˈdaɪəl]	wählen
available	[əˈveɪləbl]	(am Telefon) zu sprechen
to apologize for	[əˈpɒlədʒaɪz fə]	sich entschuldigen für
to promise	[ˈprɒmɪs]	versprechen, zusagen

70

bush	[bʊʃ]	Busch
tucker	[ˈtʌkə]	Essen
trial	[ˈtraɪəl]	Test, Prüfung
reality	[riˈæləti]	Wirklichkeit
to survive	[səˈvaɪv]	überleben
teen	[tiːn]	Teenager, Jugendliche/r
aged	[eɪdʒd]	im Alter von
Aboriginal	[ˌæbəˈrɪdʒənl]	(austral.) Ureinwohner/in
tribe	[traɪb]	Stamm
attempt	[əˈtempt]	Versuch
insect	[ˈɪnsekt]	Insekt
obese	[əʊˈbiːs]	fettleibig
producer	[prəˈdjuːsə]	Produzent/in
experiment	[ɪkˈsperɪmənt]	Versuch, Experiment
relationship	[rɪˈleɪʃnʃɪp]	Beziehung, Verhältnis
to reach	[riːtʃ]	erreichen
adulthood	[ˈædʌlthʊd]	Erwachsenenalter
channel	[ˈtʃænl]	Kanal, (TV-)Programm
participant	[pɑːˈtɪsɪpənt]	Teilnehmer/in
dump	[dʌmp]	Kippe, Deponie
half of	[ˈhɑːf əv]	die Hälfte von

71

quiz	[kwɪz]	Quiz
to land	[lænd]	landen
settler	[ˈsetlə]	Siedler/in
musical	[ˈmjuːzɪkl]	Musik-
instrument	[ˈɪnstrəmənt]	(Musik-)Instrument
underwater	[ˌʌndəˈwɔːtə]	Unterwasser-
sheep	[ʃiːp]	Schaf(e)

72

travel agency	[ˈtrævl eɪdʒənsi]	Reisebüro
to arrange for	[əˈreɪndʒ fə]	organisieren
EU	[ˌiː ˈjuː]	Europäische Union
autistic	[ɔːˈtɪstɪk]	autistisch
creek	[kriːk]	Bucht, Bach
to notice	[ˈnəʊtɪs]	(be)merken
immediately	[ɪˈmiːdiətli]	sofort, umgehend

72 (Fortsetzung)

volunteer	[ˌvɒlənˈtɪə]	Freiwillige/r
motorbike	[ˈməʊtəbaɪk]	Motorrad
tracker dog	[ˈtrækə dɒg]	Suchhund
to jump on	[ˌdʒʌmp ˈɒn]	springen auf
to camp	[kæmp]	zelten, campen
happily	[ˈhæpɪli]	glücklich
portable	[ˈpɔːtəbl]	transportabel, tragbar
completely	[kəmˈpliːtli]	völlig
to ignore	[ɪgˈnɔː]	ignorieren, nicht beachten
glad	[glæd]	froh

73

adverb	[ˈædvɜːb]	Adverb, Umstandswort
to taste	[teɪst]	schmecken
in italics	[ɪn ɪˈtælɪks]	kursiv
angrily	[ˈæŋgrɪli]	ärgerlich, wütend

74

solo	[ˈsəʊləʊ]	allein
bay	[beɪ]	Bucht
whale	[weɪl]	Wal
Atlantic	[ətˈlæntɪk]	Atlantik
wave	[weɪv]	Welle
cape	[keɪp]	Kap
tanker	[ˈtæŋkə]	Tanker
exciting	[ɪkˈsaɪtɪŋ]	aufregend, spannend

76

Kiev	[ˈkiːef]	Kiew
oyster	[ˈɔɪstə]	Auster
boatbuilder	[ˈbəʊtbɪldə]	Bootsbauer/in
boss	[bɒs]	Chef/in
secretary	[ˈsekrətri]	Sekretär/in
experienced	[ɪkˈspɪəriənst]	erfahren
woodworking	[ˈwʊdwɜːkɪŋ]	Holzbearbeitung
to study	[ˈstʌdi]	studieren
chisel	[ˈtʃɪzl]	Meißel
nail	[neɪl]	Nagel
saw	[sɔː]	Säge
tape measure	[ˈteɪp meʒə]	Bandmaß
timber	[ˈtɪmbə]	(Bau-)Holz, Nutzholz
to carve	[kɑːv]	schnitzen, (be)hauen

77

barbecue	[ˈbɑːbɪkjuː]	Grillparty
g'day	[gdeɪ]	guten Tag
to grill	[grɪl]	grillen
not yet	[nɒt ˈjet]	noch nicht
to fancy	[ˈfænsi]	mögen
soda	[ˈsəʊdə]	Mineralwasser
to practise	[ˈpræktɪs]	(ein)üben
conversation	[ˌkɒnvəˈseɪʃn]	Gespräch, Unterhaltung

78

abroad	[əˈbrɔːd]	im Ausland
chance	[tʃɑːns]	Chance, Gelegenheit, Möglichkeit

Chronologisches Wörterverzeichnis

fixed	[fɪkst]	fest(gesetzt)
relaxing	[rɪˈlæksɪŋ]	sich erholend
visa	[ˈviːzə]	Visum, Sichtvermerk
accommodation	[əˌkɒməˈdeɪʃn]	Unterkunft
discount	[ˈdɪskaʊnt]	Rabatt, Skonto, Nachlass
applicant	[ˈæplɪkənt]	Bewerber/in
citizen	[ˈsɪtɪzn]	Bürger/in
level	[ˈlevl]	Niveau
fee	[fiː]	Gebühr
to imagine	[ɪˈmædʒɪn]	sich vorstellen

79

firefighter	[ˈfaɪəfaɪtə]	Feuerwehrmann, -frau
North Carolina	[ˌnɔːθ kærəˈlaɪnə]	Bundesstaat der USA
member	[ˈmembə]	Mitglied
fellow	[ˈfeləʊ]	Kamerad
scene	[siːn]	Szene
nearby	[ˈnɪəbaɪ]	nahe gelegen, in der Nähe
kid	[kɪd]	Kind
disadvantage	[ˌdɪsədˈvɑːntɪdʒ]	Nachteil, Schaden
gym	[dʒɪm]	Turnhalle, Fitnessstudio
membership	[ˈmembəʃɪp]	Mitgliedschaft
breathing apparatus	[ˌbriːðɪŋ ˌæpəˈreɪtəs]	Atemschutzgerät
advantage	[ədˈvɑːntɪdʒ]	Vorteil, Vorzug
easily	[ˈiːzəli]	leicht, einfach
crucial	[ˈkruːʃl]	entscheidend
to search for	[ˈsɜːtʃ fə]	(ab)suchen nach
ruin	[ˈruːɪn]	Ruine
survivor	[səˈvaɪvə]	Überlebende/r
fire department	[ˈfaɪə dɪpɑːtmənt]	Feuerwehr

80

firefighting	[ˈfaɪəfaɪtɪŋ]	Feuerbekämpfung
colleague	[ˈkɒliːg]	Kollege/Kollegin

81

catastrophic	[ˌkætəˈstrɒfɪk]	katastrophal
event	[ɪˈvent]	Ereignis
normally	[ˈnɔːməli]	normalerweise

82

rooftop	[ˈruːftɒp]	Dach
rescue	[ˈreskjuː]	Rettung
plastic	[ˈplæstɪk]	Plastik, Kunststoff
drainpipe	[ˈdreɪnpaɪp]	Abflussrohr
roof	[ruːf]	Dach
courage	[ˈkʌrɪdʒ]	Mut
to borrow	[ˈbɒrəʊ]	borgen, leihen
ladder	[ˈlædə]	Leiter
to calm down	[ˌkɑːm ˈdaʊn]	(sich) beruhigen
fire brigade	[ˈfaɪə brɪgeɪd]	Feuerwehr
to rescue	[ˈreskjuː]	retten
edge	[edʒ]	Rand, Kante
bridge	[brɪdʒ]	Brücke

84

to cancel	[ˈkænsl]	streichen, absagen
Dear Sir or Madam	[ˌdɪə sɜː ɔː ˈmædəm]	Sehr geehrte Damen und Herren

Alphabetisches Wörterverzeichnis Deutsch – Englisch

A

Deutsch	Englisch
Abbildung	illustration
(ab)drucken	to print
Abendessen	dinner
Abenteuer	adventure
Abfall	rubbish
Abfertigung(sgebäude)	terminal
Abflussrohr	drainpipe
abgesehen von	apart from
abholen	to pick up
eingeben, ablegen	to file
Ablenkung	distraction
abnehmen	to lose weight
Abneigung	dislike
abreißen	to knock down
absagen	to cancel
Abschluss	qualification
(einer Ausbildung)	
abschreiben	to copy
addieren	to add
Admiral	admiral
adoptieren	to adopt
Afrika	Africa
afrikanisch	African
ähnlich	similar
Aktivität	activity
Algebra	algebra
allein	solo
allerdings	though
allgemein	general
allmählich	gradually
Alter, im ~ von	aged
altmodisch	old-fashioned
amerikanisch	American
anbieten	to offer
anderer Meinung sein	to disagree
anderswo	elsewhere
Anfang	beginning
Angeln	fishing
angreifen	to attack
Angst	fear
Angst haben	to be worried
Angst haben vor	to be frightened of, to be afraid of
anheben	to lift
Anlass	cause
Ankörner	centre-punch
Anmerkung	annotation
Anrufer/in	caller
Anweisung	instruction
anwenden	to apply
Anzahlung	deposit
Anzeige	advert
anziehen	to attract
(sich) anziehen	to dress
Anziehung(spunkt)	attraction
ärgerlich	angrily
Ärmel	sleeve
Armut	poverty
Art	type
Artikel	item
Aschenbecher	ashtray
asiatisch	Asian
Asien	Asia
Assistent/in	assistant
Atemschutzgerät	breathing apparatus
Atlantik	Atlantic
aufbauen	to set up
Aufkleber	label
aufregend	exciting
Aufsatz	composition
aufschließen	to unlock
(auf)sparen	to save
Auftrag als (Foto-)Modell	modelling job
aufwachen	to wake up
Ausbilder/in	supervisor
Ausdruck	expression, term
Auseinandersetzung	argument
Ausflug	trip
Ausgang	exit
Ausgangssperre	curfew
ausgeben für	to spend on
ausgezeichnet	excellent
ausladen	to unload
Auslagern (von Arbeitsprozessen)	outsourcing
Ausland, im ~	abroad
ausländisch	foreign
Auspuff(rohr)	exhaust
Ausrüstung	equipment
Aussage	statement
außer	apart from
außerdem	plus
(aus)tauschen	to exchange
Auster	oyster
austragen	to deliver
Australien	Australia
australisch	Australian
australischer Busch	outback
Auswahl	choice
Auszeichnung	award
Auszubildende/r	apprentice
autistisch	autistic
Autobahn	motorway

B

Bach	creek
Bäcker/in	baker
Bäckerei	baker's shop, bakery
Bad	bath
Bad(ezimmer)	bathroom
Bahnhof	station
Ballaststoff	fibre
Bandmaß	tape measure
Barkeeper	barman
Barmann	barista
Bauer, Bäuerin	farmer
Bauernhof	farm
(Bau-)Gerüst	scaffolding
(Bau-)Holz, Nutzholz	timber
Bauunternehmer/in	builder
Beamter/Beamtin	officer
bedauern	to regret
bedeuten	to mean
Bedeutung	meaning
Bedienungs-	operating
Bedienungsanleitung	handbook
Bedingung	condition
sich befassen mit	to deal with
Behälter	container
(körper)behindert	disabled
Bein	leg
bekannt, sehr ~	well known
bekommen	to receive
Beleuchtung	lighting
beliebt	popular
bemerken	to notice
bequem	comfortable
bereuen	to regret
Bericht	report
beruflich	vocational
(sich) beruhigen	to calm down
berühmt	famous, well known
Besatzung	crew
beschädigen	to damage
beschädigt	damaged
beschäftigen	to employ
beschäftigt	busy
Beschäftigung	activity
Beschreibung	description
Beschwerde	complaint
(sich) beschweren	to complain
beseitigen	to remove
Besitzer/in	owner
besonders	especially
bestätigen	to confirm
bestehen (ein Examen)	to pass (an exam)
bestimmt	particular
Besucher/in	visitor
bevor	before
bevorzugen	to prefer
bewachen	to guard
bewältigen	to manage
Bewerber/in	applicant
bewundern	to admire
(sich) bewusst werden	to realize
Bezeichnung	term
Beziehung	relationship
Bibliothek	library
Billard	pool
billig	cheaply
Bindewort	connector
Binnensee	lake
Bluse	blouse
Blut	blood
Boden, (Fuß-)~	floor
Bohne	bean
bohren	to drill
Bohrer	drill
Boot	boat
Bootsbauer/in	boatbuilder
borgen	to borrow
böse	angry
Botschafter/in	ambassador
Boutique	boutique
Brand	fire
Brauerei	brewery
breit	broad
Bremse	brake
Brille	glasses
Brötchen	roll
Brücke	bridge
buchstabieren	to spell
Bucht	bay, creek
Bühne	stage
Bühnenarbeiter/in	rigger
Bundesstaat der USA	North Carolina
Bürger/in	citizen
Büroklammer	paper clip
Busch	bush

C

Camping	camping
Chef/in	boss
Chefkoch/köchin	chef
chinesisch	Chinese
Cocktail	cocktail
Computertechnik	information technology

D

Deutsch	Englisch
Dach	roof, rooftop
danach	afterwards
Decke	ceiling

Alphabetisches Wörterverzeichnis — Deutsch – Englisch

Deutsch	Englisch
dehnen	to stretch
Designer/in	designer
desinfizieren	to disinfect
Dialog	dialogue
dick	thick
doppelt	double
Druck	pressure
dunkel	dark
dünn	thin
Durchsage	announcement
Durchschnitt	average
durchschnittlich	average
durchsuchen	to search

E

Deutsch	Englisch
echt	real
Ehefrau	wife
Ehemann	husband
Eidechse	lizard
eigen	of one's own
Eigenschaftswort	adjective
einbauen	to fit
Einfärbung	colouring
eingeben	to file
einheimisch	local
Einkauf	purchase
Einkäufe	shopping
einladen	to invite
einschließlich	including
sich einsetzen (für)	to campaign
eintragen	to fill in
eintragen lassen	to register
Einwanderer/in	immigrant
einzig	single
Eisen	iron
Empfangsmitarbeiter/in	receptionist
Endspielteilnehmer/in	finalist
Endung	ending
Energiequelle	power source
entfernen	to remove
Entfernung	distance
enthalten	to contain
entladen	to unload
entscheidend	crucial
sich entschuldigen für	to apologize for
entsetzen	to horrify
entspannen	to relax
entweder	either
Entwurf	design
Erbe	heritage
Erbse	pea
Erdbeere	strawberry
Ereignis	event
erfahren	experienced
Erfolg	success
erfolgreich	successful
erfreut, (sehr ~)	delighted
erhalten	to receive
sich erholen	relaxing
sich erinnern (an), daran denken	to remember
erkennen (wieder)	to recognize
erklären	to explain
erleichtern	to relieve
Ernährung	nutrition, diet
ernst(haft)	serious
erreichen	to reach
Ersatz-	spare
ersetzen	to replace
erste Hilfe	first aid
Erwachsenenalter	adulthood
Essstörung	eating disorder
Esszimmer	dining room
europäisch	European

F

Deutsch	Englisch
Fabrik	factory
Fachmann/frau	expert
fahren (mit dem Auto)	to drive
Fahrer/in	driver
Fahrt	journey, voyage
Fall, auf keinen ~	no way
falsch	false
fangen	to catch
Farbe	paint
Fass	barrel
fehlen	to miss
fehlend	missing
Fehler	mistake
Fenster	window
fest	sturdy
fest(gesetzt)	fixed
fettleibig	obese
Feuer	fire
Feuerbekämpfung	firefighting
Feuerwehr	fire brigade/department
Feuerwehrmann, -frau	firefighter
Filiale	branch
Firma	firm, business
Flasche	bottle
Fleck(en)	spot
Fliege	fly
Flitterwochen	honeymoon
Flüchtling	refugee
Flug	flight
Fluggast	passenger
Flughafen	airport
Flugzeug	plane, aircraft
Fluss	river
folgen	to follow
folgende/r/s	following
Form	form
fortfahren	to proceed
Frankreich	France
französisch	French
Frau	Mrs
Freiwillige/r	volunteer
Freizeit	leisure
fremd	foreign
sich freuen auf	to look forward to
friedlich	peaceful
frisch	fresh
Frist	limit
Frisur	haircut
froh	glad
furchtbar	horrible, terrible
führen zu	to result in
sich fürchten vor	to be afraid of
füttern	to feed

G

Deutsch	Englisch
Garantie	guarantee
Gasherd	gas cooker
Gaspedal	accelerator
Gasse	lane
Gast	guest
Gaststätte	pub
Gebäude	building
gebraten	fried
Gebühr	fee
Geburt	birth
geeignet	appropriate
gefährlich	dangerous
Gefäß	container
gegen	against
Gegenteil	opposite
Gegenwart	present
Geländewagen (mit Vierradantrieb)	SUV
Gelegenheit	chance
Gemüse	vegetable
genau	exactly, closely
Geometrie	geometry
Gepäck	baggage, luggage
geradeaus	straight ahead
Gerät	machine
gern haben/tun	to enjoy
Geschäft	business
Geschichte	history
Geschwindigkeit	speed
Gespräch	conversation
Gesundheit(szustand)	health
Gesundheitsfürsorge	healthcare
Getreideflocken	cereal
Gewinn	profit
Gewinner/in	winner
gewöhnlich	usually
giftig	poisonous, toxic
Gipser/in	plasterer
glatt	slippery
Glück haben	to be lucky
glücklich	happily
glücklicherweise	luckily
Grab	tomb
graben	to dig
Grafik	diagram
Grenze	limit
grillen	to grill
Grillparty	barbecue
Grog	grog
groß	great
Größe	size
Grund	cause
grundsätzlich	basically
Gurke	cucumber
gut aussehend	handsome

H

Deutsch	Englisch
Haarschnitt	haircut
haben, etw dagegen ~	to mind
Hafen(stadt)	port
Hähnchen	chicken
Hälfte, die ~ von	half of
Hamburger	hamburger
Hammer	hammer
Handel	trade
handgemacht, -gefertigt	handmade
Handschuh	glove
hassen	to hate
hässlich	ugly
Hausarbeit(en)	housework
Haustier	pet
Hauswirtschaft	domestic science
Haut	skin
heiraten	to marry
Heizung	heating
Hemd	shirt
Herstellung	production
Herz	heart
heutzutage	nowadays
hilfreich	helpful

Alphabetisches Wörterverzeichnis Deutsch – Englisch

Himmel	sky
Hinweis	tip
historisch	historic
Hitze	heat
Hochzeitsreise	honeymoon
hoffentlich	hopefully
Holz	wood
Holz-, aus Holz	wooden
Holzbearbeitung	woodworking
Hose(n)	trousers
hübsch	pretty
Huhn	chicken
hungrig	hungry

I

ignorieren, nicht beachten	to ignore
Immobilienmakler/in	estate agent
infizieren	to infect
insbesondere	especially
installieren	to fit
sich interessieren für	to be interested in

J

Jacke	jacket
Jagd	hunt
Jäger/in	hunter
japanisch	Japanese
jedenfalls	anyway
jedoch	though

K

Käfig	cage
Kalzium	calcium
Kambodscha	Cambodia
Kamerad	fellow
kämpfen	to campaign
Kanal	canal, (TV) channel
Kaninchen	rabbit
Kap	cape
Kapitän	captain, skipper
Kasse	cash desk
katastrophal	catastrophic
Katze	cat
Kaugummi	chewing gum
Kaution	deposit
Keks	biscuit
Kellner	waiter
Kellnerin	waitress
Kind	kid
Kippe	dump
Kirche	church
Klammern, in ~	in brackets
Klasse	category
kleiden	to dress
Kleidung	clothing
Kleinmotorrad (mit Kickstarter)	mokick
Klimaanlage	air conditioning
Klinik	clinic
klirren	to shake
Koch, Köchin	cook
Kochkunst	cuisine
Koffer	suitcase
Kohle(n)hydrat	carbohydrate
Kollege/Kollegin	colleague
kompliziert	complicated
König	king
Kontakt aufnehmen zu	to contact
sich konzentrieren auf	to concentrate on
Kopfschmerzen	headache
körperlich	physical
Körperpflege	bodycare
Kosmetik(a)	cosmetics
Kosmetiker/in	beautician
Krampf	cramp
krank	sick
Krankenhaus	hospital
Krankenpfleger/in	nurse
Krankheit	illness, sickness
Kreis	circle
Kreuzung	crossroads, junction
Krieg	war
Krieger/in	warrior
Krokodil	crocodile
Küche	kitchen, cuisine
Kuh	cow
sich kümmern	to care
Kunde/Kundin	client, customer
Kunststoff	plastic
Künstler/in	artist
Kupplung	clutch
Kurs	course
kursiv	in italics
kurz	short
Küste	coast

L

lachen	to laugh
Laden	store
landen	to land
langsam	slowly
lass/t uns	let's
Lastwagen	lorry
laut	noisy
Lebensstil	lifestyle
leer	empty
Lehrling	apprentice
leiden an	to suffer from
leider	unfortunately
leihen	to borrow
leisten, (es) sich ~ (können)	to afford
Leiter	ladder
Leiter/in	manager
Lenkrad	steering wheel
Leser/in	reader
letzte/r/s	final
liebe/r	dear
Lieferant von Fertiggerichten und Getränken	caterer
lindern	to relieve
Lücke	gap
Luft	air
Luftfilter	air filter
lügen	to lie
Lunge	lung
Luxus	luxury

M

mächtig	powerful
Magenschmerzen	stomach ache
mager	lean
Magersucht	anorexia
Mahlzeit	meal
makellos	spotlessly
Maler/in	painter
männlich	male
massiv	sturdy
Maßstab	scale
Maurer/in	bricklayer
Mechaniker/in	mechanic
Medien	media
Meißel	chisel
meistens	mostly
Meisterdiplom	master certificate
Meisterschaft	championship
messen	to measure
Messing	brass
Miete	rent
Milch-	dairy
Minenfeld	minefield
Mineralwasser	soda
Mischung	mixture
Mit freundlichen Grüßen	Yours sincerely
Mitarbeiter	personnel
Mitglied	member
Mitgliedschaft	membership
Mittag, Mittags-	midday
Mittagessen	lunch
Möbel(stücke)	furniture
Mode	fashion
modisch	fashionable
mögen	to fancy
Möglichkeit	chance
Motor	engine
Motorrad	motorbike
müde	tired
Müll	rubbish
Müllwerker	dustman
multikulturell	multi-cultural
München	Munich
Musikkapelle	band
Muskel	muscle
Mut	courage

N

Nachname	surname
Nachbar/in	neighbour
Nachforschung(en)	research
nachmittags	p.m.
Nachsorge	aftercare
Nachteil	disadvantage
Nagel	nail
Nähe, in der ~	nearby
nass	wet
Natur	nature
Naturforscher/in	naturalist
Netz	net
Netzkabel	power cord
neueste	latest
nicht ... mehr	not ... anymore
nicht passend	odd
Nichtbeachtung	failure to follow
Nichtraucher-	non-smoking
Niveau	level
noch nicht	not yet
Norden	North
nördlich	northern
normalerweise	normally
Notfall	emergency
Null	zero
Nuss	nut
nützlich	useful
nutzlos	useless

O

ob	whether
Ober-	upper
Obst	fruit
Öffnungszeiten	opening times

Alphabetisches Wörterverzeichnis   Deutsch – Englisch

Deutsch	English
Ohr	ear
Ohrenschützer	ear protectors
Öl	oil
Onkel	uncle
organisieren	to arrange for, organize
östlich	East

P

Paar	couple
Packung	packet
Papa	dad
Passagier/in	passenger
passen (zu)	to fit (in)
passend	appropriate
Pause	break
Personal	personnel
Pferd	horse
Pfleger/in	attendant
Pier	dock
Pirat	pirate
Plünderer, Schänder	raider
Politiker/in	politician
Porträt	profile
Praktikum	placement, work experience
praktisch	practical
Preis	prize
Prinz	prince
pro	per
Produzent/in	producer
produzieren	to produce
Prominente/r	celebrity
Prüfung	exam
Pumpe	pump
Pumpenhaus	pump house

Q

Quadratmeter	square metre
Qualität	quality

R

Rabatt	discount
Rad	wheel
Rahmen	frame
Rand	edge
Rat(schlag)	advice
Ratte	rat
rauchen	to smoke
Raucher-	smoking
Raum	space
räumen	to clear
Raumschiff	spaceship
Rechtschreibung	spelling
Regel	rule
regelmäßig	regular
Regisseur/in	director
reich	rich
Reifen	tyre
Reihenfolge	order
reinigen	to clean
Reinigungskraft	cleaner
Reise	journey, voyage
Reisebüro	travel agency
Reisebus	coach
Reklamation	complaint
Reklametafel	billboard
Religion(sunterricht)	religious education
renovieren	to renovate
Renovierung	renovation
Reparatur	repair
Reporter/in	reporter
Reiseführer	guide
Reservierung	reservation
respektieren	to respect
retten	to rescue
Rettung	rescue
(Koch-)Rezept	recipe
richtig	correct, proper, true
riechen	to smell
riesig	giant
Rinderhack(fleisch)	minced beef
ringen	to wrestle
Risiko	risk
Riss	crack
Rock	skirt
Rollstuhl	wheelchair
Ruf	reputation
ruhig	peaceful
Ruine	ruin
rumhängen	to hang out
Rundfunk	radio
Rundreise	tour
rutschig	slippery

S

Saft	juice
Säge	saw
Salat	salad
Salz	salt
Sänger/in	singer
sauber	clean, spotless
schäbig	shabby
Schaf(e)	sheep
Schal	scarf
Schauspieler	actor
Schauspielerin	actress
Schiff	ship
Schiffahrts-	maritime
Schinkenspeck	bacon
schlafen	to be asleep
Schlafsack	sleeping bag
Schlafzimmer	bedroom
Schlange	snake
schlechter	worse
schlechteste	worst
Schlussverkauf	sales
Schlüssel	key
schmecken	to taste
Schmerz(en)	pain
schmerzhaft	painful
Schmiermittel	lubricant
Schminke	make-up
Schmuck	jewellery
Schmutz	dirt
schmutzig	dirty
Schnäppchen	bargain
Schnecke	snail
Schnee	snow
Schnell-	express
Schnitzeljagd	treasure hunt
schnitzen	to carve
schnurlos	cordless
schockieren	to shock
schön	beautiful, lovely
Schottland	Scotland
Schraube	screw
Schraubenzieher	screwdriver
schrecklich	horrible, terrible
Schreibtisch	desk
Schriftsteller/in	writer
Schritt	step
Schulabgänger/in	school-leaver
schuldbewusst	guilty
Schulfach	subject
Schulheft	exercise book
Schüler/in	pupil
Schulung	training
Schutz-	protective
Schutzbrille	goggles
schützen	to protect
Schutzhelm	helmet
Schutzmaske	cup mask
schwer	heavy
Seemann	sailor
Segeln	sailing
segeln	to sail
Sehr geehrte Damen und Herren	Dear Sir or Madam
Sekretär/in	secretary
Sendung	programme
servieren	to serve
sicher	safe
Sicherheit	safety, security
sicherlich	certainly
Siedler/in	settler
Sieger/in	winner
Sitzplatz	seat
Skala	scale
Skelett	skeleton
Skonto	discount
Skorbut	scurvy
sofort	immediately
Sonnenbrille	sunglasses
sonnig	sunny
spalten	to split
spannend	exciting
spenden	to donate
spezialisiert	specialized
speziell	special
(nach)spielen	to act
sprechen, (am Telefon) zu ~	available
springen auf	to jump on
Sprungbrett	springboard
Stachelrochen	stingray
Stadion	arena
Stahl	steel
Stamm	tribe
stark	strong
Startbahn	runway
Staub	dust
stechen	to stab
stecken bleiben	to get stuck
stehlen	to steal
steigern	to increase
Stein	stone
Steinmetz	stonemason
Stellring	adjusting ring
Stern	star
Stiefel	boot
Stock	stick
Stoff	material, substance
stöhnen	to groan
stolz	proud
Strafe	sentence
Strand	beach
Strecke	route
strecken	to stretch
Streifen	stripe
Streit	argument
(sich) streiten	to argue
Stress	stress
Stroh	straw
Stromschlag	electric shock
Strumpfbandnatter	garter snake
studieren	to study
suchen nach	to search for
Suchhund	tracker dog
Süd-	south
südlich	southern

Alphabetisches Wörterverzeichnis — Deutsch – Englisch

Deutsch	Englisch
(End-)Summe	total
Synagoge	synagogue
Szene	scene

T

Deutsch	Englisch
Tabelle	table
täglich	daily
Tanz	dance
Taschengeld	pocket money
Taschenlampe	flashlight
Tasse	cup
Tätowierer/in	tattooist
Tätowierung	tattoo
Tatsache	fact
tatsächlich	actually
tausend	thousand
Techniker/in	technician
technisches Zeichnen	technical drawing
Teilnehmer/in	participant
teilweise	partly
Teller	plate
Termin	appointment
Thema	topic
tief	deep
Tier	animal
Tierarzt, -ärztin	vet
tierärztlich	veterinary
Tierwelt	wildlife
Tischler/in	woodworker
Tod	death
tödlich	deadly
Ton	sound
töten	to kill
traditionell	traditional
tragbar	portable
Transporteur	handler
Traum	dream
Treibstoff	fuel
trennen	to disconnect
Treppe(n)	stairs
trocken	dry
Türklingel	doorbell
Turnhalle	gym
typisch	typical

U

Deutsch	Englisch
üben	to practise
übergewichtig	overweight
überleben	to survive
Überlebende/r	survivor
übernehmen	to take over
überprüfen	to check
überraschen	to surprise
Überraschung	surprise
übersetzen	to translate
Ureinwohner/in (austral.)	Aboriginal
umfassen, umschreiben	to include
umschreiben	to rewrite
umsiedeln	to relocate
unabhängig	independent
unbegrenzt	unlimited
unbequem	uncomfortable
unerwartet	unexpected
Unfall	accident, crash
unfreundlich	unfriendly
ungeduldig	impatient
ungewöhnlich	unusual
unglücklicherweise	unfortunately
unordentlich	untidy
Unterkunft	accommodation
unterstützen	to support
untersuchen	to examine
Unterwasser-	underwater
unwahr	untrue
usw.	etc.

V

Verabredung	date, appointment
verbessern	to improve
verbieten	to ban
verbinden	to connect, to link
Verbindung, (sich) in ~ setzen mit	to get in touch with
verbittert	bitter
verdienen	earn
Vereinte Nationen	United Nations
vergessen	to forget
Vergleich	comparison
vergleichen	to compare
Verhältnis	relationship
Verkäufer/in	sales assistant
verladen	to load
Verlaufsform	progressive
verletzen	to injure
verletzt	hurt
Verletzung	injury
Verlierer/in	loser
vermeiden	to avoid
Vermittlung	mediation
vernünftig	sensible
verrutschen	to slip
Versorgung mit Speisen und Getränken	catering
versprechen	to promise
Versuch	attempt, experiment
Vertiefung	indentation
vertrauen	to trust
Vertrieb, Vertriebs-	marketing
verursachen	to cause
vervollständigen	to complete
Vierradantrieb	four-wheel drive
Visum	visa
voll	full
völlig	completely
vollständig	full
vor	in front of
vorbereiten	to prepare
Vorbereitung	preparation
Vorbild	idol
vorhergehend	previous
vorschlagen	to suggest
Vorschrift	rule
vorsichtig	careful
sich vorstellen	to imagine, to introduce oneself
Vorteil	advantage

W

Deutsch	Englisch
wählen	to dial
während	while, throughout
Wahrheit	truth
Wal	whale
Wandschmierereien	graffiti
warnen	to warn
Warnung	warning
Warteschlange	queue
Wartezimmer	waiting room
Wegbeschreibung	direction
weiblich	female
weit (geschnitten)	loose
weiter	further
weiterfahren	to proceed
Welle	wave
Werbung	advertising
Werkstatt	workshop, garage
Werkzeug	tool
wert sein	to be worth
westlich	west
wie folgt	as follows
wieder aufbauen	to rebuild
wiedergeboren	reborn
Wiederherstellung	restoration
wiegen	to weigh
wild	wild
Windschutzscheibe	windscreen
Wirklichkeit	reality
Wirt	landlord
Wohltätigkeit	charity
Wohnung	apartment
Wohnwagen	trailer
Wohnzimmer	living room
Wortschatz	vocabulary
wunderbar	wonderful
Wurfscheibe	Frisbee
Wurm	worm
Wurst, Würstchen	sausage
wütend	angry

Z

Deutsch	Englisch
zählen	to count
Zahn, Zähne	tooth, teeth
Zapfenstreich	curfew
Zapfhahn	tap
zeichnen	to draw
Zeitschrift	magazine
Zeitverschwendung	waste of time
Zelt	tent
zelten	to camp
Zentimeter	centimetre
Ziegel(stein)	brick
Ziel	purpose
zischen	to hiss
Zitrone	lemon
zittern	to shake
Zucker	sugar
zufolge	according to
Beispiel, zum ~	for example
zuordnen	to match
zusammenbrechen	to collapse
Zusammenfassung	summary
zusätzlich	extra
zustellen	to deliver
Zuteilung	ration
zutreffend	true
Zweck	purpose
Zwiebel	onion
Zwinkern	wink

Alphabetisches Wörterverzeichnis — Englisch – Deutsch

Dieses Wörterverzeichnis enthält alle Wörter aus Job fit Englisch in alphabetischer Reihenfolge.
Hier sind jedoch die Wörter, die zum Grundwortschatz gehören, nicht aufgeführt.

A

Aboriginal 70 (austral.) Ureinwohner/in
abroad 78 im Ausland
accelerator 36 Gaspedal
accident 17 Unfall
accommodation 78 Unterkunft
according to 22 zufolge, laut, nach
to act 15 (nach)spielen, aufführen
acting 46 schauspielerisch
activity 44 Aktivität, Beschäftigung
actor 45 Schauspieler
actress 45 Schauspielerin
actually 32 tatsächlich
to add 9 addieren, zusammenzählen
adjective 57 Adjektiv, Eigenschaftswort
adjusting ring 37 Stellring
admiral 66 Admiral
to admire 45 bewundern
to adopt 52 adoptieren, (die Patenschaft) übernehmen
adulthood 70 Erwachsenenalter
advantage 79 Vorteil, Vorzug
adventure 60 Abenteuer
adverb 73 Adverb, Umstandswort
advert 26 Inserat, Anzeige
advertiser 45 Inserent/in, Werbefirma
advertising 48 Werbung, Reklame
advice 14 Rat(schlag), Ratschläge
to afford 26 (es) sich leisten (können)
afraid, to be ~ of 12 Angst haben vor, sich fürchten vor
Africa 8 Afrika
African 52 afrikanisch
aftercare 42 Nachsorge, -behandlung
afterwards 26 danach, hinterher
against 39 gegen
aged 70 im Alter von
air 10 Luft
air conditioning 34 Klimaanlage
air filter 34 Luftfilter
aircraft 18 Flugzeug(e)
airport 18 Flughafen
algebra 8 Algebra
ambassador 52 Botschafter/in
American 54 amerikanisch
angrily 73 ärgerlich, wütend
angry 14 böse, wütend
animal 6 Tier
annotation 21 Anmerkung
announcement 18 Durchsage
anorexia 39 Magersucht
anymore, not … 42 nicht … mehr
anyway 30 jedenfalls, wie dem auch sei
apart from 37 außer, abgesehen von
apartment 47 Wohnung, Apartment
to apologize for 69 sich entschuldigen für
applicant 78 Bewerber/in
to apply 37 anwenden
appointment 26 Termin, Verabredung
apprentice 51 Lehrling, Auszubildende/r
appropriate 38 geeignet, passend
arena 31 Arena, Stadion
to argue 55 (sich) streiten
argument 15 Streit, Auseinandersetzung
to arrange for 72 organisieren
artist 42 Künstler/in
as follows 37 wie folgt
ashtray 14 Aschenbecher
Asia 52 Asien
Asian 57 asiatisch
asleep, to be ~ 12 schlafen
assistant 6 Assistent/in, Helfer/in
Atlantic 74 Atlantik
to attack 22 angreifen
attempt 70 Versuch
attendant 6 Pfleger/in
to attract 62 anziehen, anlocken
attraction 31 Anziehung(spunkt), Attraktion
Australia 21 Australien
Australian 21 australisch
autistic 72 autistisch
available 69 (am Telefon) zu sprechen
average 54 Durchschnitt, durchschnittlich
to avoid 30 (ver)meiden
award 62 Auszeichnung, Preis

B

bacon 65 Schinkenspeck
badly 41 schwer, schlimm
baker 59 Bäcker/in
baker's shop 23 Bäckerei
bakery 23 Bäckerei
to ban 52 verbieten
band 31 (Musik-)Kapelle
barbecue 77 Grillparty
bargain 54 (günstiges) Angebot, Schnäppchen
barista 23 Barmann
barman 23 Barkeeper
barrel 66 Fass, Tonne
basically 45 im Grunde, grundsätzlich
bath 24 Bad
bathroom 26 Bad(ezimmer)
battery 34 Batterie
bay 74 Bucht
beach 20 Strand
bean 24 Bohne
beautician 50 Kosmetiker/in
beautiful 32 schön
bedroom 26 Schlafzimmer
before 16 bevor
beginning 9 Anfang, Beginn
billboard 39 Reklametafel, Werbeplakat
birth 47 Geburt
biscuit 25 Keks
bitter 16 verbittert
blood 39 Blut
blouse 58 Bluse
boat 30 Boot
boatbuilder 76 Bootsbauer/in
bodycare 53 Körperpflege
boot 36 Stiefel
to borrow 82 borgen, leihen
boss 76 Chef/in
bottle 10 Flasche
boutique 54 Boutique
bracket, in ~s 7 in Klammern
brake 36 Bremse
branch 24 Filiale, Zweigstelle
brass 37 Messing
break 59 Pause
breathing apparatus 79 Atemschutzgerät
brewery 33 Brauerei
brick 32 Ziegel(stein), Backstein
bricklayer 32 Maurer/in
bridge 82 Brücke
broad 12 breit
builder 61 Bauunternehmer/in
building 18 Gebäude
bush 70 Busch
business 34 Geschäft, Firma
busy 12 beschäftigt

Alphabetisches Wörterverzeichnis — Englisch – Deutsch

C

cage 6 Käfig
calcium 66 Kalzium
caller 29 Anrufer/in
to calm down 82 (sich) beruhigen
Cambodia 52 Kambodscha
to camp 72 zelten, campen
to campaign 21 kämpfen, sich einsetzen (für)
camping 34 Camping
canal 30 Kanal
to cancel 84 streichen, absagen
cape 74 Kap
captain 31 Kapitän
carbohydrate 63 Kohle(n)hydrat
to care 52 sich kümmern
career 39 Karriere, Laufbahn
careful 12 vorsichtig
carefully 12 vorsichtig
to carve 76 schnitzen, (be)hauen
cash desk 43 Kasse
cat 11 Katze
catastrophic 81 katastrophal
to catch 21 fangen
category 53 Kategorie, Klasse
caterer 23 Lieferant von Fertiggerichten und Getränken
catering 50 Versorgung mit Speisen und Getränken
cause 46 Grund, Anlass
to cause 38 verursachen
ceiling 32 (Zimmer-)Decke
celebrity 45 Prominente/r, Berühmtheit
centimetre 12 Zentimeter
centre-punch 37 (An-)Körner
cereal 64 Getreideflocken, Müsli
certainly 27 sicherlich, bestimmt
championship 24 Meisterschaft
chance 78 Chance, Gelegenheit, Möglichkeit
channel 70 Kanal, (TV-)Programm
charity 48 Wohltätigkeit
cheaply 56 billig
to check 7 (über)prüfen, kontrollieren
chef 28 Chefkoch/köchin, Küchenchef/in
chewing gum 14 Kaugummi
chicken 26 Huhn, Hähnchen
China 56 China
Chinese 56 chinesisch
chisel 76 Meißel
choice 61 Auswahl
church 32 Kirche
circle 68 Kreis
citizen 78 Bürger/in
clean 10 sauber
to clean 6 reinigen, säubern
cleaner 18 Reinigungskraft
to clear 6 räumen
client 65 Kunde/Kundin
clinic 6 Klinik
clip 48 (Video-)Clip, kurzer (Werbe-)Film
closely 42 genau
clothing 58 Bekleidung, Kleidung
clutch 36 Kupplung
coach 47 Reisebus
coast 34 Küste
cocktail 23 Cocktail
to collapse 39 zusammenbrechen
colleague 80 Kollege/Kollegin
colouring 45 Einfärbung
coma 39 Koma
comfortable 30 bequem, wohl
to compare 9 vergleichen
comparison 57 Vergleich, Steigerung
to complain 24 (sich) beschweren
complaint 18 Beschwerde, Beanstandung, Reklamation
to complete 7 vervollständigen, ergänzen
completely 72 völlig
complicated 32 kompliziert
composition 44 Aufsatz
to concentrate on 38 sich konzentrieren auf
condition 38 Bedingung
to confirm 44 bestätigen
to connect 69 verbinden
connector 49 Bindewort
to contact 26 Kontakt aufnehmen zu, sich wenden an
to contain 63 enthalten
container 67 Behälter, Gefäß
to control 50 kontrollieren, regeln
conversation 77 Gespräch, Unterhaltung
cook 23 Koch, Köchin
to copy 7 abschreiben, kopieren, übertragen
cordless 37 schnur-, kabellos
correct 7 richtig
cosmetics 53 Kosmetik(a)
to count 59 zählen
couple 26 Paar, Ehepaar
courage 82 Mut
course 24 Kurs, Lehrgang
cow 10 Kuh
crack 61 Riss, Sprung, Spalt(e)
cramp 39 Krampf
crash 46 Unfall
creek 72 Bucht, Bach
crew 66 Besatzung, Mannschaft
crocodile 21 Krokodil
crossroads 29 Kreuzung
crucial 79 entscheidend
cucumber 63 Gurke
cuisine 61 Küche, Kochkunst
cup 39 Tasse
cup mask 36 Schutzmaske
curfew 14 Ausgangssperre, Zapfenstreich
customer 24 Kunde/Kundin

D

dad 14 Papa, Vater
daily 64 täglich
dairy 63 Milch-
to damage 37 beschädigen
damaged 38 beschädigt
dance 15 Tanz
dangerous 21 gefährlich
dark 26 dunkel, düster
darts 61 Darts, Pfeilwurfspiel
date 30 Verabredung, Rendezvous
deadly 21 tödlich
to deal with 18 sich befassen mit, bearbeiten
dear 11 liebe/r
Dear Sir or Madam 84 Sehr geehrte Damen und Herren
death 17 Tod
deck 66 Deck
deep 41 tief
definition 64 Definition
delighted 48 (sehr) erfreut
to deliver 6 austragen, zustellen
deposit 26 Anzahlung, Kaution
description 18 Beschreibung
design 32 Entwurf, Konstruktion
designer 54 Designer/in
desk 12 (Schreib-)Tisch, Schalter
diagram 68 grafische Darstellung, Grafik
to dial 69 wählen
dialogue 15 Dialog
diet 65 Ernährung, Diät(kost)
to dig 34 graben
digital 60 digital
dining room 26 Esszimmer
dinner 24 Abendessen
direction 29 Wegbeschreibung
director 46 Regisseur/in
dirt 24 Schmutz, Dreck
dirty 24 schmutzig
disabled 48 (körper)behindert
disadvantage 79 Nachteil, Schaden

Alphabetisches Wörterverzeichnis — Englisch – Deutsch

to disagree 14 anderer Meinung sein, nicht zustimmen
to disconnect 38 trennen, herausziehen
discount 78 Rabatt, Skonto, Nachlass
to disinfect 66 desinfizieren
dislike 54 Abneigung
distance 38 Entfernung, Abstand
distraction 38 Ablenkung
dock 31 Pier, Kai
dollar 48 Dollar
domestic science 9 Hauswirtschaft
to donate 48 spenden
doorbell 12 Türklingel
double 11 doppelt, zweimal
drainpipe 82 Abflussrohr
to draw 12 zeichnen
dream 24 Traum
to dress 38 (sich) anziehen, kleiden
drill 37 Bohrer
to drill 37 bohren
to drive 34 (mit dem Auto) fahren
driver 34 Fahrer/in
dry 34 trocken
dump 70 Kippe, Deponie
dust 34 Staub
dustman 24 Müllwerker

E

ear 15 Ohr
ear protectors 36 Ohrenschützer
earn 22 verdienen
easily 79 leicht, einfach
East 46 östlich
eating disorder 41 Essstörung
edge 82 Rand, Kante
egg 65 Ei
either 44 entweder
electric shock 38 Stromschlag
elsewhere 56 anderswo, woanders
emergency 51 Notfall
to employ 18 beschäftigen
empty 26 leer
ending 9 Endung, (Satz-)Ende
engine 36 Motor
to enjoy 7 gefallen, gern haben/tun
equipment 34 Ausrüstung
especially 21 besonders, insbesondere
estate
    agent 27 Immobilienmakler/in
etc. 34 usw.
EU 72 Europäische Union
Europe 18 Europa
European 56 europäisch

event 81 Ereignis
exactly 34 exakt, genau
exam 8 Prüfung, Examen
to examine 10 untersuchen
example, for ~ 6 zum Beispiel
excellent 61 ausgezeichnet, hervorragend
to exchange 7 (aus)tauschen
exciting 74 aufregend, spannend
exercise book 7 (Schul-)Heft
exhaust 36 Auspuff(rohr)
exit 51 Ausgang
experienced 76 erfahren
experiment 70 Versuch, Experiment
expert 14 Fachmann/frau, Experte Expertin
to explain 43 erklären, erläutern
express 43 Schnell-
expression 64 Ausdruck
extra 6 zusätzlich

F

fact 12 Tatsache, Fakt
factory 51 Fabrik
failure to follow 38 Nichtbeachtung
false 6 falsch
famous 21 berühmt
to fancy 77 mögen
farm 10 Bauernhof
farmer 52 Bauer, Bäuerin
fashion 39 Mode
fashionable 42 modisch, schick
fear 12 Angst, Furcht
fee 78 Gebühr
to feed 10 füttern
fellow 79 Kamerad
female 44 weiblich
fibre 64 Faser, Ballaststoff
to file 10 eingeben, ablegen
to fill in 41 eintragen, -setzen
final 7 letzte/r/s, End-
finalist 24 Endspielteilnehmer/in
fine 11 gut, in Ordnung
fire 17 Feuer, Brand
fire brigade 82 Feuerwehr
fire department 79 Feuerwehr
firefighter 79 Feuerwehrmann, -frau
firefighting 80 Feuerbekämpfung
firm 17 Firma
first aid 51 erste Hilfe
fishing 30 Angeln
to fit 34 installieren, einbauen
to fit (in) 8 passen (zu)
fitness 64 Fitness, Kondition

fixed 78 fest(gesetzt)
flashlight 34 Arbeitsleuchte, Taschenlampe
flight 19 Flug
floor 18 (Fuß-)Boden, Flur
fly 34 Fliege
to follow 29 folgen
following 12 folgende/r/s
foreign 56 ausländisch, fremd
to forget 26 vergessen
form 7 Form
four-wheel drive 34 Vierradantrieb
frame 32 Rahmen
France 63 Frankreich
French 39 französisch
fresh 10 frisch
fried 65 gebraten
frightened, to be ~ of 21 Angst haben vor
Frisbee 64 Wurfscheibe
front, in ~ of 21 vor
fruit 28 Obst
fuel 34 Treibstoff
full 68 voll, vollständig
furniture 32 Möbel(stücke), Möblierung
further 61 weiter

G

g'day 77 guten Tag
gap 59 Lücke
garage 34 (Auto-)Werkstatt
garter snake 12 Strumpfbandnatter
gas cooker 34 Gasherd
general 18 allgemein, normal
geometry 8 Geometrie
giant 39 riesig
glad 72 froh
glasses 36 Brille
glove 36 Handschuh
goggles 38 Schutzbrille
gradually 37 allmählich, nach und nach
graffiti 18 Wandschmierereien, Graffiti
grammar 7 Grammatik
great 44 groß
to grill 77 grillen
to groan 16 stöhnen
grog 66 Grog
guarantee 56 Garantie
to guard 18 bewachen
guest 23 Gast
guide 31 (Reise-)Führer
guilty 60 schuldbewusst
gym 79 Turnhalle, Fitnessstudio

Alphabetisches Wörterverzeichnis — Englisch – Deutsch

H

haircut 19 Haarschnitt, Frisur
half of 70 die Hälfte von
hamburger 30 Hamburger
hammer 37 Hammer
handbook 24 Bedienungsanleitung, Handbuch
handler 18 Transporteur
handmade 56 handgemacht, -gefertigt
handsome 46 gut aussehend
to hang out 14 rumhängen, sich rumtreiben
happily 72 glücklich
to hate 7 hassen
headache 68 Kopfschmerzen
health 64 Gesundheit(szustand)
healthcare 53 Gesundheit(sfürsorge)
heart 21 Herz
heat 34 Hitze
heating 26 Heizung
heavy 64 schwer
hectic 61 hektisch
helmet 36 (Schutz-)Helm
helpful 15 hilfreich, nützlich
heritage 31 Erbe
Hindi 53 Hindi
to hiss 12 zischen
historic 31 historisch
history 31 Geschichte
hobby 44 Hobby
honeymoon 21 Flitterwochen, Hochzeitsreise
hopefully 41 hoffentlich
horrible 52 schrecklich, furchtbar
to horrify 39 entsetzen
horse 10 Pferd
hospital 10 Hospital, Krankenhaus
housework 64 Hausarbeit(en)
hungry 26 hungrig
hunt 21 Jagd
hunter 21 Jäger/in
hurt 17 verletzt
husband 15 (Ehe-)Mann

I

icon 46 Ikone, Symbol
ideal 39 ideal
idol 46 Idol, Vorbild
to ignore 72 ignorieren, nicht beachten
illness 40 Krankheit
illustration 35 Abbildung
to imagine 78 sich vorstellen
immediately 72 sofort, umgehend
immigrant 56 Einwanderer, Einwanderin
impatient 54 ungeduldig
to improve 64 verbessern
to include 26 umfassen, einschließen
including 39 einschließlich, inbegriffen
to increase 37 steigern, erhöhen
indentation 37 Vertiefung, Delle
independent 48 unabhängig
India 53 Indien
to infect 67 infizieren, anstecken
information 7 Information(en), Angaben
information technology 9 Computertechnik
to injure 52 verletzen
injury 38 Verletzung
insect 70 Insekt
instruction 11 Anweisung
instrument 71 (Musik-)Instrument
interested, to be ~ in 8 sich interessieren für
to introduce oneself 32 sich vorstellen
to invite 30 einladen
Irish 15 irisch
iron 37 Eisen
Italian 39 italienisch
italic, in ~s 73 kursiv
item 36 Artikel, Gegenstand

J

jacket 58 Jacke, Jackett
Japanese 57 japanisch
jeans 54 Jeans
jewellery 38 Schmuck
journey 67 Reise, Fahrt
juice 66 Saft
to jump on 72 springen auf
junction 29 (Straßen-)Kreuzung

K

key 28 Schlüssel
kid 79 Kind
Kiev 76 Kiew
to kill 21 töten
kilo 39 Kilo
king 43 König
kitchen 23 Küche
to knock down 61 abreißen

L

label 53 Aufkleber, Etikett
ladder 82 Leiter
lake 30 (Binnen-)See
to land 71 landen
landlord 61 Wirt
landmine 52 Landmine
lane 47 Gasse, Weg
latest 58 neueste
to laugh 14 lachen
lean 64 mager
leg 39 Bein
leisure 35 Freizeit
lemon 63 Zitrone
let's 8 lass/t uns
level 78 Niveau
library 44 Bücherei, Bibliothek
to lie 15 lügen
lifestyle 64 Lebensstil, Lifestyle
to lift 12 (an-, hoch)heben
lighting 50 Beleuchtung, Licht
limit 15 Grenze, Frist
to link 14 verbinden
live 61 live
living room 26 Wohnzimmer
lizard 21 Eidechse
to load 18 (ver)laden
local 16 hiesig, einheimisch
to look forward to 11 sich freuen auf
loose 38 weit (geschnitten), lose
lorry 61 Lastwagen, Lkw
loser 17 Verlierer/in
lovely 58 schön, hübsch
lubricant 37 Gleit-, Schmiermittel
luckily 59 glücklicherweise, zum Glück
lucky, to be ~ 40 Glück haben
luggage 18 Gepäck
lunch 8 Mittagessen
lung 36 Lunge
luxury 48 Luxus

M

machine 18 Maschine, Gerät
magazine 14 Zeitschrift, Magazin
magnesium 66 Magnesium
make-up 14 Make-up, Schminke
malaria 48 Malaria
male 44 männlich
to manage 11 bewältigen, fertig werden mit
manager 16 Leiter/in
maritime 31 Schiffahrts-
marketing 16 Vertrieb, Vertriebs-
to marry 25 heiraten
master certificate 32 Meisterdiplom
to match 9 zuordnen
material 12 Material, Stoff
meal 23 Essen, Mahlzeit

Alphabetisches Wörterverzeichnis — Englisch – Deutsch

to mean 8 bedeuten
meaning 15 Bedeutung
to measure 12 messen
mechanic 34 Mechaniker/in
media 45 Medien
mediation 19 Vermittlung, Dolmetschen
megapixel 60 Megapixel
member 79 Mitglied
membership 79 Mitgliedschaft
metal 37 Metall
metalwork 9 Werken mit Metall, Metallarbeit
microphone 50 Mikrophon
midday 65 Mittag, Mittags-
Milan 56 Mailand
million 39 Million
minced beef 30 Rinderhack(fleisch)
to mind 65 etw dagegen haben
minefield 52 Minenfeld
to miss 16 fehlen
missing 7 fehlend
mistake 7 Fehler, Irrtum
mixture 66 Mischung
modal 33 Modal(verb)
model 39 Model
modelling job 39 Auftrag als (Foto-)Modell
mokick 6 Kleinmotorrad (mit Kickstarter)
moped 5 Moped, Mofa
mostly 9 meistens
motorbike 72 Motorrad
motorway 61 Autobahn
mountain bike 5 Mountainbike
Mr 7 Herr
Mrs 7 Frau
multi-cultural 31 multikulturell
multinational 48 multinational
Munich 32 München
muscle 64 Muskel
museum 31 Museum
musical 71 Musik-

N

nail 76 Nagel
naturalist 21 Naturforscher/in
nature 21 Natur
nearby 79 nahe gelegen, in der Nähe
neighbour 6 Nachbar/in
net 48 (Moskito-)Netz
New Zealand 44 Neuseeland
newly 61 neu
no way 26 auf keinen Fall, kommt überhaupt nicht in Frage
noisy 61 laut, lärmend
non-smoking 44 Nichtraucher-
normally 81 normalerweise
North 65 Norden
North Carolina 79 Bundesstaat der USA
northern 44 nördlich
to notice 72 (be)merken
nowadays 56 heutzutage
nurse 10 Krankenpfleger/in
nut 63 Nuss
nutrition 64 Ernährung

O

o'clock 12 um ... Uhr
obese 70 fettleibig
odd 8 nicht passend
to offer 64 (an)bieten
officer 18 (Polizei-)Beamter/Beamtin
oh 11 Null
oil 66 Öl
old-fashioned 14 altmodisch
onion 30 Zwiebel
opening times 59 Öffnungszeiten
operating 37 Bedienungs-
operation 12 Operation, Eingriff
opposite 7 Gegenteil
order 11 Reihenfolge
to organize 30 organisieren
original 56 Original
outback 34 australischer Busch
outsourcing 56 Auslagern (von Arbeitsprozessen)
overweight 64 übergewichtig
own, of one's ~ 11 eigen
owner 10 Besitzer/in
oyster 76 Auster

P

p.m. 11 nachmittags
packet 14 Packung, Päckchen
pain 16 Schmerz(en)
painful 39 schmerzhaft
paint 32 Farbe
painter 32 Maler/in, Anstreicher/in
paper clip 14 Büroklammer
participant 70 Teilnehmer/in
particular 27 bestimmt
partly 66 teilweise, zum Teil
to pass (an exam) 8 (ein Examen) bestehen
passenger 18 Passagier/in, Fluggast
patient 12 Patient/in
pea 53 Erbse
peaceful 61 friedlich, ruhig
per 26 pro
personnel 18 Personal, Mitarbeiter
pet 10 Heim-, Haustier
physical 64 körperlich
to pick up 11 abholen
pirate 56 Pirat
placement 59 Praktikum
plane 18 Flugzeug
plasterer 32 Gipser/in
plastic 82 Plastik, Kunststoff
plate 28 Teller, Platte
plus 26 außerdem
pocket money 6 Taschengeld
poisonous 12 giftig
Polish 34 polnisch
politician 45 Politiker/in
pool 61 (Pool-)Billard
popular 21 beliebt, populär
port 31 Hafen(stadt)
portable 72 transportabel, tragbar
poverty 52 Armut
power cord 38 Netz-, Stromkabel
power source 38 Energiequelle
powerful 48 mächtig, einflussreich
practical 8 praktisch
to practise 77 (ein)üben
to prefer 27 bevorzugen
preparation 21 Vorbereitung
to prepare 8 vorbereiten
preposition 25 Präposition, Verhältniswort
present 5 Gegenwart
pressure 37 Druck
pretty 57 hübsch
previous 42 vorhergehend, früher
prince 32 Prinz
to print 14 (ab)drucken
private 23 privat
prize 16 Preis, Gewinn
to proceed 37 (weiter-, fort)fahren
to produce 34 produzieren
producer 70 Produzent/in
product 45 Produkt, Erzeugnis
production 57 Produktion, Herstellung
professional 32 professionell, berufstätig
profile 10 Profil, Porträt, (Berufs-)Bild
profit 34 Profit, Gewinn
programme 21 Sendung, Programm
progressive 27 Verlaufsform
to promise 69 versprechen, zusagen
properly 28 richtig, korrekt
to protect 21 schützen
protective 36 Schutz-

Alphabetisches Wörterverzeichnis — Englisch – Deutsch

protein　63　*Protein*
proud　62　*stolz*
pub　26　*Gaststätte, Lokal*
pump　32　*Pumpe*
pump house　32　*Pumpenhaus*
pupil　9　*Schüler/in*
purchase　60　*(Ein-)Kauf*
purpose　38　*Zweck, Ziel*

Q
qualification　8　*Abschluss (einer Ausbildung)*
quality　54　*Qualität*
queue　60　*(Warte-)Schlange*
quiz　71　*Quiz*

R
rabbit　11　*Kaninchen*
radio　32　*Radio, Rundfunk*
raider　52　*Plünderer, Schänder*
rat　12　*Ratte*
ration　66　*Ration, Zuteilung*
to reach　70　*erreichen*
reader　14　*Leser/in*
real　10　*echt, richtig*
reality　70　*Wirklichkeit*
to realize　52　*(sich) bewusst werden*
rebel　46　*Rebell*
reborn　61　*wiedergeboren*
to rebuild　61　*wieder aufbauen*
to receive　62　*erhalten, bekommen*
receptionist　44　*Empfang(smitarbeiter/in)*
recipe　30　*(Koch-)Rezept*
to recognize　45　*(wieder) erkennen*
refugee　52　*Flüchtling*
to register　52　*eintragen lassen*
to regret　42　*bedauern, bereuen*
regular　66　*regelmäßig*
relationship　70　*Beziehung, Verhältnis*
relative pronoun　67　*Relativpronomen*
to relax　68　*entspannen*
relaxing　78　*sich erholend*
to relieve　68　*lindern, erleichtern*
religious education　9　*Religion(sunterricht)*
to relocate　21　*umsiedeln*
to remember　7　*sich erinnern (an), daran denken*
to remove　18　*entfernen, beseitigen*
to renovate　32　*renovieren*
renovation　33　*Renovierung*
rent　26　*Miete*

repair　32　*Reparatur*
to replace　56　*ersetzen, austauschen*
report　51　*Bericht*
reporter　16　*Reporter/in*
reptile　21　*Reptil*
reputation　32　*Ruf*
rescue　82　*Rettung*
to rescue　82　*retten*
research　42　*Nachforschung(en)*
reservation　28　*Reservierung, (Tisch-)Bestellung*
to respect　32　*respektieren*
rest　6　*Rest*
restoration　33　*Wiederherstellung, Restaurierung*
to result in　38　*führen zu, zur Folge haben*
to rewrite　11　*umschreiben, neu schreiben*
rich　21　*reich*
rigger　50　*Bühnenarbeiter/in*
risk　38　*Risiko*
river　21　*Fluss*
roadie　50　*Roadie*
roll　30　*Brötchen*
Rome　56　*Rom*
roof　82　*Dach*
rooftop　82　*Dach*
route　29　*Strecke, Weg*
routine　42　*routinemäßige Tätigkeit*
Royal Navy　66　*Königliche Marine*
rubbish　24　*Abfall, Müll*
ruin　79　*Ruine*
rule　38　*Vorschrift, Regel*
rum　66　*Rum*
runway　18　*Start-, Landebahn*
to rush　39　*schnell bringen*

S
safe　38　*sicher*
safety　34　*Sicherheit*
to sail　66　*segeln*
sailing　30　*Segeln*
sailor　66　*Seemann, Matrose*
salad　30　*Salat*
sales　60　*Schluss-, Ausverkauf*
sales assistant　58　*Verkäufer/in*
salt　64　*Salz*
sand　20　*Sand*
sandwich　26　*Sandwich, belegtes Brot*
satellite　34　*Satellit*
sausage　63　*(Brat-)Wurst, Würstchen*
to save　6　*(auf)sparen*
saw　76　*Säge*

scaffolding　50　*(Bau-)Gerüst*
scale　9　*Skala, Maßstab*
scene　79　*Szene*
school-leaver　32　*Schulabgänger/in*
Scotland　65　*Schottland*
Scouser　31　*Liverpooler/in*
screw　37　*Schraube*
screwdriver　37　*Schraubenzieher, Schrauber*
scurvy　66　*Skorbut*
to search　18　*(durch)suchen*
to search for　79　*(ab)suchen nach*
seat　32　*(Sitz-)Platz, Stuhl*
secretary　76　*Sekretär/in*
security　18　*Sicherheit*
sensible　14　*vernünftig*
sentence　7　*Satz, Strafe*
series　21　*Serie, Sendereihe*
serious　17　*ernst(haft)*
seriously　41　*ernst(haft)*
to serve　62　*servieren, anbieten*
to set up　50　*aufbauen*
settler　71　*Siedler/in*
shabby　61　*schäbig*
to shake　61　*klirren, zittern*
shampoo　53　*Shampoo*
sheep　71　*Schaf(e)*
ship　31　*Schiff*
shirt　58　*Hemd*
to shock　39　*schockieren*
shocking　39　*schrecklich, schockierend*
shopping　6　*Einkäufe*
short　46　*kurz*
sick　16　*krank*
sickness　17　*Krankheit*
silly　14　*töricht, albern*
similar　29　*ähnlich*
singer　45　*Sänger/in*
single　16　*einzig*
size　39　*Größe*
skeleton　39　*Skelett*
skilled　33　*gelernt, ausgebildet, Fach-*
skin　66　*Haut*
skipper　47　*Kapitän*
skirt　58　*Rock*
sky　58　*Himmel*
sleeping bag　34　*Schlafsack*
sleeve　42　*Ärmel*
to slip　37　*verrutschen*
slippery　51　*glatt, rutschig*
slowly　12　*langsam*
to smell　14　*riechen*
to smoke　14　*rauchen*
smoking　44　*Raucher-*
snail　63　*Schnecke*

Alphabetisches Wörterverzeichnis   Englisch – Deutsch

snake   12   *Schlange*
to sneak   14   *klauen, stibitzen*
snow   6   *Schnee*
soda   77   *Mineralwasser*
solo   74   *allein*
sound   50   *Ton*
south   44   *Süd-*
southern   48   *südlich*
space   66   *Raum*
spaceship   67   *Raumschiff*
Spain   8   *Spanien*
Spanish   8   *Spanisch*
spare   34   *Ersatz-*
special   34   *speziell*
specialized   33   *spezialisiert*
speed   37   *Geschwindigkeit*
to spell   44   *buchstabieren*
spelling   7   *Rechtschreibung*
to spend on   6   *ausgeben für*
to split   37   *spalten, platzen*
spot   12   *Fleck(en), Punkt*
spotless   42   *sauber, makellos*
spotlessly   42   *makellos*
springboard   5   *Sprungbrett*
sqm   26   *Quadratmeter*
square metre   27   *Quadratmeter*
to stab   21   *stechen*
stage   50   *Bühne*
stairs   64   *Treppe(n)*
standard   16   *Standard*
star   45   *Star, Stern*
statement   6   *Aussage*
station   26   *Bahnhof*
to steal   14   *stehlen*
steel   50   *Stahl*
steering wheel   36   *Lenkrad*
step   19   *Schritt*
stick   39   *Stock, Stecken*
stingray   21   *Stachelrochen*
stomach
   ache   16   *Magenschmerzen*
stone   32   *Stein*
stonemason   32   *Steinmetz*
store   54   *Laden, Geschäft*
straight ahead   29   *geradeaus*
straw   12   *Stroh*
strawberry   63   *Erdbeere*
stress   30   *Stress*
to stretch   68   *strecken, dehnen*
stripe   12   *Streifen*
strong   66   *stark, kräftig*
stuck, to get ~   34   *stecken bleiben*
studio   42   *Studio*
to study   76   *studieren*
sturdy   61   *massiv, fest*
subject   8   *(Schul-)Fach*
substance   51   *Substanz, Stoff*

success   21   *Erfolg*
successful   41   *erfolgreich*
to suffer from   39   *leiden an*
sugar   39   *Zucker*
to suggest   30   *vorschlagen*
suitcase   18   *Koffer*
summary   12   *Zusammenfassung*
sunglasses   57   *Sonnenbrille*
sunny   16   *sonnig*
super   60   *super, großartig*
supervisor   51   *Ausbilder/in*
to support   48   *unterstützen*
surname   44   *Nach-, Familienname*
surprise   17   *Überraschung*
to surprise   17   *überraschen*
to survive   70   *überleben*
survivor   79   *Überlebende/r*
SUV   34   *Geländewagen (mit Vierradantrieb)*
synagogue   32   *Synagoge*

T

table   7   *Tabelle*
to take over   21   *übernehmen*
tank   34   *Tank, (Benzin-)Kanister*
tanker   74   *Tanker*
tap   33   *Zapfhahn*
tape measure   76   *Bandmaß*
to taste   73   *schmecken*
tattoo   42   *Tätowierung*
tattooist   42   *Tätowierer/in*
technical drawing   9   *technisches Zeichnen*
technician   50   *Techniker/in*
teen   70   *Teenager, Jugendliche/r*
teenage   14   *für Teenager, Teenage-*
Tenerife   16   *Teneriffa*
tent   34   *Zelt*
term   55   *Bezeichnung, Ausdruck*
terminal   18   *Abfertigung(sgebäude)*
terrible   17   *schrecklich, furchtbar*
Thai   61   *Thai(länder/in)*
thick   38   *dick*
thin   39   *dünn*
though   34   *allerdings, jedoch*
thousand   52   *tausend*
throughout   59   *die ganze Zeit hindurch, während*
tiger   10   *Tiger*
timber   76   *(Bau-)Holz, Nutzholz*
tip   15   *Hinweis, Tipp*
tired   26   *müde*
toast   65   *Toast*
tomato   30   *Tomate*
tomb   52   *Grab*
tool   38   *Werkzeug, Gerät*

tooth, teeth   66   *Zahn, Zähne*
topic   8   *Thema*
total   9   *(End-)Summe*
touch, to get in ~ with   44   *(sich) in Verbindung setzen mit*
tour   34   *Tour, Rundreise*
toxic   51   *giftig, toxisch*
tracker dog   72   *Suchhund*
trade   52   *Handel*
tradition   66   *Tradition, Brauch*
traditional   61   *traditionell*
traditionally   60   *traditionell*
trailer   34   *Wohnwagen*
trainer   64   *Trainer/in*
training   24   *Schulung, Training*
transfusion   39   *Transfusion*
to translate   55   *übersetzen, übertragen*
transport box   12   *Transportbox*
travel agency   72   *Reisebüro*
treasure hunt   30   *Schatzsuche, Schnitzeljagd*
treat   14   *etw Besonderes*
trial   70   *Test, Prüfung*
tribe   70   *Stamm*
trip   34   *Ausflug, Reise*
trouble, to get into
   ~   14   *Probleme bekommen*
trousers   58   *Hose(n)*
true   6   *richtig, zutreffend*
to trust   14   *vertrauen*
truth   15   *Wahrheit*
tucker   70   *Essen*
Turin   56   *Turin*
type   12   *Art*
typical   10   *typisch*
tyre   36   *Reifen*

U

ugly   46   *hässlich*
uncle   7   *Onkel*
uncomfortable   61   *unbequem, ungemütlich*
underwater   71   *Unterwasser-*
unexpected   16   *unerwartet*
unfortunately   46   *unglücklicherweise, leider*
unfriendly   7   *unfreundlich*
United Nations   52   *Vereinte Nationen*
unlimited   32   *unbegrenzt*
to unload   18   *entladen, ausladen*
to unlock   60   *aufschließen*
untidy   38   *unordentlich, unaufgeräumt*
untrue   49   *unwahr*

Alphabetisches Wörterverzeichnis — Englisch – Deutsch

unusual 21 ungewöhnlich, unüblich
upper 42 Ober-
USA 8 die Vereinigten Staaten von Amerika
useful 6 nützlich
useless 7 nutzlos, sinnlos
usually 25 gewöhnlich, meistens

V
vegetable 28 Gemüse
verb 7 Verb
vet 10 Tierarzt, -ärztin
veterinary 6 tierärztlich, Veterinär-
visa 78 Visum, Sichtvermerk
visitor 21 Besucher/in
vitamin 63 Vitamin
vocabulary 41 Wortschatz
vocational 32 beruflich
vodka 14 Wodka
volunteer 72 Freiwillige/r
voyage 31 (See-)Reise

W
waiter 23 Kellner, Ober
waiting room 12 Wartezimmer
waitress 23 Kellnerin, Serviererin
to wake up 12 aufwachen
war 52 Krieg
to warn 40 warnen, darauf hinweisen
warning 15 Warnung
warrior 21 Krieger/in, Aktivist/in
waste of time 8 Zeitverschwendung
wave 74 Welle
to weigh 39 wiegen
weight, to lose ~ 64 abnehmen
well known 21 sehr bekannt, berühmt
west 46 westlich
wet 38 nass, feucht
whale 74 Wal
wheel 36 Rad
wheelchair 48 Rollstuhl
whether 30 ob
while 38 während
wife 15 (Ehe-)Frau
wild 21 wild
wildlife 21 Tierwelt
window 25 Fenster
windscreen 36 Windschutzscheibe
wink 15 Zwinkern, Blinzeln
winner 16 Gewinner/in, Sieger/in
wonderful 16 wunderbar, wundervoll
wood 32 Holz
wooden 67 aus Holz, Holz-
woodwork 9 Werken mit Holz, Holzarbeit
woodworker 32 Tischler/in
woodworking 76 Holzbearbeitung
work experience 51 Praktikum
workshop 34 Werkstatt
worm 12 Wurm
worried, to be ~ 14 Angst haben
worse 57 schlechter, schlimmer
worst 17 schlechteste, schlimmste
worth, to be ~ 54 wert sein
to wrestle 21 ringen
writer 45 Schriftsteller/in, Autor/in

Y
yet, not ~ 77 noch nicht
Yours sincerely 11 Mit freundlichen Grüßen

Z
zero 39 Null
zoo 10 Zoo, Tierpark

Bildquellen

RF-Fotos
Alamy: S. 42 / EyecandyImages;
CV: S. 36 (1–6)
Istockphoto: S. 5/1.1, S. 5/2.1, S. 5/3.1, S. 5/4.1, S. 5/5.1 u 2, S. 5/6.1; S. 6 (1–6 unten); S. 12; S. 13/1; S. 24; S. 63/1,3,9; S. 71/4; S. 72/2;
Gettyimage: S. 8;
Shutterstock: S. 5/1.2, S. 5/2.2, S. 5/6.2, S. 6/1, S. 6/2, S. 13/2, S. 13/4, S. 13/5; S. 14/3; S. 16; S. 23/4; S. 34; S. 53 (1–9); S. 63/2, 3, 4, 5, 6, 7; S. 71/3, 6, 8; S. 72/5, 6; S. 76 (1 oben, 1–6 unten);
V. Maly: S. 6.3, S. 14/1, S. 14/2

RM-Fotos
Alamy: S. 14/4 / drinkAlanKing; S. 18/1 / D. Lander, S. 18a / C. Pillitz, S. 18c / Caro / Sorge, S. 18d / M. Goldwater; S. 20 / K. Kreder; S. 21 / Photo 12; S. 23/2 / A. Segre, S. 23/3 / J. Roper, S. 23/6 / R. Wilkinson; S. 26/1 / Magwitch; S. 28/1 / Sunny photography; S. 31/1 / Colin Palmer Photography, S. 31/2 / Topix, S. 31/3 / D. Toase, S. 31/4 / Factory Hill; S. 32/1 / I. Mac Donald, S. 32/2 / J. Woodhouse; S. 50/1 / Acestock, S. 50/2 / R. Hutchings, S. 50/3 / J. Greenberg, S. 50/4 / J. Greenberg, S. 50/5 / ABN Stock Images, S. 50/6 / R. Hutchings; S. 56/1 / P. Canova, S. 56/2 / P. Horree; S. 61 / A. Segre; S. 64 / IE103 / Image Source Black; S. 66 / R. Walls; S. 71/1 / L. Authors, S. 71/2 / Dallas Heaton, S. 71/5 / E. Davies, S. 71/7 / D. Ball; S. 72/1 / S. Levis; S. 72/3 / Farlap; S. 72/4 / M. Scott; S. 77 / image 100; S. 79 / Tom Tracy Photography;
Fotofinder: S13/3 Joker / J. Loeffke, S. 13/6 / T. Roetting / transit; S. 18b / Bilderbox / E. Wodicka; S. 23/1 / Bilderbox / E. Wodicka; S. 23/5 / Argum / F. Heller; S. 26/2 / VarioImages, S. 28/2 / VarioImages, S. 28/3 / A1PIX, S. 28/4 / VarioImages, S. 28/5 / Caro / Oberhaeuser; S. 72/1oben / Outdoor Archiv / D. Wilmar; S. 82 / Das Fotoarchiv A. Pohl,
Picture Alliance: S. 39 / A. Motte; S. 45/1 / Haribo, S. 45/2 / EPA / Riera, S. 45/3 / F. Mächler, S. 45/4 / dpa / PA; S. 46 / Bandphoto; S. 48/1 / PA Photos / Rui Vieira, S. 48/2 / Keystone / K. Grobl; S. 52/1 / L. Mc Carten, S. 52/2 / I. West; S. 58 / M. Gambarini; S. 70 / H. Wiedl; S. 74